Lawrence E. Thompson

The Person of Christ

BOOKS BY G. C. BERKOUWER

MODERN UNCERTAINTY AND CHRISTIAN FAITH

THE TRIUMPH OF GRACE IN THE
THEOLOGY OF KARL BARTH

RECENT DEVELOPMENTS IN ROMAN CATHOLIC
THOUGHT

THE SECOND VATICAN COUNCIL AND THE NEW
CATHOLICISM

STUDIES IN DOGMATICS SERIES —

THE PROVIDENCE OF GOD

FAITH AND SANCTIFICATION

FAITH AND JUSTIFICATION

FAITH AND PERSEVERANCE

THE PERSON OF CHRIST

GENERAL REVELATION

DIVINE ELECTION

MAN: THE IMAGE OF GOD

THE WORK OF CHRIST

Studies in Dogmatics

The Person Of Christ

BY

G. C. BERKOUWER

PROFESSOR OF SYSTEMATIC THEOLOGY
FREE UNIVERSITY OF AMSTERDAM

WM. B. EERDMANS PUBLISHING COMPANY
GRAND RAPIDS, MICHIGAN

Set up and printed, April 1954
Fifth printing, January 1973

Library of Congress Number 53-8143

ISBN 0-8028-3031-5

This American Edition is published by special arrangement with the Dutch publisher

J. H. KOK — KAMPEN

This volume translated by John Vriend

PHOTOLITHOPRINTED BY GRAND RAPIDS BOOK MANUFACTURERS, INC.
GRAND RAPIDS, MICHIGAN, UNITED STATES OF AMERICA

Contents

Introduction

CHAPTER I

Introduction

WHEN in 1871 Dr. Abraham Kuyper gave his lecture on "Modernism: A Mirage in the Sphere of Christianity," he drew a parallel between the inspiring optical phenomenon to be observed at the Strait of Messina — and Modernism; at this time he characterized the movement as fascinatingly beautiful, as having arisen by a definite logic, but as being devoid of all objective reference. Thus he sharply condemned the modernism of the nineteenth century and posited an irreconcilable antithesis between Modernism and the Christian faith. He pointed out specifically that heresies arise on Christian territory by a fixed law, as does a mirage in the atmosphere. They are, according to him, a "necessary deflection of the light of Christianity in the spiritual atmosphere of a given age." Every age produces its peculiar heresy in the church of Christ, and since the nineteenth century occupies a place of honor in the history of man, it was inevitable, by the logic of history, that in this age a resounding heresy should rise to the surface.

When Kuyper referred to Modernism as "bewitchingly beautiful," he doubtlessly recalled the fascination which the modernism of Scholten had exerted on him as a student. He acknowledges in 1871 that he too had once dreamed the dream of Modernism.[1] And when at the age of eighty he addressed the students of the Free University,[2] he harked back to the

---

1. A. Kuyper, *Fata Morgana*, page 52.
2. *Nog in den band van voorheen*, 1907.

"unspiritual presumption" which had caused him to slip. "At Leiden I joined, with great enthusiasm, in the applause given Professor Rauwenhoff when he, in his public lectures, broke with all belief in the Resurrection of Jesus." "Now when I look back," he writes, "my soul still shudders at times over the opprobrium I then loaded on my Savior."[3] Kuyper concludes his lecture with a reference to the Incarnation of the Word and points out the unfathomable cleavage between the church of Christ and Modernism. Now that endorsement of Rauwenhoff's negation and criticism has given way to adoration of the Son of Man, Kuyper recognizes in Arianism the image of the Modernism of his own day.[4] "One merely has to write other names and other dates into the history of the Arian heresy, and, provided one takes it in broad outline, the course of Modernism is repeated."

From these remarks it appears clearly that Kuyper finds in this Christological conflict not a dispute on some purely theoretical point of divergence but a religious and existential conflict of absolutely determinative significance. The point at issue, according to him, is heresy aimed at the heart of the church; and for this reason Kuyper joins the company of Athanasius who fought Arius consciously with a view to the wellbeing of the church. In this heresy the Christian perspective is lost: "Why not stop using the word 'prayer'? What you call prayer is a fanatic self-exaltation, a ventilation of your own hearts, a dialogue with your own soul."

*   *   *

Contained in this reference to Kuyper lies, to our mind, a pointer for all the problems which will occupy us in this study. Here we feel, more than anywhere else, that theology is not practised in a corner apart from the faith of the church, from the religion of faith, prayer, and adoration. In the

3. A. Kuyper, *Nog in den band van voorheen*, 1907, page 34.
4. *Fata Morgana*, pages 50-51.

various dogmatic distinctions touching also the Christ of God this connection must be maintained, and it should be brought out clearly that in scientific analysis Christ cannot be made the "object" of a neutral interest. The pre-commitment of faith or unfaith has always determined the Christological conflict. And this pre-commitment brings about also that in Christology there will be implicitly audible a Christian admonition, even when theological discussion does not change into preaching. This state of affairs has not always been sharply perceived. At times, however, there was a recognition on opposite sides of a debate of the fact that something more than the products of scientific analysis was at stake. We are thinking in this connection of the passionate indictment aimed by Kuyper at the remarkable figure of Allard Pierson, who has been called — and not without reason — the "enfant terrible" of Modernism. This disciple of Opzoomer felt obliged to push the empiricism of his master to its logical conclusion and so became the sceptic of Modernism. He began to doubt the much-lauded synthesis between faith and knowledge, and finally resigned his office as minister in the Reformed Church. In his farewell letter, dating from the year 1865, he stressed that the only reason for his departure lay in the nature of the Reformed Church as seen in the light of his own principles. The concept of a supernatural revelation has become for him a chimera. Hence Pierson feels he is compelled to make a practical decision. Confronted by the question whether his critical point of view permits him to continue his work in the church with unreserved honesty, he replies in the negative.[5] His farewell is a matter of conscience with him. Asking the church to extend its boundaries is equivalent to asking the church to

5. *Allard Pierson aan zijn laatste gemeente*, page 19; Boersema, *Allard Pierson*, page 235; cf. Kuenen, *Het goed recht der moderne richting*, 1886, page 4, where he says that formerly only "confessionals" used to deny modernists the right to remain in the church but now modernists themselves dispute that right. See further, J. Lindeboom, *Geschiedenis van het vrijzinnig Protestantisme*, 1933, II, 109.

sign its own death-warrant To remain in the church is unthinkable for a man of principle, and so there remains only the
possibility of a break for anyone who has perceived the incompatibility of Modernism with ecclesiastical Christianity.
Pierson deemed it impossible to construct a theology on
modernistic presuppositions. The modern consciousness starts
out — does it not? — with the absolute causal categories of
nature, categories by which the possibility of supernatural entities or of miracles is excluded. And since supernaturalism
is a *conditio sine qua non* for the church, the antithesis must be
openly and honestly acknowledged. Pierson refuses any longer
to play with the old terms of orthodoxy and then to give these
terms a modern content. He wishes to be consistent in his
scientific credo and places modernists before the pivotal question whether Modernism can, by rights, be called Christianity.

Allard Pierson and Kuyper were directly opposed in their
respective faiths but on one point at least they agreed: on the
incompatibility of Modernism and the Christian faith. Kuyper
was attacked in his day because he refused to be reconciled,
and Pierson because he doubted that a synthesis could be found.

*   *   *

In these historical reflections we touch on one of the most
important questions in the sphere of dogmatics. For it is
apparent that these problems have gone far beyond the
boundaries of the nineteenth century. Since that time, in
numerous variations, these problems have continued to occupy
the minds of men. The modernism of the nineteenth century
cannot, simply, it is true, be equated with that of the twentieth,
but anyone who has penetrated into the Christological views of
our day will speedily note that the conflict continues in numberless new forms. Again and again the points at issue range
themselves round the one central question: What think ye
of the Christ? And again one can say: Names and dates
change, but the conflict remains the same. A truly mysterious

reality manifests itself in this richly variegated interest in Jesus Christ. And often we notice, also now, something of the existential nature of the decisions made at this point. Again we hear words of hope in view of an expected synthesis, but at the same time we hear a witness to an irreconcilable antithesis between modern thought and the Christian faith.

* * *

During Christ's sojourn on earth, widely divergent ideas of him were already current. "Who do men say that the Son of man is?" Christ asked his disciples. As answer to this question we learn that one man discovers in him John the Baptist, another Elijah, or Jeremiah, or one of the prophets. But then, ignoring all these surmises, Christ directs the question at his disciples: "But who say ye that I am?" Not that Christ wishes to hear still another conjecture in addition to the ones already aired; on the contrary, what he wants now is a decision of another sort, a personal and practical decision which will correspond directly with the truth concerning his person; what he wants now is an answer which will transcend mere theorizing, the only answer possible in view of the reality confronting them. And that answer was then and there given him. "Thou art the Christ, the Son of the living God." Upon this answer Christ presses his emphatic *imprimatur*. Now follows his benediction and a reference to the mysterious origin of this confession: "Blessed art thou, Simon Bar-Jonah: for flesh and blood hath not revealed it unto thee, but my Father who is in heaven" (Matt. 16:17).

This conviction or this confession is immediately referred back to a divine revelation, to an *apokalupsis*. It is not to be explained from the lofty heights or profound depths of some rational insight, nor by referring it to some infallible intuition, but by tracing it to a miraculous gift of God. Here we get some inkling of what Christ meant when he said on another occasion: "No one knoweth the Son, save the Father" (Matt. 11:27).

The whole subject matter of Christology is most intimately related to the secret of revelation. Involved is a revelation of God, the enlightenment of the eyes; and the entire, age-long conflict about the Christ is exposed to the fierce light-beam of John's original witness to Christ: "Whosoever believeth that Jesus is the Christ is begotten of God" (I John 5:1).

For this reason the confession of the church touching Jesus Christ can never be a knowledge such that, with it, the church can elevate itself above the world. It is precisely within the church that people will have to remind themselves that this knowledge is a gift and a miracle which did not arise out of flesh and blood. This humility and this awareness of the origin of our confession that Jesus is the Christ do not exclude the testimony of the church but, on the contrary, press the church to it. "He that hath not the Son of God hath not life" (I John 5:12). This message of the church often sounds like a proud threat to one who is a stranger to the life of grace. But in reality it arises, just as with John, from the conviction that in Christ alone we have life.

*   *   *

The conflict over the identity of Christ, as well as over his program on earth, assumes various forms in different ages. In this connection we may observe that there are crescendoes in this conflict, namely, when the church's central confession is attacked and disputed. We are thinking without excluding other periods, of the fourth, the fifth, the nineteenth, and twentieth century. In the twentieth century particularly the dispute has come to a climax. Now more than ever the question has become acute as to whether modern thought is compatible with the Christian faith. How will the Christian confession sound in the spiritual atmosphere of our age? Is there going to be room for it, and if so, what place will be assigned to it after the development of the science of comparative religion, after the clash over the absoluteness of Christianity, and after the rise of the phenomenology of religion? Has the chasm of which Pierson and Kuyper speak been filled in or has it become deeper? There is every reason, in a period of fearful relativism, to confront ourselves with these questions; for people are already telling us of a new world-outlook which is utterly different, in its contours, from that in which the message of Christ — as Lord and Son of God — was broadcast over the earth. And we must ask whether this altered world-picture possibly brings with it an altered view of him who for centuries formed the content of the church's confession.

We are now thinking particularly of the supremely relevant issue of the "Entmythologisierung" (process of removing the myths from — Tr.) of Christianity, of which Rudolf Bultmann is the best-known representative. When the gospel of Jesus Christ has been disinfected of its "mythological" characteristics, the question is whether anything is left of that message with which the infant church in its apostolic activity stormed into the world, asserting that God had prepared the salvation which eye saw not, and ear heard not, and which entered not into the heart of man (I Cor. 2:9). Is it still possible, if one wishes to be and to remain an honest Christian in this age, to enter the world as a missionary? Can missions, in a world of evolving religions, still be based on an unchanging formula, or does the church, with all its missionary passion, finally flap its wings in a void? It is not for nothing that we introduce missions at this point: for it is clear that reflection on the gospel of Christ is not independent of the courage displayed by the church in its absolute witness!

The following are inseparable: the veracity of Christ's sacred claims, of his witness to himself, the truth of the apostolic witness, *and* the pretension — the affectionate and modest pretension — which the church carries into the world. Whoever undermines the first cannot avoid undermining the second. Missions and dogma join hands in the old question: Who do men say that I am? A weakening witness to Christ has far-reaching consequences for the mission-consciousness of the church. When on the home front the sound of true doxologies dies away, the mission spirit on the landing-beaches of the world will be broken by the encounter with its enormous resistance.

When Troeltsch, in 1906, wrote his treatise on missions in a changed world, he inquired into the influence of the new science of religion on the mission-mindedness of the church. The old view of Christianity and paganism was declared invalid.

"There is no question of a general, darkened as well as sinful, mass of lost and damned people — outside of Christendom — who from pity and with a view to salvation must be converted to inherit eternal bliss."[6] Orthodoxy, according to Troeltsch, had to buttress itself with this theory in order to be able to maintain its unique claim to truth. But now that this theory has been thrown into the dustbin, this "most simple and most urgent motive for missions, the duty of compassion and of extending a saving hand" goes out with it. Not conversion but uplift is now the rallying cry. Troeltsch does not believe, however, that this new orientation does away with the call to missions. For the adherent of an ethical and religious world-view will always have the courage for propaganda and expansion and, in addition, he will need missions for his own development. Here Christology and missions, in their interdependence, are in visible crisis. The fervor of the absolute challenge, and the claims of the "only Name given among men," are gone. Not a vestige is left of the conviction that the way, the only way of salvation, coincides with the Christ.

---

6. E. Troeltsch, *Die Mission in der modernen Welt*, Gesamm. Schr. II, page 789.

For this reason the church is called upon to re-think its confession. If the church wishes, in the face of falsehood and denial, to testify to the truth, it will have to be more than ever convinced of the reliability of its message. The church must not stutter when it answers, as it should answer, the question of the Hindu professors, the question "why we Christians assert that Jesus Christ alone is the Redeemer."[7] And in answering it the church will always have to fall back on the witness concerning the disclosure in Caesarea Philippi. The church must know what it is about when it defends the ancient creeds. And in this defense it will not be enough merely to extend a protective hand over the common property of tradition, but if it is to speak with the ring of sincerity, it will have to show something of the necessity which is laid upon it.[8] In the life of the church there should be a reflection of the knowledge that its secret did not proceed from flesh and blood but that it is a gift, as is also the possession of enlightened eyes. Orthodoxy — what else can it be than to live in continuity with a vibrant past, not indeed a continuity which is a mere thoughtless progression on the trusted paths of tradition but one which is full of the mystery of Caesarea Philippi — of the benediction of Christ.

---

7. E. Brunner, *Missionarische Eindrücke von einer Asienreise.* Evang. Missions-magazin, 1951, page 40.

8. Compare I Cor. 9:16; also Grundmann in Kittel's *Theol. Worterbuch* under *ananke*: "a divine must lies on him, from which he cannot withdraw himself."

The Crisis in the Doctrine of the Two Natures

CHAPTER II

The Crisis in the Doctrine of the Two Natures

PREOCCUPATION with the many problems which, in the course of history, have arisen around the person of Jesus Christ is bound to reveal the undeniable fact that one can speak without exaggeration of a far-reaching crisis in the dual-nature doctrine. The old confession of the church, the confession that Jesus Christ was truly God and truly man, has increasingly become the object of radical criticism. From its earliest infancy the church confessed the secret of salvation in Jesus Christ and defended it in the teeth of numerous heresies — against the denial of Christ's divine and human nature. This defense took place, not just in the sphere of theory and dispassionate analysis, but with the earnest words of warning uttered by the church, which appealed to the exhortation of John to the effect that he who does not confess that Jesus Christ is come in the flesh is led by the spirit of the Anti-Christ (I John 4:3).

Precisely in the light of this warning does the conflict over Jesus Christ become so serious; and for this reason too the crisis of the church's confession merits a good measure of our attention. Now we note, however, that many who object to the dual-nature doctrine, do not in the least feel hit by the admonition of John, because they think that the doctrine of the church, rather than they, has gone up a dead alley and, under the influence of a number of philosophical ideas, has dissociated itself from the New Testament witness. Hence it is of supreme importance to inquire into the background of this crisis. Particularly since the eighteenth century objections have been raised from different directions against the doctrine of the church, objections which gradually led to a definite critical tradition in which, as a matter of course, the presuppositions of the creeds were dubbed as untenable.

In the nineteenth century especially one can speak of a frontal assault on the doctrine of the two natures. People were pretty generally agreed that "the figure of the Savior," as given in the creeds, was unreal, unimaginable, and untenable in the light of genuinely religious reflection. The decisions of the ancient councils were called in question and fresh Christological thinking forced its way into the public eye. This modern Christological current was ushered in, as it were, by Socinianism, which has strongly influenced the development of the critical tradition. Socinianism is known particularly for its fierce attack on the doctrine of the vicarious suffering and death of Christ but no less for its criticism of the dogma of the dual nature. Whoever studies the discussion of proof-texts for the divinity of Christ in the Socinian Catechism Racoviensis will observe to what extent this criticism forms a prelude to the arguments of the modernistic criticism of the nineteenth century.[1] One senses in it a determined rationalism and a profound estrangement from the biblical testimony concerning Jesus Christ. The Trinity, atonement, and the divinity of Christ — all these are subjected to sharp criticism. Without ado the union of the two natures in Christ is dismissed as unthinkable. The full consequences of this criticism, it is true, were not accepted in all respects, for the Socinians still believed that Christ was supernaturally begotten by way of the virgin birth, but the results of their criticism would soon be visible in every point and sub-point of church doctrine. The end-result of this development was going to be the reduc-

---

1. Compare A. D. R. Polman, *De Strijd om het dogma,* in *Christus de Heiland,* 1948, page 140.

tion, in the doctrine of the church, of the Savior to the historical man Jesus of Nazareth.

The course of Christological development has, however, been very complicated. Rationalistic criticism did do its surreptitious work but it left the hearts, by and large, cold and dry. And it need not surprise us that various efforts were made to maintain Christ, in one way or another, as the true center of the Christian faith. It is certainly incorrect to brand the whole critical tradition as simply rationalistic. We are thinking, for instance, of Schleiermacher who was sharply opposed to the coarse rationalism of his day. Over against the primacy of human reason he pleaded for the exceptional value of feeling in the realm of religion. In this connection it is worth noting the consequences of this attitude for his views on the doctrine of the two natures. His evaluation is based on the standard of the Christian consciousness. From this point of view he wishes to strip away all that which, in the course of the centuries, had occupied a central place in the conflict but which does not belong to the essence of the matter.[2] When Schleiermacher examines the confessional stipulations of the church, he finds in them "almost nothing against which no protest should be registered."[3] He protests, first of all, against the use of the term "nature" with reference both to the divine and to the human. For that which is "natural" is finite and finitude is not applicable to God. With reference to "nature" and "person" he asks: "How can a genuine, vital unity consist with a duality of natures without a yielding of the one to the other when the one presents a larger, and the other a narrower, orbit; or without amalgamating when both systems of modes and laws of action become genuinely united in the one life? when nonetheless our speech is to be concerning one person, that is, an ego which in all successive moments remains constant?"

---

2. Schleiermacher, *Der Chr. Glaube,* paragraph 95.
3. *Ibid.,* par. 96.

From the fact that again and again the two natures of Christ were either separated or run together Schleiermacher infers that this construction of the church is itself mistaken. The sterility of the doctrine appears most patently in the problem of the two wills in Christ. It was inevitable that out of this construction "a complicated and artificial procedure should arise." This theory is of very little value for use in the church. We need to find another solution for the formulation of the impression we receive "of the peculiar dignity of the Redeemer." Schleiermacher is concerned to have a blending of the human and divine of Christ. And the solution he offers shows that his concern is not merely with the terms used in the creeds but with the problem itself. This solution may be reproduced by saying that the Redeemer is similar, in virtue of the self-identity of human nature, to all other men, "but distinguished from all other men by the constant vigor of his God-consciousness, which was a genuine indwelling of God in him."[4] Thus Christ is brought nearer to us than it was possible in the creeds and can become the object of our faith and adoration.

Besides the change desired in church doctrine by Schleiermacher, there is the Christology of Ritschl.

Ritschl placed all emphasis upon the historical revelation in Christ and vigorously opposed the influence of metaphysics in religion and theology. Characteristic of this metaphysics is that it operates with ontological instead of with value judgments and thus stabs religion at its core. Since the doctrine of the dual nature of Christ introduces a complete ontology into theology, it is on the face of it untenable. This criticism had the enthusiastic endorsement of Ritschl's disciples. Out of his school arose numerous historians of dogma, like Harnack and Loofs, who interested themselves in the origin of Christological doctrines and thought themselves able to point out the

---

4. Schleiermacher, *op. cit.*, par. 94.

vitium originis. Philosophical influences had been determinative for Christological dogma and had removed it, by successive stages, from the religious depth of the New Testament witness. These dogmatico-historical views have greatly strengthened and stimulated the critical tradition. Increasingly it seemed that from this point of view one could "see through" Christological dogma as being founded, not in true religion, but in a cosmological system. And for this reason the attempt to purify Christology of these so-called ontological categories became more and more determined.

Consciously people turned away from the old confession of the church. Harnack views the logos-doctrine as a pagan, metaphysical invasion in the sphere of Christianity, by which the truly human picture of Christ is petrified and mutilated; and Chalcedon is criticized for its cold, negative definitions.[5]

Of the one subject Christ, church doctrine made two subjects, and unity was lost in the fatal struggle against the monophysite theory. The dogma thus lost its practical significance for personal piety.[6] Similar strictures may be found in others. One gets the impression that they are all eager to champion the unity of the Christ-figure threatened by church doctrine. Loofs says it is impossible, upon serious reflection, to imagine "that a divine person should have become the subject of a human life limited by time and space." By various routes the rationalistic arguments come back like the surf upon the beach of orthodoxy. We may read the sum of the matter in Nitzsch: "A true man cannot at the same time in a metaphysical sense be truly God." That is the argument throughout the nineteenth century: the confession of the church "vere Deus, vere homo" is impossible.

It is worth our while to note in what way the nineteenth century has tried to find substitutes for this impossible doctrine. Any number of modern formulations may be observed in

---

5. Harnack, *D. G.* II, page 397.
6. J. Kaftan, *Dogmatik,* page 424.

this century. One of the most striking is undoubtedly that of the so-called speculative Christology. It was controlled by the philosophical influence of Hegel who became to many "the mainstay of the renewal of church dogma."[7] For an example of this Christology we can take Biedermann who acknowledges his indebtedness to Hegel for a large part of his philosophical thinking. This indebtedness is true of his Christology. It was the intent of the Hegelian philosophy to point out the unity of the human and the divine. Biedermann felt attracted to the dogma of the Word become flesh. This "becoming" in particular drew the attention of Hegelian philosophers. Divine being, they reasoned, does not remain locked up within itself but undergoes a process, or evolution, or revelation. This revelation takes place in the realm of the finite, in history with its variegated riches but also with its limitations. The human does not stand in contrast with the divine but is a revelation of it. Thus the theology influenced by Hegel began to speak boldly of the humanization of God and to reflect on the relationship between this humanization of God and the dogma of the church. Immediately, however, we encounter sharp criticism of the dogma of the Incarnation of the Word because it limits the humanization of God to the person of Christ.

The teaching of the church, so this Christology goes, must be understood in its necessity and generality. Humanization in Christ is not at all something new but rather the illustration of a general idea. Christ is not the God-man but a sublime revelation of the unity of the human and the divine. All of humanity as the Son of God is the realization of an idea. The idea has not been perfectly realized in any single individual, not even in Christ. Strauss, a follower of Hegel, formulates this idea sharply: "It is not at all natural for the idea, in process of self-realization, to pour out its whole contents into

---

7. A. E. Biedermann (1819-1855), *Chr. Dogmatik*, 1869, page VIII.

one exemplar."[8] The "once-for-all" taught by the church must
be generalized. And a distinction must be made, moreover,
between the Christian principle and the person of Christ. The
principle, the root-idea of the Christian religion, may not be
identified with the person of Christ. The religious life of
Christ is, indeed, the "first self-realization of the principle in
a world-historical personage."[9] On this basis one can accept
the relative value of the creeds. That the Sonship of Christ
was understood by the church as a metaphysical relationship
between the pre-existing ego of Christ and God, and that thus
the church arrived at the unity of his being and his true
humanity — all that was an expression, in the given conceptual
form, of the truth of the Christian idea. Even the idea that
Christ was "before the foundation of the world" can to a
certain extent be called true. For it is "the imaginative and
therefore mythologizing expression of the truth that the self-
revelation of the absolute Spirit in the finite spirit has already
been given in the being of the former."

In this speculative manner the doctrine of the church is led
to the executioner's block. We are already confronting at this
point what amounts to a program of "Entmythologisierung."
For if the idea is to be grasped with precision, it will be
necessary to strip from these creedal conceptions their mythological character.

* * *

In addition to the speculative Christology there is another
form of Christological thought which has been very influential
in the nineteenth century and in which there is again observable
a critical shift in the doctrine of the two natures. We are
referring to the so-called *kenosis*-Christology. It too is con-

8. Strauss, who was consistent in his historical criticism, asserted that
it is impossible, by the means of historical research, to ascribe to Jesus
of Nazareth a "supreme value," uniqueness, or absoluteness. Compare K.
Barth, *David Fr. Strausz als Theologe*, page 26. Also: "Humanity is
the absolute, the real content of Christology."
9. Biedermann, *Op. cit.*, page 593.

vinced of the difficulties implicit in the traditional point of
view, but wishes nonetheless to accommodate itself to certain
high points in the development of Christology and discovers
various traces in that development which point in the direction
of a particular *kenosis*-doctrine. This group does not want
simply to drop the dual-nature doctrine but to remove from
it those parts which are offensive to modern thought and in the
end to purify and reform the dogma of the church.[10] Its name
is owing to the term *kenosis* as used in Scripture and is intended to denote the Scriptural nature of the doctrine (Phil.
2:7). The *kenosis*-idea became the point of departure for a
new Christological movement. The core, for this Christology,
lies in the difficulties necessarily entailed in the doctrine of
"two natures in one person." It wishes, to a degree impossible
within the traditional framework, to have a unified image of
Christ and teaches, with this end in view, that the "logos
asarkos" parted voluntarily, either wholly or in part, with
his divinity and, by way of *kenosis* or "emptying," *became*
man. For a genuine assumption by the Son of God of a human
nature there is no room on this view. In place of this assumption has come a change of some sort — as expressed by
Thomasius: *"Kenosis* is the exchange of one form of existence
for another."[11] In the doctrine of the two natures, exponents
of the *kenosis*-theory contend, one runs perpetually into a
duality — in the consciousness, in the actions, and in the life
of Christ. One can escape this duality, according to Thomasius, only by conceiving *kenosis* as a genuine emptying of the
divine form by an act of self-denial and self-limitation. This
would not mean, the exponents of the theory assert, that the

---

10. Compare E. Gunther, *Die Entwickelung der Lehre von der Person
Christi im* 19. *Jahrhundert;* S. Faut, *Die Christologie seit Schleiermacher;*
O. Benson, *Die Lehre der Kenose;* J. J. Muller, *Die Kenosisleer in die
Kristologie sedert die Reformatie;* M. Waldhauser, *Die Kenose und die
moderne protestantische Christologie;* F. W. Korff, *Christologie,* Vol. I,
pages 270ff.
11. Thomasius, *Christi Person und Werk,* II, page 151.

divine being itself is given up.   To teach it would be a "Scrip-ture-contradicting error."

The Logos surrenders the glory and the attributes of the divine mode of being without parting with divine being.   By this distinction Thomasius seeks to escape the danger of doing less than justice to the ancient teaching that in God there is no change.   Hence he distinguishes between the immanent and the relative attributes of God.   The relative attributes have reference to the world; the immanent, to God's essence. And at the incarnation the Logos retains the immanent attrib-utes but lays aside the relative.

We are evidently vis-a-vis an effort to rise above the diffi-culties of the "God-man" doctrine; an effort, moreover, to build up a Christology in which a genuine unity is both possible and conceivable.   But there is in all this a noticeable hesitation. For if the *kenosis*-theologians were consistent in their talk of the humanization of God, the problem of the dualism would be solved.   But from such consistency the majority shrink back, with the result that the problem, be it in another form, is right with us again.   The relative attributes may have been shed, but of the immanent attributes this cannot be said; hence the problem of the divine attributes in the man Jesus Christ re-mains.   It is not hard to understand that some adherents of the *kenosis*-theory, dissatisfied with this dualism, have pro-ceeded to teach a laying-aside of all the divine attributes.   The Logos then *becomes* man in the full sense of the word, and the problem seems to be solved.   The Godhead, says Gess, is trans-muted into humanity.   Godet also concludes from the freedom of God that God is not inseparably bound to his divine mode of being.   Thus we observe that this Christology, when consistent, arrives at a view which leaves room for nothing but the man Jesus Christ.   Behind this man may lie the mystery of his origin — nonetheless he is fully humanized. Duality is can-celled by a pure humanity.   The problem discovered in the dogma of the church is resolved by the expedient of eliminating one of the constituents. The motive for the *kenosis*-theory lies in the desire to have in full view the unity of Christ's consciousness; but if this is to be attained by way of a *kenosis*-doctrine so construed, it is no longer evident that it is truly God who comes to us in Christ. A genuine union is then out of the picture. The core of Korff's criticism of the *kenosis*-doctrine is that it precludes the actual coming of God into the world — the secret of Christology.[12] With good reason Baur passes judgment upon this Christology: "This complete self-renunciation is in fact the complete self-dissolution of dogma." Any effort to transcend the duality of Christ leads inevitably to the doctrine of the mutability of God.

*   *   *

It is plain that this doctrine is in direct conflict with the confession of the church. For any real relationship between the two natures is excluded on this view; it champions a humanization of God, a transition from the divine mode of being into a human, which replaces a union of the two natures. This doctrine is condemned, implicitly and explicitly, by the decisions of the councils. Hence we read in the Athanasian creed that in the Incarnation there takes place, not a metamorphosis of deity into flesh, but an assumption of humanity.[13] And, to mention no others, the Belgic Confession is pronouncedly anti-kenotic when it asserts that each nature retains its attributes.

The *kenosis*-theory, rather than an elucidation of the dual nature doctrine, violates and dissolves it. The theory is a symptom of the serious crisis which the dogma of the church is undergoing. Dorner, among others, attacked it with a view to maintaining the immutability of God. He mentioned the theopaschitic doctrine, earlier called patripassianism, which

12. Korff, *Christologie*, I, page 289.
13. "Unus autem non conversione divinitatis in carnem, sed assumptione humanitatis in deum."

teaches that the divine essence — a true trinity being denied — suffered in the flesh. Dorner does acknowledge the religious motive in the *kenosis*-theory, namely, that in Christ one can observe the work of the divine, redemptive, suffering love take place.[14]   There is a desire to do justice to a genuine becoming and development in Christ and to implicate the Logos in that process. But if *kenosis* be understood as a transmutation and a laying aside, whether consistently or not, of divine attributes, then Dorner adverts to the Pauline dictum: God cannot deny himself (II Tim. 2:13). And he confronts, with this text, especially those who argue from the freedom of God to the possibility of abdicating the divine mode of being.

The *kenosis*-doctrine did not point the way out of the impasse supposedly present in the dogma of the church. The question remained urgent whether Christ was and could be truly God and truly man. At the end of the road, when the reconstruction of Christology was undertaken, arose the danger of the complete humanization of Christ.[15]

*   *   *

In the same century still other difficulties appeared on the horizon, namely, from the side of the "historical-critical" school. Its efforts led to the acceptance by many of a "historical Jesus" — the real Jesus, absolved from the distortions of the creedal formulations. People were content with the man Jesus Christ and did not wish to be bothered with any doctrine of theanthropy. However high the qualities ascribed to this historical Jesus, it was nonetheless impossible that in this movement the problem of the two natures should arise, for

---

14. J. A. Dorner, *Jahrbucher fur deutsche Theol.*, I, page 379.

15. Compare D. M. Baillie, *God was in Christ*. An essay on Incarnation and Atonement, 1947; on the *kenosis*-theory: "If taken in all its implications, that seems more like a pagan story of metamorphosis than like the Christian doctrine of Incarnation, which has always found in the life of Jesus on earth God and man in simultaneous union — the Godhead 'veiled in flesh' but not *changed into* humanity," page 96.

the simple reason that the divine nature, the genuine divinity of Christ, had been eliminated on principle. An enormous conflict has, since that time, raged around the liberal picture of Jesus. In our time we may say that the stock of liberal theology as regards its idea of Jesus no longer rates very high. Many scholars have denied that it is possible, on the basis of the New Testament witness, to construe a historically reliable picture. More and more the idea gained ground that in the gospels we do not possess historically reliable evidence — by means of which we can conjure up the historical Jesus — but rather that there we have the witness of faith and the voice of the pulpit; and now one can no longer get behind this wall of apostolic testimony to a historical Jesus.

In this manner it was possible, to a large extent, to endorse the criticism of the gospels. Sometimes these "testimonies of faith" were understood to have nothing to do with historical accuracy and to have significance only as "interpretation" of the life of Jesus — in the light of his Resurrection — by those who believed in him.

At issue, in the appraisal of the liberal view, was the historicity of the life of Jesus. Criticism varied from moderate to radical points of view, but on one point it was agreed: namely, that the gospels are intended, not to teach the humanity of Jesus in a faith-founding sense, but to sketch the Christ as pictured in the early church — a picture indicative of the arch-belief of the Christian church but in no respect biographical. By this route it was thought possible to maintain one's critical orientation and still give a true account of the significance of the church's witness.

It is therefore of extraordinary interest to ask whether the shift from the "historical" Jesus — the Jesus who is in fact a man of like passions as we are — to the Christ of the infant church has had any effect on the crisis of the dual nature doctrine.

For many people this shift was a liberation; it gave them perspective amid the endless difficulties spawned for them by the historical-critical school. Historical criticism used to have the function of rendering uncertain what had previously been established. What was left, after all, when the gospel of John proved to be unauthentic? and when it became evident that the gospel writers had pictured Jesus in the light of the Resurrection? In that period it was still customary to rid the gospel picture of the accretions for which the early church was responsible. That was the "uncertain" path to the historical Jesus — and a wavering way it was.

In this situation the change which took place in New Testament research was that the gospel witness, the witness of faith, was no longer accorded a priori disqualification. It was Kähler in particular who, in the confusion of historical research, pointed the way to the kerygma. His major premise was that we do not have reliable sources on the life of Jesus. "I view the entire 'Life-of-Jesus movement' as going up a dead alley." It is simply impossible to get behind the witness of the gospels. One cannot return from the biblical Christ to a historical Jesus.[16] If this were possible, faith would be completely dependent on scientific research. But no — the gospels are testimonies of faith. They are not intended to inform us, biographically, on the historical Jesus but rather to generate faith in Jesus Christ. They are not a piece of historical reporting but "Urkunde" on which preaching is based.[17] This solution of Kähler, says Althaus, is "the liberating answer" which frees us from the historical-critical school. Doubts could now be vanquished, since belief was no longer contingent on historical research. One simply had to listen to the preaching of this biblical Christ. The earlier historical approach thus stands discredited by the idea of "testimony." Here the true Christ confronts us. Historical problems lose much of their

---

16. M. Kähler, *Der sogenannte historische Jesus und der geschichtliche, biblische Christus*, second edition, 1928.
17. *Ibid.*, page 22.

frightening difficulty.[18] Without exaggeration it can be said
that the basic theory of Kähler has been, and is still, very
influential. Whoever reads Brunner, for instance, and finds
him ready to agree rather cordially with the results of higher
criticism and nonetheless eager to think and speak positively
in line with the New Testament kerygma, will perceive unmistakable echoes of Kähler's original theory.

And on this basis, we may ask, what happens to Christology?
For — this much is clear to everyone — not all difficulties are
thus easily solved. Even the kerygmatic conception of the
gospels leaves us with the troublesome question to what extent
we are facing the true, historical Christ in these testimonies
of faith. An inquiry as to the authority of one who brings a
message is always in order. While one may not always demand evidence for the truth of a given testimony, the point of
its authority can be significantly raised. It is not surprising,
therefore, that Christology, also where the kerygmatic point of
view has almost universal sway, remains completely at the
mercy of whatever conclusions are drawn from this kerygma-
concept.

But more remains to be said about this problem. It is
undeniable that the gospels do not enable us to write the life
of Jesus and that they were consciously written to summon
people to faith in Jesus Christ. Ridderbos has conclusively
demonstrated from the synoptic gospels that they must be
understood as "the proclamation of the Christ to posterity."[19]
"Not the *when* but the *that,* not the biographical but the Christ-
proclaiming motif dominates."[20]

At the same time Ridderbos points out that the problem is
not thus swept aside. For "the real and the deeper question
at issue concerns the relation between the kerygma and the
history of which it speaks; in other words, are we, in the

18. P. Althaus, *Der "Historische Jesus" und der biblische Christus,*
Theol. Aufs., II, pages 162ff.
19. H. N. Ridderbos, *Zelfopenbaring en Zelfverberging,* page 32.
20. *Ibid,* page 33.

gospels, confronted by the person of Jesus Christ as he existed in the belief of the church and as he was then read back into the life of Jesus of Nazareth — or is the Christ of the early church also the Christ of history, the Christ therefore who in fact preached to the multitudes, performed miracles, suffered, died, and rose again from the dead?"

The answer to this question involves the reliability of the gospel. The historical record may have been strongly influenced by its kerygmatic purpose, but the final purpose of the gospel nonetheless is to demonstrate the truthfulness of what has been said of the Christ.[21] One need not object when it is said that the gospels have been written out of faith; this faith, after all, is the conviction that the historical Christ is the Son of God. No one escapes the difficulties of historical criticism by means of a formal kerygma-concept. We need not be surprised, therefore, that the conflict about Jesus Christ and the confession of the church, despite the kerygma-theory, continues unabated.

The central problem of the nineteenth century, that of faith and science (historical science included), affected also later conceptions of the gospel of Jesus Christ.

He who seeks detachment from history in a speculative theology and renders the historical relative by making it general — the historical, that is, in the person of Christ — can ignore these problems. In idealistic fashion he has laid aside the problems of theanthropy. The solution of the kerygma is not solution, at least, not for anyone who has granted the historical Christ a central place in his faith and theology. In the kerygma-scheme the same questions recur, the more since we are now face to face with the preaching of responsibility and with testimonies of faith which are considered basic to Christology. The old difficulties are inescapable — consider, for example, the theories of Bultmann in which the crisis of the dual nature doctrine stands out sharply against the backdrop

---

21. *Ibid,* page 33.

of the kerygma-concept. Bultmann speaks of the kerygma of the primitive church and that of the hellenistic church.[22] But this witness Bultmann now subjects to a critical analysis. The primitive witness is not such that modern man can simply accept it. And this analysis led him ever more clearly to a program of myth-removal.[23] This program is needed, says he, because myth has an important place in the kerygma. Preaching in a modern world must be honest. And the encounter between gospel and the modern man has a peculiar complexity because the world-picture of the New Testament is mythological in character.

This mythology proceeds from the assumption of a heaven in which dwells God while earth is the arena of conflict between supernatural forces, between God and his angels on the one hand, and Satan and his demonic assistants on the other. Now here, now there, they interrupt the natural course of events. At present this world is still under demonic management but this situation will be terminated when the heavenly judge appears in the Resurrection of the dead.

It is Bultmann's conviction that the Christian account of the events of redemption accord with this mythological world-picture. Ideas like "the fulness of time," and God sending his Son, who appears on earth both as a pre-existent divine being and as a human being, who bears sin and brings reconciliation, overcomes demons, dies and rises from the dead in order, at some later date, to reappear as World-Judge on the clouds of heaven — all this belongs to the mythological mind, says Bultmann, and he adds that this world-picture has ceased to be of force to us. Hence the problem of myth-removal.

"The present-day Christian pulpit faces the question therefore whether, when it demands faith of man, it expects him

---

22. R. Bultmann, *Theol. des N. T.*, pages 34 and 64.
23. *N. T. und Mythology. Das Problem der Entmythologisierung der N. T. Verkundigung,* beitr. zur evang. Theol., 1941, pages 27ff.

to acknowledge this past, mythological world-picture."[24]   If this be an unreasonable request, as Bultmann thinks it is, then the next question is whether there is nonetheless truth in the New Testament witness — dependent as it is on this mythological cast of thought. If there is, it is the task of theology to peel off the mythological wrappings and present the true contents of the Christian message, a message which need no longer outrage the sensibilities of modern man. What sense is there to the confession: "descended into hell, and ascended into heaven," when we no longer take seriously the world-picture of which this confession forms an integral part? "And so we are done with the stories of Christ's descent into hell and ascent into heaven; done, too, with the expected return, on the clouds of heaven, of the Son of man and with the expected 'rapture' of believers who were to meet him in the air."

Honesty is the watch-word here, says Bultmann. Just as in the Orient mythological religion is on the way out in proportion to the spread of medical and hygienic care, so the New Testament mythology will cease to satisfy us to the extent we live by other conceptions. The church may not be left in doubt as to what it is to regard as true and what not. The only way out is that of myth-divestment — and the New Testament itself points more or less in this direction.[25] The question is meanwhile whether one can strip away the mythical material without injuring the core of the kerygma. Since such misconstrual of the kerygma often took place in the past, the question is of no small moment. What remains of the "events of Redemption" once we set our feet on this road? Is there in the kerygma a message which remains true even for myth-scorning modern man? If one dissociates himself from a conceptual world of myth and from the ideas of late-Jewish apocalyptic literature and of gnosis, can he still preach anything with

---

24. Bultmann, *Op. cit.,* page 29 compare W. Klaas, *Der moderne Mensch in Theologie R. Bultmanns,* pages 4ff.
25. *Ibid.,* page 37.

authority? Can one speak of "Christian" events, of God acting in Christ without lapsing, whether in thought or word, into mythology?[26]

In the New Testament the Christian events are always pictured mythologically but is such procedure necessary? A peculiarity of the New Testament, says Bultmann, is that in it mythology and history are intertwined. Jesus Christ, as Son of God and pre-existent divine being, is a mythical personage; but at the same time, as Jesus of Nazareth, he is a historical personage. His father and mother are known and still he is pre-existent. On the one hand we have the Cross — which is historical; and on the other, the Resurrection — which is mythological. That is the problem preoccupying Bultmann. To Paul this juxtapostion of the historical and mythical is precisely the mystery which enshrouds the Christ: God revealed in flesh. But Bultmann cannot see it that way. He believes that the mythological (pre-existence, among other things) is intended to accentuate the importance of the person of Christ. This intent appears in the Cross and the Resurrection. In the New Testament the Cross is a mythical event, because it is the preexistent Son of God who is crucified, and because his blood has substitutionary and death-destroying significance. All this is unacceptable to the modern mind. In the New Testament, however, the historical event of the Cross is "elevated to a position of cosmic dimensions."[27] In reality it is an historical event but the record of the event places it in decisive and eschatological perspective.

And therefore to remove the mythical husk from the New Testament witness is not necessarily to destroy the witness itself. On the contrary: the historical event, cast in mythological mold, enables us to discover the meaning of the Cross in which God, full of grace and forgiveness, comes to this world, In reality the Cross is not a mythical but an historical event of

26. *Ibid.*, page 59.
27. *Ibid.*, page 61.

great significance. The mythical entourage hints at this significance, but need not itself be accepted by us.

The Resurrection is another matter. For now we are given
no more, according to Bultmann, than "an expression of the
importance of the Cross." The story points to the fact that
the Cross of Christ must not be viewed as a purely human
death, but "as the liberating judgment of God upon this
world." Hence the interconnection between Cross and Resurrection. They are not to be understood as two consecutive
high-points in the history of redemption. The Resurrection is
not a miracle, as it is pictured in the New Testament — for
instance, in the legends of the empty tomb and post-Resurrec-
tion appearances. But these are later forms of which Paul
knew as yet nothing. Neither is the Resurrection an historic
fact — no one returned from the dead — but it is rather an
object of faith. "The Easter-event understood as Resurrection
is not historical; only the Easter-faith of the disciples is intelligible as an historical event."[28] For this reason, Christian
faith is not interested in the historicity of the Resurrection.
The pivotal point here is the meaning of God's action in the
Cross. Easter-faith points in that direction — even though
the form of this reference must indeed be viewed as historical,
as it is in St. Paul. But this is fatal reasoning. For we are
interested not in an historical resurrection but in the meaning
of the Cross. It is here that God acts and his action is not
mythical but historical. It is not a supernatural act but historical reality. God has reconciled the world to himself.
Therefore the historical man Jesus must be preached in his
redemptive-historical meaning. He is the eschatological word
of God to the world. That is the skandalon, the offense, which
can be overcome only by faith. It is an act or gift of God. In
this act death and resurrection belong together. To see the
connection is to understand St. Paul. He refers to the Resurrection of Christ as "objective fact," and supports its his-

---

28. *Ibid.*, page 66.

toricity by citing many witnesses.[29]   He interprets the death
of Christ in the categories of gnostic myth, but the modern
mind is not to be reached in this manner, for acceptance of this
interpretation would require the credibility of the previously
announced facts of pre-existence, incarnation, and resurrection.
Facts however do not have the power to address us.   We are
interested, not in gnostic fineries, but in the meaning of the
Cross.   The word of the Cross alone can penetrate the heart
of man for it places him before a decision concerning the
redemptive acts of God.   This is the truth of the ages — a
truth which remains valid even when the New Testament has
been divested of its mythical coloring.

*   *   *

In the theology of Bultmann we are undoubtedly at the
critical nadir of the doctrine of theanthropy.   This theology
pretends to approach the New Testament witness under the
aspect of pastoral honesty toward modern man — a man ac-
customed to a cosmic environment differing from that in which
the New Testament arose.   There is here no preaching of a
historical Jesus, as was the case in the nineteenth century, when
the attempt was made to display the man Jesus in a blaze of
glittering qualities; on the contrary, the New Testament
teachings of pre-existence, incarnation, historical resurrection
and ascension, are fully acknowledged.   There is not even an
effort to show, for instance, that pre-existence in the New
Testament should be understood in different terms — on the
hypothesis that the sacred authors had conceived it as other
than the pre-mundane existence of the Logos.   But at the end
all this is cast aside as myth.

The consequences for the dogma of the church are plain.
Nothing remains of it but the historical Jesus who becomes
the crucified one.   This cross, however, is not the failure of

29. Bultmann, *Theol. des N. T.*, pages 290-299.

the man Jesus but God acting to reconcile the world. Not a shred remains of the *"vere deus, vere homo."* In John's Gospel the prologue ends with the revelation of the Logos who "became flesh," but Bultmann explains: "The argument is in the idiom of mythology."[30] A major part of gnostic salvation-mythology is that a divine being, the Son of the Supreme God assumed the form of a man, veiled himself in human flesh and blood, to bring revelation and redemption.

The mystery in the Son of man, as confused by Paul and the church, is no more. The mythical residue in the New Testament witness has been drained out. It is evident by now that the "liberating answer" which many a man saw in the kerygmatic view of the gospels cannot, in the least, be called a way out of the impasse. The problems surrounding the person of Christ remain.

It is not hard to perceive, in Bultmann's position, the decisive influence of modern scientific thought. The differences between him and the nineteenth century may be considerable but not so great as to exclude the influence of a rationalism which in effect shuts God out of a mechanistically conceived nature. In Bultmann we encounter precisely the same arguments as those used by modernist theologians in the nineteenth century against the possibility of the Incarnation and of the Resurrection. It is on the basis of this philosophical point of view that Bultmann came to the necessity of myth-debunking. The fact that he proceeds from a pastoral and missionary motive — namely, to preserve modern man from rejecting the New Testament because of its mythical structure — does not diminish by one iota the theological presumption of this undertaking. The conflict over the church's dogma of the two natures ends here with a declaration that what the church regards as Christ's essence is myth. What in the dogma of the church are regarded as God's acts in history are devalu-

---

30. Bultmann, *Das Evang. des Johannes,* page 38.

ated by Bultmann to the status of a religious fancy. Theology can sink no farther. The witness of the Scriptures and the dogma found on them are pushed aside and the cross is made into the irrational fact of a decision in which man comes to know himself. At a given moment everything is at stake; the history of redemption is condensed into the "meaning" of the cross. But the cross is stripped of its entire context. And thus God can still act meaningfully while we retain our modern world-picture. The biblical Jesus Christ, whom the kerygma-the-ologians wished to find, is bidden adieu at the suggestion that now the mythical world-view has become untenable.[31]

In conclusion we wish to devote our attention to the forms which the crisis of the dual-nature doctrine assumed in Dutch theology during the nineteenth and twentieth century.

This crisis is most patent in the polemics conducted, for about a century, by and against modernism in the Netherlands. The crisis came to the fore particularly in the theology of Scholten, the father of the modern movement, who purposed to develop Christology along Reformed lines. At first blush he seems to maintain the doctrine of the two natures. He brings on the carpet both the heresies condemned by the early church and the decisions made at Nicea and Chalcedon. Then he posits the important question whether Protestantism has preserved and applied the principles established at these councils

---

31. Without entering fully upon a discussion of Bultmann's position, we would stress one point in which his view emerges as clearly untenable. When Bultmann says that John uses the gnostic mythology of redemption to build up his picture of the person and work of Christ (*Theol. des N. T.*, page 387), he is obliged to add immediately that John does not view the incarnation — in gnostic fashion — as a cosmic phenomenon. Besides this, he has to concede many other points of difference (*Ibid.*, page 387). In this same connection he observes that John polemicizes against the gnostic heretics whom he believes to be allied with the Anti-Christ. "It is exactly because John employs the gnostic redeemer-myth for his picture of the person and work of Jesus, that delimitation over against the gnosis is to him such a pressing assignment" (*Ibid.*, page 287).

In connection with these differences — which are far from peripheral — Gaugler is of the opinion that the gnostic myth was not present to John's mind, because "the decisive features are missing" (E. Gaugler, in *Jesus Christus im Zeugnis der H. Schrift und der Kirche*, page 53).

— a question which Scholten answers in the negative. Lutheranism, for instance, has definite monophysite tendencies, while Reformed Christology (Calvin) was unable to rise above the Nestorian idea of separation.[32]

Its Christology, though intended to be anti-Nestorian, remained deficient. Hence, says Scholten, we must try to overcome these deficiencies by concentrating on the great and determinative Christological principle of "the unity of the divine and human nature in Christ in accordance with the teaching of John that the Word became flesh." We must seek for a unity transcending the Lutheran and Reformed Christologies, and the search will be rewarded only if we desist from thinking of God and man as opposites. For in Christ appears the unity of the divine and the human. He is the God-man, but as such he is not unique, nor is he isolated. For what Christ was, this his church must become in and through him.[33] Thus we observe, at the beginning of the development of modern theology in the Netherlands, the strong influence of speculative Christology. The unity of the divine and the human is elevated, in Hegelian style, above the confession of the church that Christ was truly God and truly man. And so we can understand why Scholten sets his jaw especially against Docetism. He defends the humanity of Christ because it forms the basis on which the unity of the divine and the human can be attained.

*   *   *

In the subsequent development of modernism in the Netherlands the dogma of the two natures in Christ remained a rock of offense. Observable everywhere was the tension between the Christian faith and the modern idea of science. The result was the rejection of church dogma. Had modernism remained on this level, there would be no purpose to any further re-

---

32. Scholten, *L. d. H. K.,* II, page 303.
33. *Ibid.,* page 355.

flection on other modernist theologians. But now we face the
fact that in this century a reaction has set in against the old
modernist Christology.

When Roessingh began to tabulate the distinguishing features of this new movement, he referred to a dualism — over
against the monism of the old modernists — a resistance to
the anti-supernaturalism of the older movement, and the intent to be specifically Christian. He spoke of a shift in
modernism and was aware that this shift was intimately related to its confession of Christ. Roessingh began to speak
again of a Christ-centered theology, and to construct a Christology, be it on a critical foundation. He resumed rapport with
the Christian tradition because there the tragic opposition
between sin and grace was more profoundly experienced, said
he, than in the old modernism, which softpedalled this dramatic
antithesis.[34] Our hearts go out again, Roessingh admits, to
this Christian tradition and, "in the high-points of our preaching, we find ourselves returning, almost willy-nilly, to the
old home of orthodoxy."[35]

At the same time Roessingh is conscious that in many respects his views are very close to the liberal tradition of a
century ago. On the one hand he tries to escape the old
modernistic anti-supernaturalism as well as monism, and the
iron causalities of natural law which leave no room for personality and religion; for there is a break in the causal net of
events, an incursion of the other world into our world, or,
to put it religiously, a reciprocal action between man and God;
but, on the other, this does not mean that the Scriptural miracle
is to resume its place of honor. The expansion of the idea of
causality does not yet justify caprice and, further, Roessingh
has scruples about accepting the miraculous world of the New
Testament. His opposition to monism is intended merely to
open the way for the possibility of an individual religious life,

---

34. Roessingh, *Verz. Werken* I, page 193.
35. *Ibid.*, page 194.

which has nothing to do, meanwhile, with the broad spaces of history. Roessingh's supernaturalism leads to no historical consequences. The moment he thinks he has rescued a reciprocal action between God and man, the strong pressure of historical criticism becomes noticeable.

Of particular importance are his remarks about the specifically Christian character of this new modernism. He finds himself placed before the doctrine of the dual nature and tries, without forfeiture of his modernistic point of view, to construct a Christology. In all this he is far from satisfied with the old liberal picture of Jesus. In this picture, that which is central in Christianity, namely, the grace of God in Christ, is missing. However critical we may be of the Bible stories, Christ is nevertheless experienced again and again as the power of God. He is a reality, and "more reality than anything else in history."[36] This confession, however, posits the problem of the relationship between faith and history — a problem which began increasingly to preoccupy Roessingh. What has the Christ-picture of the primitive church to do with our personal faith? This burning question Roessingh found himself unable to escape and his answer is noteworthy: "My two-fold answer is: Nothing and everything. The 'nothing' distinguishes me from the mainstream of orthodox theology; the 'everything,' from a large number of liberals." He who understands this "everything" and "nothing" has grasped the core of Roessingh's Christology. The "nothing" registers dissent from every effort to direct faith to some immovable point of reference in the midst of the relativity of history. This road, Roessingh declares with emphasis, he cannot travel.[37] The foundation of truth which is to undergird our faith cannot be found within history. "History means nothing to me any more as regards faith." From this position one might

36. Compare *Verz. Werken,* II, page 304: ". . . Christ, not as I view him or as somebody else views him, but as he is, in his timeless absoluteness."
37. *Ibid.,* page 308.

draw the conclusion that the historical, also in Christ, to Roessingh, could be at best a symbol or illustration, in idealistic fashion, of eternal truth. To do justice to him, however, we must notice also the "everything." How can it co-exist with the "nothing"? What is the meaning of this paradoxical answer, as he himself calls it?

It is a fact that Roessingh, after he has declared history useless to one's faith, nonetheless proceeds to the re-instatement of history. He wonders whether it is conservatism or a coincidence that religion orientates itself recurrently to the historical. There is an intuitive sense of the meaning of history. History is "metaphysically lit up, and something more is operative in it than causally related coincidence." In it the Spirit is struggling to realize itself. We must of course transcend an orthodoxy which knows exactly where this takes place. Modern man cannot believe that normativity, absolute validity, or perfect value, can be fully bound up in one empirical fact.[38]

There are nevertheless — and this cannot be denied — certain "centers of divine life" on which we live. Roessingh is now about to render his confession of Christ: "To me Christ is the center of history. And this means that I am forced to confess — forced by my view of the spiritual movements of the past, by my reaction to the totality of things — that in Christ I find the highest value present to me in history; in him I find revealed, to a high degree, the metaphysical contents of cosmic reality; in Christ I finally grasp something of the tragic mystery of human life and of this world. And so I choose him. I may be wrong: people have often been wrong in their evaluations. But that is the risk which insures that our relationship to history will always be vital and presses us ever forward to new conquests; the centralization of our faith in Christ remains an act which must ever be repeated."[39] And therefore Roessingh speaks of placing oneself at the dis-

38. *Ibid.*, page 311.
39. *Ibid.*, page 312.

posal of "that historical revelation out of which there comes
to us the voice of God. That to me is Christ."

Center of history, turning-point in my life, unique concentration of values, embodiment of normativity: "I would be
cutting the ground from under my life and work, if with all
these I should now shrink from the risk."[40] In this position he
believes he has preserved continuity with the core of the Christology of all time. Christ is Lord of all, of the world: he is
the cosmic Christ in the history of the world. Indeed, he is
"God in the world." The impression Roessingh receives of
Christ from the New Testament is so potent that, on this
point at least, he wants to limit the competence of a special
science like theology. But at the same time he displays a certain hesitation. Uncertainty concerning the Christ remains.
Hence Roessingh admits that the distance between the Christ
of the New Testament and the Christ of history is considerable.
His Christology fails in the end to remain in touch with the
historical Jesus of Nazareth. But should we lose the guarantee
of historicity, Christ would nonetheless remain "the value-
center" of history. Radical scepticism of the New Testament
does not in the least seem necessary to Roessingh but he is
prepared in principle to take this scepticism with complete
seriousness.

Tension between this reality, "which is greater than anything else in history," and historical relativity is the pivotal
problem of Roessingh's Christology. In it we are faced with
a moving struggle between the biblical witness and modern
thought, which is opposed to a completely historical revelation.
In 1924 Roessingh wrote a letter which highlights this struggle: "I am in search of a synthesis between the principles of
idealistic philosophy and the principles of the Christian Reformation."[41] But he immediately adds: ". . . perhaps such
a synthesis cannot be found at all. . . ."

---

40. *Ibid.*, page 313.
41. *Verzamelde Werken* I, XII; Heering, *Geloof en Openbaring* I,
page 259.

With these words, spoken in the last phase of his theological development, Roessingh accurately characterizes his own thinking. In the history of Christology the Idealistic current has always tended to disavow the significance, the decisive significance, of history.[42] The absolute revelation of God in history always seemed to Idealism a threat to the autonomy of the human spirit; for then it would be subordinated to a position of dependence on historical fact. Roessingh too admitted that his concern was for this autonomy. It was his intent to rescue personality and religion from the clutch of monism; but in this passionate struggle he viewed the authority of the Holy Scriptures and the determinative value of the facts of redemption as an intolerable threat to human autonomy. Not without benefit Roessingh had followed the lectures of the teacher Hermann, a champion fighter against all heteronomy.

Roessingh was out to find a synthesis between Idealism and the Reformation. And however hesitant he may be in his conclusions, his search is unflagging. In dialectical theology he admires the heavily underscored paradoxical nature of sin and grace but his appreciation is limited: "Our ancestral head is Erasmus and, whether we like it or not, we cannot banish him." And in characterizing Liberalism, he expressed himself with great clarity: "The Roman Catholic Church and other dogmatically bound groups may now be far ahead, and may have been ahead for a long time, in the psychological control and guidance of the masses, but at the bottom, in the central rationale of their great systems, they are no longer true — they are spent, and obsolete." The entire development of modern philosophy, our knowledge of history, and Bible-criticism, has made imperative an absolute break with all these old, though strong and fruitful, traditions.[43]

---

42. Compare H. Groos, *Der deutsche Idealismus und das Christentum,* pages 178ff.

43. Roessingh, *Op. cit.,* IV, page 405.

To Roessingh's mind, in our opinion, the greatest conflict existed between the concept of autonomy and the revelation of God in the historic Christ. His Christology, and his appraisal of the cosmic Christ, is determined by his autonomy.[44] In essence it is the same old problem which occupied Scholten when he stated his views on the Reformed doctrine of the testimony of the Spirit. This testimony as interpreted by Scholten is antithetic to all external authority.[45] And Roessingh too arrives at that conclusion: "The final criterion, the last authority, to which I must defer, consists in the testimony of my own spirit." The most telling aspect of Roessingh's struggle is his uncertainty whether a synthesis between Idealism and the Reformation would be possible.

*   *   *

It was Roessingh who tossed up the problem of Modernism versus Orthodoxy, also in connection with Christology: and when he died at the age of thirty-nine (1925), in the midst of his theological development, one naturally wondered what the development of his type of modernism would be. W. J. Aalders wrote concerning Roessingh's conception of Christ: "We are in the twilight: who knows whether it is the twilight of the evening or that of dawn?" The answer came from Heering who provided the next stage of this neo-modernistic trend. His theology was the more interesting because he was a fairly strong critic of Roessingh whose theology, says he, does not offer sufficient foothold and lacks the basic categories of faith and revelation.

Roessingh did not adequately ground his theology in the Gospel — in the biblical kerygma — and could not avoid embarrassment in the end.[46] Heering does concur with Roessingh in his conception of autonomy, and to him also ortho-

---

44. *Ibid.*, IV, page 237.
45. Scholten, *Op. cit.*, page 183.
46. Heering, *Geloof en Openbaring*, I, page 269.

doxy is on the wrong track.   But one need not continue to
totter on the edge of complete scepticism.   There is a foothold
and a foundation in the Gospel.   Heering seems at first blush
to have advanced far beyond Roessingh in his Christology.
And this impression is strengthened when Heering tells us
that to him the basic motifs of Roessingh's Christology —
Christ as "value-center" and "image of totality" — are much
too feeble.   Heering who wishes to get far beyond this point
speaks of Jesus' coming into the world — of the appearance
of the Eternal One in history.   What he is after is the revelation of God in history, the revelation of his great redemptive
act of love by which he condescends, in human form, to draw
to his great heart a poor and lost humanity.   But the acknowledgement of this truth of revelation is by no means dependent,
according to Heering, on the acceptance of the dogma of the
Incarnation.   On the contrary, this teaching clashes with the
reality of religious experience.   The doctrine of Incarnation
as a theory arose gradually in the early church and its origin
must be attributed, not to the New Testament, but to the
church-father Irenaeus.   It is unknown to the synoptic gospels.
And when Heering encounters the Gospel of John in the course
of his ruminations, he feels obliged to reject its prologue.   It
may be a profound meditation of the revelation of God in
Christ, but it cannot itself be revelation.   The church, giving
asylum to this speculative theory, first established the deity of
Christ, then his humanity, and finally the unity of the two
natures.   This doctrine represents an effort to enter into
the secrets of God.   Heering would rather speak of the divinity
than of the deity of Jesus because the word "deity" is too
reminiscent of the second person of the Trinity.

   With great clarity he formulates his point of view: "However illuminating this truth (namely, the eternity, holiness,
and divinity of Jesus Christ) may be, and although we too
believe in the Son in this sense, we can honestly confess that
we have never felt any religious need to reflect on the origin

and pre-existence of Jesus, or on the Incarnation of the Word, in short, on all that is bound up in the old doctrine of the church with the Incarnation."[47]   Seldom flowed a more devastating judgment from a modern pen.   But this non-reflection is the more unjustified because over against it we have Heering's Christology, which designates Christ as "the embodiment of God's Spirit."   It is noteworthy that in Heering's theology an appeal is made to reverence mystery.   This respect for mystery forbids us to conceive the sonship of Christ, as does the doctrine of the church, in realistic and biological terms. Christ's being and appearance are mysteries.[48]

With an appeal to the reality of mystery the modernism of Heering turns its back upon the mystery of which the Scriptures speak and of which the church has always devoutly stammered. It is unnecessary to say much more of Heering's views.   We prefer the practically permanent hesitation which marks the course of Roessingh's thought. In Heering there is no hesitation whatever; and his complaint that Roessingh's theology is without normativity and without foundation boomerangs upon himself.   This criticism of Heering is as unfair a verdict as ever was issued in the history of Modernism, at least as viewed in the light of his own dogmatic creations.   Heering's theology has a still smaller claim to be associated with historic Christianity than has Roessingh's.   The twilight which Aalders mentioned has now changed into dark night.

*   *   *

Having pointed out a few high-points in the crisis enveloping the doctrine of theanthropy, we are now in a position to sketch a few reactions to this crisis.   Let no one think that the onslaughts of criticism went unchallenged.   Apart from the defenses offered by Reformed theology in the nineteenth and twentieth centuries, there were evidences in many direc-

---

47. *Ibid.*, II, page 157.
48. *Ibid.*, II, page 149.

tions of greater understanding and purer insight. In earlier times it seemed that a mere breath of criticism of the word "nature" was enough to upset the theological mind. Nowadays it is understood by at least a few people that the truth of God is at stake — the truth of which the church had to give an account, in unavoidably human fashion, by way of dogmatic utterances. Compare, for instance, the Christology of Gerretsen and Aalders' book on the Incarnation. Gerretsen stands squarely in the critical tradition. There are no differences between Arius and Athanasius, to his mind, because both reason from a metaphysical, instead of from an ethical, conception of God. The ethical point of view proceeds from the love and the will of God, but the church bases its doctrines on the ontological: an arid wilderness from which can spring no new life.[49] The Greek mind submerged the simplicity of the Gospel with the aid of the concept "nature." In this manner ethical theology contributed its quota of destruction to the doctrine of the two natures. Since that time, however, ethical theology has struck a different note. We are thinking now of the publications of Aalders and Korff. Aalders rates Nicea as a triumph of the church over idolatry. The mystery of the person of Christ is faithfully reflected in the creeds of the church: in that of Chalcedon, for instance, whose negative stipulations are in keeping with the mystery of the Son of man. Vigorously Aalders defends the unity, as well as the duality, of Christ's natures.[50] Korff, in his Christology, is on the same track. To him also the doctrine of the church is a confession of faith and by no means speculation. God came to this world in Jesus Christ: that is the truth which the church has tried to express in its doctrine of the two natures.[51]

*   *   *

Our rejoicing would be premature were we to suppose that the time is almost past when a man can thrust aside the dogma

49. J. H. Gerretsen, *Christologie*, page 31.
50. W. J. Aalders, *De Incarnatie*, 1933.
51. F. W. Korff, *Christologie*.

of the church as so much metaphysical speculation and still get a hearing. Through various causes there was an increased interest, both in the Netherlands and elsewhere, in the Christological pronouncements of the ancient church. Dialectical theology, namely that of Barth and Brunner, was decidedly critical of the Christology of the nineteenth century and resumed the defense of the ecumenical decisions of the church. It became strongly apparent how eager these men were to dissociate themselves from the dogma-evaluation of Harnack and others; witness, for example, Brunner's resistance, in his book on the Mediator, to Harnack's point of view.[52] The situation was all the more dramatic because here was a theology which called a halt to a fierce and unsparing criticism while it did not itself wish to be considered a return to the pristine theology of the Reformation. In the Netherlands, too, new voices, emitting a new sound, were heard from modernistic quarters. An example is *"De Christologie van het Nieuwe Testament,"* produced by G. Sevenster, who came to the conclusion, in his analysis of the New Testament witness, that the old orthodox exegesis of statements made by and concerning Christ was truly based on Scripture. Sevenster rejected, for instance, the sharp cleavage which modern theology had earlier said existed between Jesus and Paul, and indicated that the unity of the New Testament is far greater than used to be believed. He acknowledged that in the Synoptic Gospels there is repeated mention of the pre-existence of Christ; and of the Christology of Adoptianism, he says, there is not a trace.[53] One can speak without exaggeration of a transformed modern exegesis. A comparison of Sevenster and Heering will bring out the striking difference between the new and the old. The change which thus took place in exegesis carried over into dogmatics. Vos, for instance, takes the confession of the two natures under his theological wings and fights off misconceptions of it. The

52. See Chapter XIII of Brunner's book.
53. G. Sevenster, *De Christologie van het N. T.,* page 106.

church speaks of two natures and thereby indicates its reverence in the presence of mystery.[54] "It is enough to believe the fact that Jesus Christ was simultaneously God and man in the unity of his person." This idea is not a projection of the church, says Vos, but a mysterious truth to which Scripture testifies. In his book returns the argument which was often employed by orthodox writers (Kuyper, among others) against the modern adoration of Jesus. This argument is based upon the self-conscious utterances of Jesus Christ about his relationship to the Father and his power to forgive sins. "Jesus speaks with divine authority and now we have to make our choice: Either he speaks the truth or he does not. If he does not, we have again two possibilities: He utters falsehood either consciously or not. Should it be deliberate falsehood, he is the greatest deceiver known to history; should it be unconscious falsehood, he is the most pathetic victim of religious megalomania known to history. Given these possibilities we prefer to believe that Jesus Christ spoke the truth and had the right to speak with divine authority simply because he was God."[55] In direct opposition to Heering, Vos posits the thesis that the doctrine of the Incarnation is soundly biblical. In his book the old, orthodox appeal to Scripture is again given its place. Quotations from all the Gospels and the Epistles, quotations full of praise for Jesus Christ, again make their appearance, while the pre-existence of Christ is viewed as integral with the New Testament witness. "One cannot avoid teaching Christ's pre-existence: if Jesus Christ be God, then he existed before he became man."[56] The irrefragable connection between Christ's Deity and his eternal pre-existence here find emphatic expression.

*   *   *

It need not surprise us that it was Heering who raised a warning cry against a weakening of the critical point of view

54. H. de Vos, *Ons algemeen Chr. Geloof,* page 191.
55. *Ibid.,* page 193.
56. *Ibid.,* page 198.

among modern theologians. He frankly expressed his profound alarm. Among other things he posited the theses: (1)
Liberal protestant theology has, during the last forty years,
re-discovered many an evangelical truth (for whose eclipse
the church was responsible as well) and for that reason it
underwent a profound change — visible especially in its Christology. This change was an internal necessity and it took
place on good critical grounds. (2) Critical responsibility,
under present-day conditions, imposes on liberal protestant
theology the duty to resist the suction of ecclesiastical tradition;
for this suction, reinforced by external circumstances, exerts
a strong pull these days.[57]
   The danger of yielding to the pull of tradition he attributes
to the spiritual confusion and insecurity of our day which
makes the troubled mind look for stability in an untroubled
tradition. The same Heering who in 1913 warned against
the superficialities of the older modernism, in 1948 issues a
ringing plea for the good rights of criticism over against the
tradition of the church. And over against a semi-critical
theology he takes up the cudgels for "the tradition of thorough
criticism and intellectual honesty." Sevenster in particular
is a thorn in his flesh because his Christology, almost from
beginning to end, adheres to the tradition which teaches that
the New Testament is controlled by a single Christology.
   The crisis in Christology is far from exhausted. Any number of Christological problems are now being broached which
prove that the conflict between orthodoxy and modernism is
by no means a thing of the past. The doctrines of the Virgin
Birth and of Reconciliation are still very much in dispute.
Here and there in modern theology is a sign of unrest and
perturbation; off and on we note a self-criticism which is
amazing. This self-criticism, on points long established in
modern liberal theology, is all the more encouraging because
it results from continued inquiry into the Scriptures. We

57. G. J. Heering, *Theologie en Praktijk,* June and July, 1948.

perceive anew something of the power of the unfettered Word
of God and of the perspicuity, confessed by the church, of the
Sacred Scriptures, by which human wisdom is put to shame.
But it has become clearer than ever that the orthodox believer
in Christ, in the midst of all the dangers that continually
beset him, is called upon to witness in this hour of confusion:
to witness to the personal relevancy of the question asked at
Caesarea Philippi: to testify that the crisis of the doctrine
of the two natures is not merely a theoretical matter but a
religious crisis. The church may not cease, even at the risk
of being accused of pride, from being earnest with the earnestness of John, nor from warning with the zeal of Paul.

Ecumenical Decisions

CHAPTER III

Ecumenical Decisions

I N Chapter II we ran repeatedly into criticism of the confession of the church which, in the eyes of many, is unable to give expression to the faith of our day. It is desirable, therefore, to acquaint ourselves somewhat with the pronouncements of the early church uttered when the church was compelled by the rise of heresies to confess its faith in concrete terms. The motives governing the church in this conflict are not hard to find. Without entering fully into the details one can say that the ancient church rose to defend both the deity and the humanity of Christ.

The Christological conflict began to rage on a large scale in the fourth century. In the year 325 at Nicea the church condemned the heresy of Arius who denied the deity of Christ. In the same century, at Constantinople in 381, the church was obliged to express its disapproval of Apollinaris who in the judgment of the church did not do justice to the truly human nature of the Savior. In the fifth century the church began increasingly to reflect on the relationship between these two natures; preoccupation with this problem led, in vigorous opposition to the heresy of Nestorius and Eutyches, to the decisive and influential fixation of Christological doctrine at Chalcedon in the year 451. This summary indicates the course of Christological development in the fourth and fifth centuries. What followed was largely explication and defense of positions taken earlier. We shall try, in brief outline, to indicate the significance both of the conflict in the church and of the decisions made by the church.

A. NICEA, 325 A. D.

The year 325 will always remain a mile-post in the development of Christological reflection in the church. At this time the simple faith of the church successfully resisted one of the most serious attacks it ever faced. The decision made at Nicea must not be confused with the so-called Nicene creed which is one of the three ecumenical symbols. For this creed embodies, not the decisions made at Nicea in 325, but those of the Nicaeno-Constantinopolitan councils of the second half of the fourth century. We are discussing now the decision in which the deity of Christ is set forth over against Arius.

The background of Arius' Christology was laid in the school of Lucian at Antioch. Harnack not without truth calls Lucian "the Arius before Arius." Lucian based his views on the Adoptionist Christology of Paul of Samosata, who taught that Christ had been adopted by God *as man*.[1] Lucian so influenced Arius that he clashed with the church. At the Council of Nicea, where passages from Arius' writings were read aloud, the rupture came. In this rupture the decisive issue was the deity of Christ which Arius had denied. Arius' argument was that, since God is eternal and one, there could not be anything beside him or subject to him but that which is created and which has its origin in the divine will. This argument applies also to the Son, who, says Arius, is not co-eternal with the Father, but a created being. We are persecuted, as Arius writes to Eusebius of Nicomedia, because we say that the Son has a beginning and that God is without a beginning. The Father was not always Father, for there was a time when the Son was not yet created and hence God was not yet Father of his Son. He did not become Father till the creation of his Son. This Son proceeds not from the being but from the will of the Father. He is not truly God but a creature, how-

---

1. Brunner calls Paul of Samosata "the first Ritschlian."

ever true it is that he is a perfect creature standing in a very special relationship to God. To demonstrate the truth of his doctrine Arius appealed to a large number of Scriptural texts; for instance, "Jehovah . . . is one. . . ." (Deut. 6:4) ; "Jehovah possessed me in the beginning of his way," (Prov. 8:22) ; ". . . the Father is greater than I," (John 14:28). The Son is inferior to the Father and does not share in the being of the Father. Arius was emphatically opposed to every form of Emanationism as well as to such expressions as "Light of Light." In view of Christ's special relationship to the Father we might call him God but this relationship does not make him truly God in his essence. Hence Arius chose consciously and consistently for a subordinationist Christology — all in the name of the monotheism to which he held and which did not tolerate another besides the one, true God.

In this connection is to be understood the fact that after much conflict Nicea came to the following formulation: "I believe . . . in one Lord Jesus Christ, the only-begotten Son of God, begotten of the Father before all worlds; God of God, Light of Light, very God of very God; begotten, not made, being of one substance with the Father. . . ." Also rejected was the view of those who say that there was a time when the Son did not yet exist. The addition by the Council of the expression "of one substance" (homo-ousios) gained peculiar significance. After all, in this specifically anti-Arian formullation the die was cast at Nicea. For Arius had denied that the Father and the Son have the same "ousia," the same substance. Hence the Nicean "homo-ousios." We stress this point because in 268 a synod was held at Antioch which explicitly rejected the term "homo-ousious." This fact was of course well-known in the period of the Arian disputes and the Semi-Arians repeatedly called attention to this Act of Synod to justify their aversion to the idea of "homo-ousios." Why, one asks, did Nicea make such decisive use of the word and make it, as it were, "a catch-word of orthodoxy"? The

question is important because Gnosticism too was fond of the
term and used it in connection with the aeons which, as cosmic
forces, emanated from God. Was it not dangerous to employ
the term at this critical juncture in the Christological conflict? This "homo-ousios" comes too close, one might say,
to the gnostic idea of emanation, just as the phrase "Light
of Light" is reminiscent of gnostic metaphors like "radiations
of the sun" and "branches of a tree."

An urgent reason must have impelled the church in 325
to embody a decision of so much consequence in this heavily
loaded term. And that reason was indeed present. The Synod
of 268, working under a different set of circumstances, had
rejected the term. It is very likely that this Synod had to
guard against the Sabellian heresy in which the distinctiveness
of the three persons was either fully or virtually denied.
This caution was confirmed in the post-Nicean period when
those who were uneasy about the term "homo-ousios" were
also wary of the Sabellian danger.

It was the mind of Nicea that against the threat of Arianism
the term "of one substance" (as well as the expression "Light
of Light") could be used to good advantage and on good
grounds. Every historical situation has its peculiar complex
of dangers. As the term "homo-ousios" was handled in 268
it was clearly recognizable heresy. But *hic et nunc,* with
Arius degrading Christ to the status of creature, and sever-
ing the essential relationship between the Father and the Son,
and teaching that Christ is a "derived creature" of an un-
derived Father, the church, to squelch this heresy at this time,
reached for the term "of one substance."[2] At Nicea the
theological situation became so clear that the Arians felt unable to maintain their position in the church as was once
possible under the compromise-formula of Eusebius of Caesarea. Also, it was now unequivocally clear that the church,
when it used the term "homo-ousios," had in mind something

---

2. Compare Karl Barth, *Kirchliche Dogmatik,* I, 1, pages 460ff.

other than a gnostic emanation. It strove mightily for the honor and deity of Christ. To this end the term used was a valuable means. We may note in passing that Athanasius, after the Council of Nicea, was very sparing in his use of the term — probably with a view to the re-emergence of Sabellianism in the person of Marcellus of Ancyra.[3] But the substance of the doctrine was fixed in his mind, as appears from the fact that in the continuing conflict with Arians and Semi-Arians the expression gains more importance. Later complaints to the effect that the term "homo-ousios" would lead inevitably to Sabellianism did not, in spite of Marcellus, greatly impress Athanasius.

And so, because the church wished to confess that Jesus Christ was truly God and to maintain that in him God himself had come to us, the "homo-ousios" became the core of the Nicene Creed."[4] In later times the conflict about this term was frequently dismissed as a conflict about metaphysical subtleties without any religious significance. This criticism, however, ignores the religious motives which drove Nicea and its exponent, Athanasius, against the Arian Christology. The religion of Nicea harks back to the witness of the Scriptures and is an echo, loaded terms notwithstanding, of the adoration with which the New Testament is imbued. Nicea intended only to give expression to what John, the apostle of love, wrote when he addressed the church with the joyous words: "This is the true God, and eternal life" (I John 5:20).

B. CONSTANTINOPLE, 381 A. D.

The conflict about the deity of Christ continued with the customary fluctuations, as illustrated in the life of Athanasius, throughout the period between 325 and 381. The result was that the confession of Nicea remained that of the church and

---

3. In his *Orationes contra Arianos,* Anthanasius used the term only once (I, 9).

4. Compare Athanasius, *Op. cit.,* I, page 22.

that Arianism, which led to a virtual polytheism, failed to get a permanent foothold inside the church of Christ. In this connection the danger was far from illusory that the church would be content with the endorsement of the deity of Christ and would see no dangers from any other quarter. The conflict of the church with Apollinaris proves that it was alert in other directions as well. For the doctrine of Apollinaris did not militate against Nicea — he was a warm defender of Nicea and an admirer of Athanasius — and nonetheless he got himself into a conflict with the church which had far-reaching influence on the subsequent course of Christological development.

The church did not, despite Apollinaris' agreement with Nicea, leave him to his own devices. The spiritual warfare waged by the church in the fourth century proves that the church proceeded, not on the basis of its own schematizations of the person of Christ, but in obedience to the Scriptural witness concerning the Christ. Apollinaris of Laodicea was preoccupied particularly with John 1:14: "And the Word became flesh." He sought to understand the unity of the person and argued on the basis of the Eternal Logos who became truly human. But this Incarnation is to him very puzzling. The most troublesome question to him is how to understand the unity of the person. Can two beings be united into one being? To solve this intellectual difficulty Apollinaris began to teach that under no circumstances could the divine Logos have united himself with a complete human being since such a union could result only in a third kind of being. Had the Logos assumed a complete human nature, he would have adopted also human variability and human sin. Since it is certain that Jesus Christ is immutable, it is by that token impossible that he united himself with a variable human spirit. A genuine union is possible only when the Logos, as the principle of self-consciousness and self-determination, *takes the place of,* instead of assuming, the human spirit. There was probably some development at this point in Apollinaris. First he operated with a dichotomous view of man and taught that the Logos assumes only a human body, and hence took the place of the soul. Later, reasoning from a trichotomy, he taught that the Logos assumed body and soul, and took the place of the human spirit. This anthropological distinction does not interest us as much as the idea of substitution which was and remained dominant in Apollinaris. The union in Christ was not, therefore, a union of the Logos with a complete nature but a union accomplished by an interpenetration of the Logos and the human nature. The Logos is the active, moving principle and human nature is the passive recipient of its action. The Logos permeates the human as organic principle. A complete human nature would carry mutability into the work of the Logos. Apollinaris insists that the divine Logos is the sole actor in the drama of salvation lest it come to nothing. The conclusion was therefore that the human nature of Christ was not the same as that of other men. All that was of any account in Christ was divine and the human was no more than passive instrument. At bottom there is but one nature and hence Apollinaris did not shrink from saying that Christ was not a complete man.

At this point, conflict with the church was inevitable. The church proved, in its contention with Apollinaris, that it had listened to the Scriptural instruction, not only as to the deity of Christ, but also as to his Incarnation and his being in all things like us his brethren, sin excepted.

Over against Apollinaris the Council of Constantinople in 381 maintained the completeness of Christ's human nature. Even before the Council convened, the Cappadocian theologians, Gregory of Nazianzen, Gregory of Nyssa, and Basil the Great, had warned Apollinaris that his theology failed to do justice to the complete humanity of Christ. Later evaluations of the great defender of Nicea were varied. Harnack, for instance, has a good deal of appreciation for Apollinaris and rightly sees in his theology an incipient monophysitism.[5] On the other hand, Harnack admits that the church, by its championing of the full humanity of Christ, "performed an incalculable service" to later generations. This tribute to the church is deserved. For it faithfully stood its ground, just after an exhausting struggle against those who denied the deity of Christ, in opposing the absorption of the human nature into the divine.

The contours of the "vere deus, vere homo" are now fully present to our minds. Not that the church wished to bind its membership to a specific anthropology, but it did reject the effort of Apollinaris to substitute the Logos for a part of human nature in order thus to make an organic synthesis acceptable to himself. One may say that in 381 the church protected the mystery of the personal union of the two natures against an idea which later, when monophysitism led to a Christology in which the deity of Christ threatened to submerge his humanity, proved so attractive. Whoever thinks that the Christological conflict was a matter of ingenious theological subtleties does not know what he is saying. Antidocetism, for the church of Christ, is a question of to be or not to be.

C. CHALCEDON, 451 A. D.

Against the background of the Christological conflict of the fourth century it is easy to understand that the church continued to be preoccupied with the relationship between the two natures of Christ. At issue in the dispute with Apollinaris was the *unio personalis,* and it remained on the agenda of the church for many centuries.

In the fifth century this problem is underscored as the church grapples with the doctrines of Nestorius and Eutyches, both

---

5. The Apollinarians opposed the Antioch theologians as the people "of the two natures." Compare E. Weigl, *Christologie vom Tode des Athanasius bis zum Ausbruch des Nestorianischen Streites,* page 10.

of whom were condemned at the Council of Chalcedon, after Nestorius had been independently condemned at Ephesus in 431.

We can sketch the development of this dispute most tellingly by recalling that the Antiochian School had held to the complete humanity of Christ in opposition to Apollinaris. They spoke, without perturbation, of the two natures of Christ. The Logos had dwelt in the complete man, Jesus Christ, they felt, and this the church had taught in 381. The nature of this indwelling was to be understood as a moral union on the analogy of God's indwelling in man, be it that the indwelling of the Logos in the man Jesus was of a special kind. In this direction Nestorius developed his thinking. As bishop of Constantinople he opposed the designation "mother of God," as referring to Mary, since she was not the mother of Christ's divine but of his human nature. The theology of Nestorius is generally mentioned as teaching that two natures imply also two persons. Later this traditional interpretation of Nestorius was called in question. Many a person believes he was unjustly condemned as heretic as a result of the political intrigues of his great opponent Cyril of Alexandria. However that may be,[6] we are now interested in the Christological rationale which impelled the church to reject Nestorianism. In any event the church wished to indicate that the two natures of Christ are undivided, and are bound together by a stronger bond than that of a moral union of friendship between two independent persons. Maintaining the complete humanity of Christ in response to Apollinaris, the church would permit no separation of the two natures when Nestorius began to offer his theological wares.

The polemic against Eutyches involved the opposite error. His thesis was that upon a union of two natures there could be only one nature — hence his monophysitism. From a duality of natures Nestorius inferred a duality of persons; and from the unity of the person Eutyches inferred a single thean-

6. Compare Polman, in *Christus de Heiland*, pages 121 ff.

thropic nature. He was justly accused of con-fusing the two
natures. At Chalcedon both the separation and the confusion
of the two natures were rejected. The decisons of Chalcedon
were strongly influenced by the well-known letter which Leo I
addressed to Flavian in the year 449. In this letter he maintained that each of the two natures has its peculiar attributes;
for this opinion he was later accused, by several, of Nestorianism.

At the so-called robber-synod of 449 Eutyches was declared
orthodox and an anathema was pronounced over anyone who
should persist in speaking of two natures. But Chalcedon, in
451, rejected both the confusion and the separation of these
natures. Antithetically opposed to the heresies, it taught that
Jesus Christ was truly God and truly man; as touching his
Godhead *homo-ousios* with the Father, and as touching his
manhood *homo-ousios* with us his brethren. Of the relationship between the two natures it declared that they were united:
without mixture and without change, without division and
without separation; to this was added that each nature, even
in the union, retains its own properties. Many writers have
complained about the negative character of the Chalcedon
Creed. These complaints evince a misunderstanding of the
fifth century conflict. Confronted by the concrete heresies
of Nestorius and Eutyches the church could not do better than
reject that which failed to do justice to the unity of the person.
Apart from the fact that Chalcedon spoke also positively, one
can say that this Council had decisive influence in later years.
Another question is — we shall consider it later — whether
the church can possibly get beyond the quadruple answer of
Chalcedon. In the light of history Chalcedon appears as being
unusually important. It has indicated directions which the
church, if it wished to safeguard the mystery of the union,
would have to avoid. It is no wonder that the heaviest critical
bombardments, in the crisis of the dual-nature doctrine outlined
above, were aimed at Chalcedon. These broadsides do not,

of course, establish the truth or value of the Chalcedon creed, but they do impel us to further reflection on the mystery which Chalcedon sought to confess.

*   *   *

The Christological conflict is, by no means, fully delineated by our mentioning the decisions of the ancient church touching Arius, Apollinaris, Nestorius, and Eutyches. But we *may* say that these decisions were fundamental and served as a compass to the church in later ages. Christological dogma continued to be discussed also after Chalcedon. This continued interest is true particularly of the stand of the church relative to the relationship between the divine and the human nature of Christ. The problem of monophysitism was the focus of centuries of conflict. Nestorianism enjoyed a re-emergence — for its rejection did not extinguish it — in the so-called Adoptianism of the eighth century. But the church was especially harried by those who sought continually to get from under the decisions of Chalcedon. Repeatedly the charge came up that Chalcedon did violence to the unity of the person of Christ. This conflict led finally, in 680, to a new decision of the church by which, at Constantinople, also monotheletism was condemned. Actually the doctrine of the one theanthropic will was a revival of monophysitism.

The position of 680 is a re-assertion, in the very formulas adopted, of Chalcedon. It did not take the church long to discover that monotheletism was "a veiled re-edition of the monophysite error,"[7] against which the Lateran Council of 649 had already spoken out. It declared that the two natures were united without mixture and without separation, and that it is a criminal heresy to believe that there was in Christ but one will and one mode of operation — a heresy by which, in the judgment of the church, the mystery of Christ is violated.

---

7. M. Schmaus, *Katholische Dogmatik* II, 1949, page 656.

At the Council of Constantinople in 680 there was a renewed discussion on the two wills in Christ. Constantinople continued in the line of Chalcedon and declared that in Christ there are two wills and two modes of acting — and these without mixture, change, division, or separation.

*   *   *

Even more than Chalcedon this pronouncement on monotheletism was the center of a protracted dispute. The objection was against a dualism which threatened the unity of the person. The objectors fail to note, however, the emphasis of this Council on the phrase "without separation." Seeberg, who like Harnack attributes the decision of the Council to the influence of politics, wrongly believes that the history of Christology, through church-politics and the logic of the concepts brought into play, ended with an "Apology of the Antiochian School."[8]

One must rather say that the church again recognized and rejected the mystical tendency to unification implicit in the monophysite theory. It saw correctly that, from a desire for a unified image of Christ's person, the monophysites would soon arrive at the complete absorption of the human nature by the divine. In maintaining the position of Chalcedon the church preserved the "vere homo" for the future and thus performed a great service to later generations.

In the history of dogma it is almost a miracle that the church, after going the full limit in its defense of the deity of Christ against Arianism and working under various political circumstances, should nonetheless, in a conflict covering many centuries, rise with might and main to the defense of the full and true humanity of Christ. The church understood the peril to itself of arriving at such a unity as would violate the mystery confessed at Chalcedon. Thus the ancient church weeded its garden and produced much fruit.

---

8. Seeberg, *D. Gesch.*, II, page 300, 302.

In later times people have tried by means of more refined concepts to override the decisions of the ancient church. But the result was nearly always that in contending with the words of the church the polemicist actually clashed with what the church intended, namely, to confess that Christ was truly God and truly man, and not to offer a scientific formulation of the mystery of the Incarnation. It is surely no sign of traditionalism to take more pleasure in the Christological conflict of the first few centuries than in nineteenth-century efforts to make the unity of Jesus Christ humanly conceivable. On the contrary, it is to have rapport with the living past in which the church went neither to the right nor to the left in defending the biblical message concerning Jesus Christ, the Word, who became flesh.

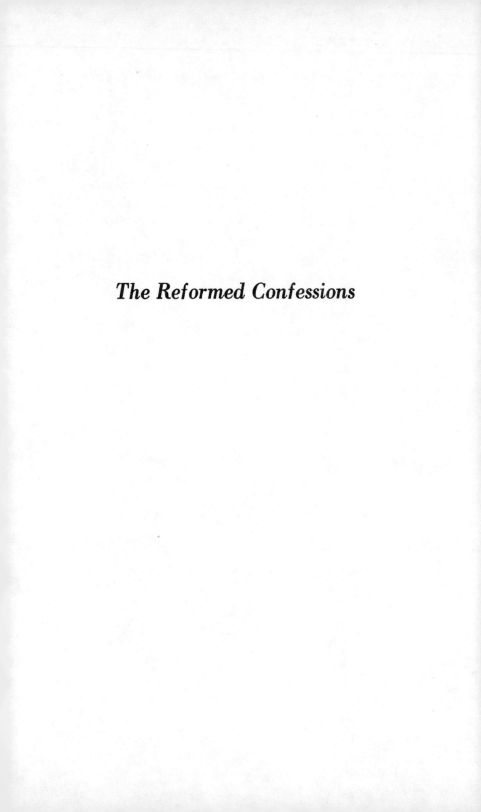

The Reformed Confessions

CHAPTER IV

The Reformed Confessions

HAVING presented a synopsis of a few highpoints in the
battle which the ancient church had to conduct to maintain, against various heresies, its confession of Jesus Christ
as the simple faith of the church, we would now stop, by way
of orientation, to consider the witness of the Reformed confessions touching the person of Christ. The churches of the Reformation, among them the Reformed churches, were not
content merely to express their agreement with the ecumenical
formulations of the ancient church but arrived themselves at
fresh fixations of Christological dogma. This development
was closely integrated with several controversies of the Reformation period, among others, with Lutherans and Anabaptists. It is immediately apparent, however, that these new
formulations are fitted into the framework of the Christological confessions of the ancient church, namely, those of Nicea
and Chalcedon. The Netherlands' confessions are a case in
point. The Heidelberg Catechism speaks of the divine and
human nature of Christ in close connection with the Trinity.
Within the context of the confession of salvation in Christ,
the only comfort in life and death, a song of praise is raised
to the faithfulness of the only Savior Jesus Christ is his holy
sacrifice for and redemption of lost mankind.[1] In the indirect
mode of argument embodied in Lord's Days 4 to 6 the ground-
work is laid for the confession of the Redeemer and Mediator,[2]
who is "a true and righteous man and yet more powerful than

---

1. Question 1.
2. Question 15.

all creatures, that is, one who is withal true God."[3] He is the
only-begotten Son of God, the one, true, and eternal God together with the Father and the Holy Spirit,[4] the Savior,[5]
ordained by the Father to be our prophet, priest, and king.[6]
In distinction from us he is called the eternal, natural Son of
God,[7] our Lord,[8] born of the virgin Mary by the operation
of the Holy Spirit,[9] and our Mediator.[10]

With reference to this Christ it is said that he is truly God
and truly man. ". . .With respect to His human nature, He is
no more on earth; but with respect to His Godhead, majesty,
grace and Spirit, He is at no time absent from us."[11] The
two natures of Christ are here plainly distinguished, while over
against the Lutherans, in Question 48, there is a polemic against
the inclusion of the Godhead of Christ in the human nature,
a confessional statement generally referred to as "extra-calvinisticum."

All these confessional utterances are placed in the same context with the redemptive work of Christ, so that it is impossible
to find even the slightest dualism between his person and work.
The entire Catechism displays for us the encouragement and
comfort of the person and work of Christ.

* * *

The Belgic Confession, in its Christological utterances also,
bears a somewhat different character from that of the Catechism. This difference appears particularly in Articles 18 and
19, but also in other articles. Here, too, the Christological confessions are presented in connection with the Trinity. Article 9
rejects those heresies of Paul of Samosata and Arius which
bear on the Christ. Article 10 confesses Christ as true and

---

3. Questions 15 and 18.
4. Questions 25 and 53.
5. Questions 29 and 30.
6. Question 31.
7. Question 33.

8. Questions 34 and 44.
9. Question 35.
10. Question 36.
11. Question 47.

eternal God, as the only begotten Son of God, "begotten from eternity, not made, nor created (for then He would be a creature), but co-essential and co-eternal with the Father, the very image of his substance and the effulgence of his glory, equal unto Him in all things." His status as the Son of God did not begin with the Incarnation but he is from eternity the Son, the Word, through which all things are made. The conclusion of Article 10 mentions concerning the Son that we invoke, worship, and serve him. Strongly in evidence, in this article, is its continuity with the formulations of the ancient church in its conflict with the Arian theory of Christ as the creature of God.

At some distance from this article on the deity of Christ come Articles 18 and 19 which treat of the Incarnation and the union and distinction of the two natures in Christ. These important articles merit special attention.

Article 18 confesses that in the Incarnation the divine promise is fulfilled. Christ's debut on the scene of history is viewed in the broad perspective of the history of redemption. Christ's appearance was not an accidental happening to which we have attached our explanations later on, but a fulfilment, a realization of ancient promises made by God. In this connection the Confession strongly emphasizes the human nature of Christ. He "became like unto man, really assuming the true human nature. . . ."[12] Whereas in Article 10 the true deity of the Son was confessed, here, in connection with the Incarnation, his humanity occupies the foreground. In order to stress this aspect the Confession adds: ". . . and did not only assume human nature as to the body, but also a true human soul, that He might be a real man." One can catalogue this confession also as sharply anti-docetic. The argumentation is quite in line with that of the ancient church: soul and body, the whole man is completely lost — hence "it was necessary that He

---

12. "et *veram* naturam humanam cum omnibus ipsius infirmitatibus, excepto peccato, *vere* assumpsit."

should take both upon Him, to save both."[13] So ran the argument of Athanasius and such was the confession of the church over against Apollinaris. But the situation of the sixteenth century is not that of the fourth and this change is reflected in the remaining formulations. Article 18 takes position, namely, against the Anabaptists. There is mention of those "who deny that Christ assumed human flesh from his mother." Various formulations pose the opposite: Christ partook of the flesh and blood of the children; he is a fruit of the lions of David after the flesh; a fruit of the womb of Mary; born of a woman. And then again: a branch of David, a shoot of the root of Jesse, sprung from the tribe of Judah, descended from the Jews according to the flesh, of the seed of Abraham. Certainly an unusual heaping up of historical aspects! It indicates the importance which the fathers ascribed to this part of their confession. They see Christ Jesus in the flesh and confess the reality of his humanity without any reservation. Although in Article 10 the fathers heavily underscore the deity of Christ, they do not permit the deity to overshadow his humanity. The Confession is not content to say that God acts in Christ; it adds that the blessings of salvation are poured out upon us by the *man* Jesus Christ.

As to this anti-docetic witness there was great unanimity in the Reformation. There was, to be sure, some disagreement in this connection between the Lutherans and the Reformed over the doctrine of the communication of attributes. And the Reformed have more than once held against the Lutherans that they fail to do justice to the true humanity of Christ. But it cannot be denied that Reformed theologians and Lutherans joined hands in rejecting the Anabaptist view of Christ's human nature.[14] We have reason to be grateful, here if anywhere, for this flash of the full-fledged ecumenical witness of the church. The Reformation, and in particular the Reformed confessions,

---

13. "necesse fuit illum utrumque assumere, ut utrumque simul servaret."
14. See the Lutheran Formula Concordiae.

saw as the background of the Anabaptistic view the dualistic doctrine that the Logos had taken his flesh and blood down from heaven. This dualism proceeds on the assumption that the Logos cannot be united with the true human nature. Over against this dualism the Reformed confessions maintained, with emphasis and explicitness, the truth and implications of the "vere homo."

* * *

In Article 19 the main subject is the union of the two natures of Christ. The core of the article consists in the pronouncement touching the inseparable union of the person of the Son with his human nature. In this personal union the idea is not a certain bond between two sons or persons but two natures united in a single person. The person of the Son and the human nature are conjoined.

Completely in the spirit of Chalcedon it says that each nature retains its own properties in the union — clearly antithetically to every attempt at deification or humanization, and to every form of monophysitism. The position that Christ would be a mixture of God and man in one theanthropic nature was forcefully rejected. Against this idea of mixture the Confession points out concretely that the divine nature is uncreated and continues to fill heaven and earth without beginning of days or end of life. The Confession knows of no inclusion of the divine nature in the human, and is therefore in complete harmony with the Heidelberg Catechism. Of the human nature it is said that it too retained its distinct properties, remained created and finite, and kept everything belonging to a true body. There is a decided concern here — that much is evident — to preserve the mystery of Chalcedon. The reality of the human nature in Christ remains unchanged. Our salvation and resurrection depend on the reality of his body. Not even death, according to the Confession, can separate the two natures of Christ; of the one Christ it remains true that he is really God and really man. Finally, a summary states that Christ was "very God by His power to conquer death; and very man that He might die for us according to the infirmity of His flesh."

* * *

The striking conformity of these Confessions to the ecumenical decisions of the church is no less evident in other creedal statements of the Reformed churches. The agreement is remarkable.[15] The Confessio Gallicana reads: "God and man in one person." Servetus is rejected because "he attributes to holy Jesus an imaginary divinity." The two natures are "truly and inseparably conjoined and united, each nevertheless remaining in its own distinction."

The divine nature is uncreated, infinite, filling all things; the human nature "has remained finite, having its form, measure, and properties." The same thing is striking in the *Confessio Helvetica posterior* of 1562, which confesses, in opposition to gnosticism, the reality (nec phantastica) of the body of Christ, which he did not, it is said, bring from heaven. United, but not mixed, these natures are — Apollinaris and Eutyches to the contrary notwithstanding. There was never any talk of a deification of human nature, while, on the other hand, the separation of the two natures, as it appears in Nestorius, is likewise rejected.[16]

In the English confessions we soon discover the same lines, namely, with reference to the inseparable union.[17] The Westminster Confession rejects "all confusion" with emphasis. Stress is laid on the unity of the person, "each Nature doing that which is proper to itself."[18]

---

15. Compare, for the Swiss Confessions: "Fidei Ratio" by Zwingli, 1530, (K. Müller, *Die Bekenntnisschriften der ref. K.*, 1903, p. 80 and the *Conf. Helvetica prior* of 1536, where Christ is called our brother (Müller, p. 103).
16. "unionem personae dissolvens."
17. Cf. E. J. Bicknell, *A Theological Introduction to the Thirty-nine Articles of the Church of England*, 1950, page 70ff.
18. Müller, p. 563, compare also the Westminster Catechism of 1647 (Müller, page 616).

The Reformed Confessions, it is evident, pursue the line laid down by Chalcedon.

*   *   *

We may not conceal from ourselves the fact that the Belgic Confession in particular was the butt of serious criticism, that is, as far as its Christological formulation is concerned. We mention here particularly the criticism of Doedes and Korff. Most interesting to us is the criticism of Korff, because it was he who emphatically defended Chalcedon in the teeth of modern criticism. He acknowledges that the Belgic Confession gives us the church's Christology as conditioned by the Reformation. But against Article 19 he has serious objections. That which is specifically Reformed was here given, he believes, its least successful form.[19] "The redaction is exceedingly faulty, almost clumsy," says he, while the content can by no means be considered satisfactory. In the first place Korff encounters here the "extra-calvinisticum" against which he entertains serious objections. The unity of the person, in the second place, is taught in an extremely obscure manner. Hence Korff consents to the criticism of Doedes who objects that at best we have dogmatic stammerings here.[20] One can ask the question why Korff puts so much emphasis on the obscure and stammering nature of the confessions. Repeatedly he himself has stressed that in the confession of the two natures we must be concerned to point out a mystery and that the ancient church clearly sensed this necessity. We should have expected therefore that he would have been more sensitive to what Article 19 intended to say in all these formulations concerning the union of the two natures in Christ.

It is evident that the confession by no means intended to give an explanation of this mystery but rather to accept whole-

---

19. Korff, *Christologie* I, page 267.
20. J. I. Doedes, *De Nederl. Geloofsbelijdenis en de Heid. Catech.*, I. 1880, p. 232.

heartedly what the ancient church taught: a union without confusion, change, division, or separation. One can agree that the confession seems to stammer; but in this stammering one thing is apparent: the rejection of every attempt to undermine Chalcedon.

*   *   *

A genuine question — now that we have witnessed the conscious aim of the Reformed confessions to operate within the limits set by Chalcedon — is whether· later developments in fact enjoyed continuity with Chalcedon or whether, particularly in the Reformed confessions, an essential change arose. According to Korff, a decided change does take place at a few points. Over against his opinion stands the view of Koopmans who calls Article 19 "the elaboration of the famous formula of the Council of Chalcedon."[21] He believes the varied expressions of Article 19 are plain to anyone who has grasped the fundamental point of view embodied in the confession of the deity and humanity of Christ. Still one wonders whether there is no development or explicit elaboration in the history of Christology which could form a basis for the position of Korff who does accept Chalcedon but not the entire course of the development of Christological dogma. We are faced here with the important question whether and to what extent we can speak of a development of this dogma. Theologians have pointed to the mystery of the unity of the person in the two natures and denied that after Chalcedon, which reverently confessed this mystery, there has been any further development or elaboration. This problem was given specific form by the views of Korff who emphatically wants to keep our Christological witness bound to the confession of Chalcedon and who denies that there was, since Chalcedon, any further development, at least no development which did not detract from the mystery of Christ. Hence we must ask ourselves: Was Chalcedon a terminal point?

---

21. J. Koopmans, *De Nederl. Geloofsbelijdenis,* 1939, p. 128.

Chalcedon A Terminal Point?

CHAPTER V

Chalcedon A Terminal Point?

A VERY important question arose — the question embodied in the title of this chapter — in discussions on
the Christology of the creeds. The question "Was Chalcedon
a terminal point?" posed by Miskotte in a critical discussion
of the Christology of Korff, conditioned many discussions
since.[1] Now that in 1951 the Council of Chalcedon was com-
memorated, the question becomes particularly timely. Korff
rather drastically brought up for discussion the cardinal point
of the problem when he provided the proposition "Chalcedon
a terminal-point" with an exclamation mark and expressed
his disapproval of all later developments. He continually
speaks of his great appreciation for the decision of 451,
since this council, in its negative predications, aimed to reverence the mystery of the person of Christ. In his opinion
Chalcedon intended, not to explain, but merely to confess the
mystery of the "very God and very man."[2] The four negatives of Chalcedon are the riches — and not the poverty —
of a modest, believing church. Its pronouncement is comparable to a double row of light-beacons which mark off the
navigable water in between and warn against the dangers
which threaten to the left and to the right. Korff infers that
one may not consider the pronouncement of Chalcedon an
"explanation," nor may one so use it, since the Church never
intended it as such. The tendency to go off in that direction

---

1. K. H. Miskotte, *Halt bij Chalcedon?* In "Woord en Wereld," 1941,
pages 23-42.

2. Korff, *Ibid.*, I, 193.

has nonetheless on several occasions been too strong both for church and theology. People then began to "work" with the formula of Chalcedon and to draw broader conclusions from it in order to make the unity and diversity in Christ at least somewhat transparent. "In studying the history of Christology one gets the impression that dogmatic thinking succumbed often, one is almost inclined to say as a rule, to this temptation."[3] People tried to enter into the nature of the personal union and used the dual-nature scheme, for instance, to light up the gospel story and to point out what Christ did with his divine and what with his human nature.

Whenever one operates with Chalcedon in that manner, one is bound to fall into one heresy or another: one either separates or else one mixes the two natures. Korff believes it to be a remarkable fact that "when people, forgetting that the dogma is no explanation, nonetheless use it as such and hence begin to operate with it, they come automatically in conflict with it." The confession that Christ was truly God and man "is a terminal-point; it cannot be a starting-point." There is little we can do with Chalcedon, thinks Korff, and we certainly cannot use it as a take-off for various dogmatic or exegetical expeditions. This view, according to him, is valid not only with reference to Christological dogma but is true for our other formulations and doctrines as well. But in relation to the central significance of Christological formulation this view is especially valuable.

To Korff, as is apparent, the issue is freighted with implications. From this point of view he criticizes the two elaborations of Christological dogma: the idea of the impersonal human nature of Christ and the decision of the church in 680 on the issue of monotheletism. These inferences seem to be perfectly logical. On the basis of Chalcedon people have tried to show how the Incarnation and the union of the two natures were possible. Korff does not deny the perfect

---

3. *Ibid.*, I, page 195.

logic of it,[4] but says that exactly at this point the church should have instantly refused to draw any inferences, "be they logical or illogical." "Inferences" inevitably lead us astray and therefore, having indicated the mystery, we should stop and leave the mystery for what it is. God has come into the world. This cannot be doubted: Christ is very God and very man. Hence, out of reverence for this mystery, Korff calls a halt at Chalcedon.

*   *   *

The problem Korff broaches has been up for discussion before and then, too, in direct connection with the negative formulation of Chalcedon. Whereas Kuyper judged that though Christological dogma had initially crystallized in the conflicts of the first few centuries it gained greater lucidity in the days of the Reformation,[5] Honig expressed himself somewhat differently when he wrote[6] that this dogma is not capable of modification and has been fully formulated. "At this point the development of doctrine has reached its limit. I do not even hesitate to say that the doctrine of the Person of the Mediator, as it has been formulated by the church, is incapable of further development." It is evident, however, that the views of Korff and that of Honig may not simply be identified, since Korff does object, and Honig does not, to the doctrine of the impersonal human nature of Christ, although Honig says later that he would prefer to avoid the *term,* lest misunderstanding arise.[7] Besides Honig there are others who place full emphasis upon the mystery confessed at Chalcedon and yet do not share Korff's objection to later "development." Aalders, for instance, sees in Chalcedon four

---

4. *Ibid.,* I, page 202.
5. Kuyper, *Loci* III, cap III, page 43.
6. A. G. Honig, *De persoon van den Middelaar in de nieuwere Duitsche dogmatiek,* 1910, page 74.
7. *Ibid,* page 75, 76; cf. Honig, *Handboek van de Geref. Dogmatiek,* page 460ff. Honig also takes the decision against monotheletism under his wings.

finger-posts placed exactly where a dike-break threatens. The Council does not say how the union between the divine and the human nature is possible, "but it does draw a line and declares how it is not possible."[8] One could speak of a confession of poverty, but it is a poverty gladly accepted and honorable. There are things which lie beyond our comprehension, "which are different, higher than we are; things we do not understand but adore as a miracle of God, as the mystery of his majesty," and immediately Aalders adds, "this is where the church calls a halt." Boundary lines are a matter of life and death for the church of Christ. Hence also a halt at Chalcedon. And still Aalders' attitude to later decisions is different from that of Korff. He thinks apparently that in these later decisions the church did not cross the *Todeslinie.* We are thus confronted by various interpretations of the stop at Chalcedon. And thus we are faced with the central question of this chapter: What is the significance for Christological dogma of this terminal point? This question is not merely of theological but also of confessional importance to the church. The question touches the monotheletic conflict and, further, the so-called extra-calvinisticum, which Korff likewise rejected as an illegitimate "inference" from Chalcedon.

It is therefore necessary to ask whether Korff takes us in the right direction in his view on mystery. We must first of all assent that the danger he mentions is real — that of rationalizing the mystery of the unity of the person and in some way or other failing to do justice to what the ancient church intended to confess. In later times this danger became reality in various efforts to get beyond Chalcedon and to make the unity of the person "conceivable." There is a "halt!" at Chalcedon which will indeed continue to sound against every form of speculation which attempts to penetrate into this mystery further than is warranted in the light of revelation. But this caution does not in the least justify the

---

8. W. J. Aalders, *De incarnatie,* 1933, page 150.

view of Korff. All depends on what is understood by the development of the dogma and inferences from this dogma. Korff apparently proceeds on the assumption that development of it means a logicistic treatment, a supremacy of rational thought over the content of Scripture which thus gradually loses the character of mystery. He does not take account, at least not sufficiently, of the possibility of an increasingly obedient understanding of the Scriptural message, issuing from an increasingly stronger attachment to the Word. If there should be only a "development" leading away from the simplicity of faith, Korff would indeed be right in calling a halt; even then it would have been better to place this warning-signal at the beginning of the church's dogmatic reflection than in 451. But the church never intended such a development, never intended to rise above a continual subjection to the Scriptures or above the inapprehensible mystery. Korff's view of the Chalcedonian halt is of course part and parcel, as he himself acknowledges, of his entire view of dogma in general. He certainly holds no brief for dogmatic indifferentism,[9] but we do perceive in his conceptions something of the older "ethical" fear of dogmatic formulation. He stresses that dogmatic activity should proceed "cautiously" — an excellent warning indeed, but he patently aims at more than caution. The danger he is especially afraid of is that of "drawing conclusions," an element which repeatedly enters into the work of the dogmatician. On his view we must not draw conclusions in an area in which we do not know "whether our inferences are valid." Salvation revolves, not around a system, but around a series of contingent acts of God by which we are led from one surprise to another. In the nature of the case "but very little room is left for syllogisms." Korff's argument is evidently conditioned by his reaction to logicism and the rationalizing systematization of God's acts. In the

---

9. Compare Korff, *Christologie*, I. page 1ff. and *De Wetenschap des geloofs*, 1932.

place of progressive thinking he wishes to introduce regressive thinking into dogmatics. This shift implies a repeated going back to the point of departure, the revelation of God. But it is clear that in this manner we do not expel the demon of confusion.

This antithesis between progression and regression cannot be maintained; it proceeds from a caricature of the development of dogma and of the confessional development of the church. The caricature is that, to Korff, progression is contraposed to a continual harking back to the revelation of God. He interprets progression to mean a growing dissociation from Scripture, which is left behind like a railway-station on a journey. Such a progression is not, indeed, imaginary, and constitutes a continual and very real danger. At this point lies precisely the issue between the Roman Catholic and the Reformation view of the development of dogma. The question here is: what constitutes the progressive? But it is something else when progression and regression are simply treated as polar opposites. The incorrectness of the dilemma is shown up by the fact that there can be a forward movement which runs true precisely *by* a continual backward reference to Scripture. Uninterrupted research in Scripture must guide the reflection and proclamation of the church: this "going back" must be the source of guidance and correction. It is our conviction that such progression has played an important role in the history of the church. The ideal of the church's reflection is not formal progression but a progression which expresses close attachment to Scripture, expresses a growing understanding of Scripture as a result of faithful reading of Scripture. Such understanding implies the recognition of heresy and its rejection. Theology must not be intent on continually saying new things because they are new; but because from age to age it is confronted by new situations — situations, too, implying an acute threat to the Gospel — the church must be ready each time to formulate the truth anew.

It does not then propose a new dogma, but tries to understand the truth of God in the new situation.   Through conflict, and under the guidance of Word and Spirit, the church often becomes more clearly aware of the riches of the salvation granted again and again.

It is this approach which, in our opinion, illumines the problem of Chalcedon as a terminal point.   In the first place, there is no reason whatever to call a halt, particularly in Christological dogma, at one specific utterance of the church. Such a halt would be meaningful only if one should interpret progression, as Korff does, in the sense of reason overpowering mystery.   Moreover, we do not encounter mystery only in Christology but in the entire dogma of the church; it all refers to and participates in mystery.   And so there is no reason to make the pronouncement of Chalcedon a final milepost in the history of the church, however gratefully we may confess its truth.   For the Scriptures are richer than any pronouncement of the church, no matter how excellent it be and how faithfully it has been formulated in subjection to the Word of God.   To acknowledge this fact is not to have a relativistic view of dogma but to have a right sense of proportion: the place of dogma is in the church, which in turn is subject in all its expressions to the Word of God.   A church which so understands itself is in no danger of going off into false directions and neither does it exclude the possibility of genuine advances.   The error of Rome does not consist in progression as such but in the presuppositions basic to its progression — presuppositions which are particularly patent in what may be called the cement of the Roman Catholic development of dogma: the equalization of Scripture and tradition.   This danger does not, however, exclude that the church, in its development amid manifold historical dangers, should be led by Scripture into greater lucidness and hence into making formulations which reflect the greatest vigilance and caution.

People have thought however that there is special reason in the case of Chalcedon to speak of a necessary halt. They have based this opinion on the negative character of the Chalcedonian pronouncement, which, it is said, tells us only how *not* to take the union of the two natures in Christ: without division, separation, mixture, or change. Do not these negative predications imply resistance to all progress?

In answering this question one must first consider whether it is right to put such one-sided stress on the negativity of Chalcedon. To anyone who reads the pronouncement with care it is clear that to qualify it as negative is to do less than justice to its contents. For in these four "negative" determinations lie positive directions; just as a fingerpost signalizing a dead-end street is positive in meaning or as the negative statements of the Bible about the new Jerusalem are positive in their import. So it is with Chalcedon; and Aalders is right in speaking of the "positive tone" emitted by Chalcedon. The positive implications of Chalcedon are not, moreover, limited to the four negatives but come to expression also in the remaining part of the Chalcedonian pronouncement. Chalcedon contains more than the four words generally quoted. They form only a part of a larger whole which confesses that Jesus Christ is truly God and truly man — "consubstantial [co-essential] with the Father according to the Godhead, and consubstantial with us according to the Manhood . . . begotten before all ages of the Father according to the Godhead, and in these latter days, for us and for our salvation, born of the Virgin Mary, the Mother of God, according to the Manhood; one and the same Christ, Son, Lord, Only-begotten, to be acknowledged in two natures, inconfusedly, unchangeably, indivisibly, inseparably; the distinction of natures being by no means taken away by the union, but rather the property of each nature being preserved, and concurring in one Person and one Subsistence. . . ."[10]

---

10. Schaff, *Creeds of the Greek and Latin Churches*, page 62.

In this utterance the four negative words clearly connote the inability of the church to fathom the mystery of the Incarnation, but the pronouncement shows too that, on the basis of Scripture, the church does make a few positive statements about that Incarnation. Witness what it says about the retention of the respective properties. It is very important to observe that in the later pronouncements of the church — the ones Korff throws overboard — it was this direct, positive formulation which determined the issue; and that Korff creates the impression at times that Chalcedon was concerned merely to say how *not* to conceive the union. This is the more noteworthy because we nowhere find in Korff the statement that Chalcedon already went too far and that, having uttered its negatives, it should have called a stop. Why did he not speak of an inference drawn from the "very God and very man" already at Chalcedon, since it declared that the properties of the two natures remain? Further, it would not be amiss to ask whether consistency does not demand of Korff that he should also fight the decision of the church against monophysitism, a decision which can also in a certain sense be called an "inference" from the "God and man" combination. Why, with a view to the mystery, monophysitism must be rejected but not monotheletism is not at all made clear.

Nor is this made clear in Korff's disavowal of the "extra-calvinisticum." With this term is meant that by the Incarnation the Logos is not included in the flesh but that, as the Catechism has it, "since the Godhead is illimitable and omnipresent, it must follow that it is beyond the bounds of the human nature it has assumed, and yet nonetheless is in this human nature and remains personally united to it."

Korff acknowledges that, strictly speaking, it is unfair to speak at this point of an "extra-calvinisticum" — as if this teaching were a specific peculiarity of Calvinism. For, says he, in itself this doctrine was not new; the "extra" was rather a common conviction found in practically all pre-Reformation theology. Athanasius already had it and Augustine gave it specific formulation when he wrote: "Christ added to himself that which he was not; he did not lose what he was." And the epistle of Leo, which profoundly influenced the decision of Chalcedon, declares that the Son, though he did descend from his abode in heaven, did not depart from the glory of his Father.[11] Korff then speaks of a peculiar accent which the doctrine gets in Reformed theology. He believes that serious objections must be registered against it, since, says he, we here reach out to a level unbecoming to us. But one can hardly assert that Reformed theology has wished to do anything other than maintain what Chalcedon says, namely, that the peculiar properties of the natures are preserved in the union. Reformed theology stressed this truth over against Lutheran theology, to be sure, but there are no grounds for the argument that the Reformation added anything essential to the old doctrine. Though Korff asserts that it did he does not prove it. We are back to the same issue: Korff views Chalcedon as exclusively negative and practically neglects what Chalcedon says about the union. One who takes seriously both the pronouncement on the union and the fourfold negation will not be able a priori to reject the later pronouncements of the church as speculative conclusions. And one certainly may not do this on the basis of an a priori concept of mystery. In our chapter on the crisis in the doctrine of the two natures we noted already how often theologians appealed to the idea of mystery as their ground for the rejection of the content of the dogma — Heering being a particularly good example. Reference to mystery does not clinch the case. From the history of Christology it is clear that people have frequently and seriously obscured the idea of mystery; it was then made a vague notion of incomprehensibility to the neglect of the Scriptural revelation which tells us that we are here concerned with the mystery of the love of God: God revealed

---

11. Epistle of Leo IV.

in the flesh. Chalcedon refers indeed to this mystery as the act of the Son of God in the assumption of human flesh. It speaks of this union in negative terms in order to fend off the attempt to make this act transparent by categories in which the unity must yield to the duality or the duality to the unity. In this manner Chalcedon combated the concrete heresies of the fifth century which formed a genuine threat to the mystery of Incarnation. But now we note that Chalcedon, precisely to express the concreteness of this confession, spoke also of the continued distinction of the two natures. This additional statement was not a second dogma subjoined to the "vere Deus, vere homo" but basically a renewed expression of the same confessional content. The union of the two natures was viewed as real only if God truly came to us in the person of Christ and in human flesh, so that either the elimination of the "truly God" or of the "truly man" would threaten the reality of the personal union. Hence it is unfair to speak of Chalcedon as being exceptional and final and thus bring all later formulations in disrepute. It is by no means true that the church in later periods used Chalcedon as a logicistic "explanation" of the sort mentioned by Korff. The so-called "extra-calvinisticum" too was intended merely as a defense of Chalcedon. It is noteworthy, moreover, that even Korff cannot quite escape thinking and speaking inferentially on the basis of Chalcedon. He writes, for instance, that in Christ we have a humanity "which reflects the Godhead" and that the Godhead puts its stamp on the humanity.[12] Why is it that Korff shies away from "explanations" and is admittedly incapable of determining the influence of the divine nature on the human, and still makes references in these directions? The reason is that Chalcedon does not refer to an incomprehensible mystery in general, a mystery on a level with other mysteries and riddles, but to the mystery of the Word become flesh, God and man in one person. The core of the problem is not a mys-

---

12. Korff, *Ibid.*, I, page 335.

terious or paradoxical union of two persons in general, a union which to our minds is a contradictory union, but an act of God in Jesus Christ.

For this reason one can blame neither Chalcedon nor later church councils for having laid full stress on the peculiar properties of the two natures. It is precisely on the basis of Chalcedon that one can maintain unreservedly that the Son of God came into the flesh without lapsing into abstract reflections on the finite and the infinite. If one in fact takes seriously the confession of the church — the *vere Deus,* and *vere homo,* that is — then he can speak about this union only, both as far as the Godhead and as far as the humanity is concerned, in the light of Revelation. The limits of dogmatic reflection on Christology lie, not in a given historical decision of the church, but in exegesis or rather in Scripture itself. In this activity the church and theology with it, warned by many deviations and speculations, must certainly be on its guard. But it may try to maintain in human formulations, amid all Christological heresy, that the core of this mystery is not a paradox, capable of being seen only in an irrational intuition of faith, but an act of God, of him who is and remains truly God, in this assumption of human nature also.

Thus it will preserve the full perspective of the biblical witness and, at the same time, be able to hold at bay all impoverishment of the Christological confession of the church. And thus it will discover too that Chalcedon is not as rich as that Scriptural fullness on which the church, in its preaching, is continually allowed to draw. This does not imply a devaluation of the church's confession but rests on the fact that the confession is not intended to replace the riches and fullness of the Scriptures. It is precisely the purpose of the confession to point out that fullness and those riches. It is the riches, not of an incomprehensible mystery to be believed in all its irrationality, but of the recollection, amidst heresy, of the Word which says that "though he was rich, yet for your sakes he became poor, that ye through his poverty might become rich" (II Cor. 8:9). This mystery the church has confessed at various times and under varying circumstances. For the church there is but one terminal point and but one limit: the limit of this revelation of him of whom it is written: ". . . no one knoweth the Son, save the Father" (Matt. 11:27).

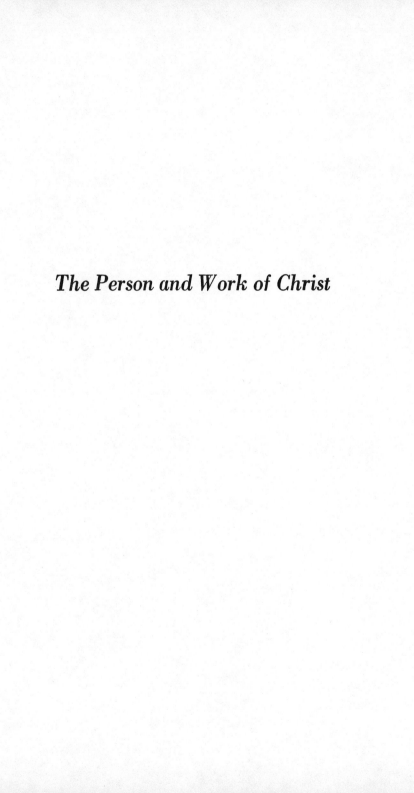

The Person and Work of Christ

CHAPTER VI

The Person and Work of Christ

B EFORE proceeding further in our discussion on the person
of Christ we are compelled to face the question whether
the distinction usually made between the person and work
of Christ can, methodically and religiously, stand on its feet.
People have criticized this distinction because, they said, the
treatment of the person of Christ would, in this division, inevitably degenerate into an abstract and speculative treatment
of the two natures. Particularly in those circles which were
sharply critical of the doctrine of the two natures this criticism,
too, was expressed. The heart of the question which engages
us at the moment is the justice or injustice of the criticism
which dismisses the confession of the two natures as metaphysical speculation.

In this connection one may profitably recall the illuminating
anecdote which Ritschl once heard from Doellinger. Benedict
XIV once paid a visit to a nunnery as Mass was sung. When
the nuns kept repeating "genitum, non factum" (begotten,
not made) the pope became impatient and interrupted the
singing with the words: "sive genitum, sive factum pax vobis-
cum," (whether begotten or made, peace be unto you). Ritschl was so excited over this anecdote that he relayed it by
letter to Harnack and commented, "a beautifully ironic comment on all dogmatics and its contentious distinctions."[1] To
Ritschl the function of dogmatics is not to provide ontological judgments but to provide value-judgments, not to discuss

---

1. We encountered the anecdote in an article by A. Gilg printed in
Jesus Christus im Zeugnis der H. Schrift und der Kirche, 1936, page 91.

ontology but salvation. This anti-ontological disposition
strongly stimulated criticism of the distinction under discussion. The idea was that the treatment of the person of Christ
would naturally be ontological and that the soteriological
would then be viewed as secondary. In the discussions on this
distinction people appealed again and again to the well-known
utterance of Melanchthon: "To acknowledge Christ is to
acknowledge his benefits, not, as is sometimes taught, to behold his natures or the modes of his Incarnation."[2]

Many in the nineteenth century appealed to this statement
in order to point out, under auspices of the Reformation, that
not the two natures of Christ or the "being" of his person is
of central interest to us but his benefactions, his grace "für
uns." Melanchthon's dictum even played a role in criticism
of the confession of Christ's deity, a confession regarded as
metaphysical and hence to be dismissed. This use of the
statement was glaringly in conflict with Melanchthon's intention. For in the same context he refers to scholastic
theology with its vain use of words and concepts through
which the gospel of grace was often gravely obscured. Over
against this Melanchthon points at the power of sin, at the
law and at grace, and declares that a knowledge of these
produces a knowledge of Christ. After that he asserts that
unless we know *why* Christ has put on human flesh, our historical knowledge will not profit us.[3] We must learn to know
Christ as medicine, as our complete salvation; which is something quite different from what the scholastics teach. Paul
does not philosophize either about the tri-unity of God or the
incarnation but he rather speaks of sin and grace and the salvation prepared for us in Christ Jesus. Cold, ontological reflections, and imaginations indifferent to salvation, are con-

2. Melanchthon, *Loci,* 1521: "hoc est Christum cognoscere, beneficia
eius cognoscere, non quod isti docent eius naturas, modos incarnationis
contueri."
3. "ni scias, in quem usum carnem induerit et cruci affixus sit Christus,
quid proderit eius historiam novisse?"

traband to Melanchthon. These ontologies may be philosophical, they are not Christian; in the person and work of Christ we are concerned with comfort for the frightened conscience. From this it is apparent that Melanchthon, far from being indifferent to the confession of Christ as being truly God and truly man, warns and protests against the unfruitful speculations of scholastic theologians. Barth has correctly pointed out[4] that Melanchthon strikes a different tone when in combat with antitrinitarians. One can put it this way: Melanchthon rises to the defense of the existential character of the knowledge of faith and declares it to be knowledge of the salvation granted us in Christ. The only justifiable use one could make of Melanchthon's statement would be against those who speculate about the person of Christ and about his natures; it certainly is no argument against the distinction between the person and work of Christ.

Luther, too, was annexed by the value-judgment apologetes. One of his utterances, which points in the same direction as that of Melanchthon, runs as follows: "Christ is not called Christ because he has two natures; what is that to me? But he bears this glorious and comforting name from the office and work which he took upon himself. That he is by nature both God and man belongs to himself, but my comfort and benefit is that he used his office on my behalf, and poured out his love and became my Savior and Redeemer."[5] This statement of Luther, too, must be taken as a reaction which he shares with Melanchthon. The way to a genuine knowledge of Jesus Christ, Luther means, does not run through speculation about his natures but through the knowledge of his grace. Not that to Luther the knowledge of Christ's deity

4. K. Barth, *Kirchliche Dogmatik,* I, 1, page 437ff.; compare J. Koopmans, *Het oudkerkelijk dogma in de Reformatie bepaaldelijk bij Calvijn,* 1938, page 19.

5. Compare Koopmans, *op. cit.,* who comments: "Such remarks in Luther are never aimed at the ancient church dogma as such, but always against the scholastic treatment of it," page 19. One can find the quotation from Luther in H. Stephan, *Glaubenslehre,* page 170.

and humanity was unimportant, for his entire work points to
the contrary. Even if one should feel obliged to object to
some extravagent expressions, which may be and have been
misunderstood, he cannot but recognize that Luther and Melanchthon were a far cry from the later idea that knowledge
of Christ consisted rather in value-judgments than in ontological judgments. They gave expression in various ways
to their conviction that Christ's benefits cannot be abstracted
from his person and they are truly "personal" benefits and
not blessings in general. It simply does not do to interpret
the Reformation by way of Ritschl. The difference between
ontological and value-judgments as a motif in the elaboration
of Christology was as completely foreign to the Christology
of the Reformation as it is to the biblical message.

In our own time Brunner built up his Christology, with
an appeal to Melanchthon, by dealing first with the work of
Christ and then with his person.[6] He says he wants to follow
the order of knowing and not that of the subject and declares:
"The person of Christ is knowable from his work." Hence
the treatment of his work should precede that of his person.
To us it seems evident that one thus proceeds, in building

---

6. "Since we, however, follow an inductive and not as elsewhere a de-
ductive method, and thus follow the order of knowing and not the order
of being, we begin, not with the person, but with the works of Christ," E.
Brunner, *Dogmatik II* page 317. Compare also K. H. Miskotte about the
order in which he confesses the Christ in *Fundamenten en Perspectieven
van Belijden*: "First what Christ *does* is dealt with, then what he *is*. The
reverse order is typical for scholasticism and also for "orthodoxy," if one
considers its doctrine and not its much more profound inner life," *De
kern van de zaak*, 1950, page 61. Somewhat later: "We do not begin with
the theanthropic being of Christ but with his *appearance;* this we try to
understand as an operation, a demonstration of power, a revelation of his
messianic glory." We do not regard this a genuine dilemma, and, in addition, it does not harmonize with article 4 of *Fundamenten en Perspectieven.* At the beginning of its Christological creed it reads: "Jesus Christ
is truly God with us." But even Miskotte says also: "The being and the
work of Christ may not, for a moment, be thought of apart from one
another." From this it is clear how little progress one makes with a
vaguely defined antithesis against ontology. It will, in my opinion, be
one of the tasks of present-day theology sharply to define the nature of
speculation in order not to lapse into a cheap handling of this term,
against orthodoxy in particular.

one's Christology, on a wrong premise. Reasoning after this fashion one could as well say that the significance of Christ's work is knowable only from his person, from the reality he represents, since it is his personal work. The fact that we can come to a true faith only by way of a knowledge of the salvation and blessings of Christ does not in the least imply that in dogmatics we must give precedence to the treatment of Christ's work.

In the Bible we continually encounter the irrefragable unity of Christ's person and work. The gospel wants us to understand what Christ does but, at the same time, who he is: the one sent by the Father, the Messiah of Israel. Without this knowledge one can only be puzzled by his work and ask: "Whence hath this man this wisdom, and these mighty works? Is not this the carpenter's son? Is not his mother called Mary? And his brethren, James, and Joseph, and Simon, and Judas? And his sisters, are they not all with us? Whence then hath this man all these things? And they were offended in him" (Matt. 13:54-57). Not to know who he is means: not to understand what his work is; and not to see his work in the right perspective is not to understand his person. One stumbles past his person and work and, offended in the Christ, passes him by. And therefore the revelation of God illumines both Christ's person and work. It is not true that one first gets to know what Christ does and then who he is. Peter is called blessed because the Father has revealed to him, concerning the Christ, that he is the Son of the living God. Nor is this revelation an abstract disclosure of Christ's identity in distinction from his work, for Peter confesses him as the Christ and in this designation is implied an open recognition of his messianic work. But one can never construe a contrast here, nor start out with his work in order thus to arrive at his person. The Scriptures everywhere teach a unity of the two. Paul speaks of Christ as existing in the form of God with immediate reference to his humiliation and exaltation (Phil. 2).

Christ came, and his coming is bound up with his purpose to seek and to save that which was lost and to destroy the works of the evil one. And one who proceeds in his dogmatics from the work of Christ, because his person is known from his work, fails to do justice to the mystery of the person, which gives to the work its eternal and universal value. It is quite impossible rightly to understand the work of Christ without revelation, that is, without understanding that it is God acting in Jesus Christ. In Brunner we note, moreover, that he fails to remain true to his starting-point. He aims to proceed from the work of Christ as a prerequisite for understanding his person, but in the section on the work of Christ he already treats of the "Würdenamen Jesu," as, e.g., "Son of God," and "Immanuel." In this context Brunner says: "Jesus is to be known in that which God does in him."[7] Hence it is merely illusion that Brunner aims to proceed exclusively from the work of Christ. Now appears, too, the methodological error of Brunner's intent. In treating Christ's work he already — and what else could he do? — discusses his offices; so that he is then no longer able to proceed, phenomenologically and inductively, from Christ's work in history. The moment one deals with the offices of Christ he is consulting the light which God's revelation casts over his person, over Christ himself in the administration of his offices. The starting point of Christology will have to be the entire witness of Holy Scripture concerning both Christ's person and his work.

*   *   *

Still there is another question to be answered here. Does not, as many assert, the knowledge of Christ which originates from the knowledge of salvation have decisive significance for the subject under discussion? This, it was said, is true for Christology. Althaus, for instance, declares that the Chris-

---

7. Brunner, *op. cit.*, page 320.

tology of the New Testament runs "from the bottom to the top,"[8] i.e., "from the reality of the man Jesus springs the certainty of the presence of God in him." From here one reasons to the thought of the Deity of Christ and infers the eternity of Christ, the Trinity, and the Incarnation of the eternal Son: that is thinking "from the top to the bottom." Althaus here uses terms like anthropocentric and theocentric and says that the way from the bottom to the top must pattern our Christology. This reasoning assumes that Christology must proceed by the light which the historical Jesus has kindled, and forgets that we no longer face the historical Jesus but the proclamation of Jesus Christ who comes to us in the apostolic kerygma.

The course of Christology cannot be deduced from the course of history. Its background is the revelation of God which illumines the humiliation and exaltation of Christ Jesus, just as the apostles after Pentecost were also witnesses of Christ's resurrection.[9]

If we, in this study, deal separately with the person of Christ, it is not at all because we cherish a one-sided interest in his person, as if we would consider his work of secondary interest. Precisely such a distinction between "primary" and "secondary" is out of place in the reality with which the Gospel confronts us. One who starts off with the person of Christ can assume this point of departure because in the revelation of Scripture touching the person and work of Christ he observes God acting

---

8. P. Althaus, *Grundriss der Dogmatik*, II, page 85. Compare W. Elert, *Der Christliche Glaube*, 1940, page 355ff.

9. In this connection one can point at any number of faulty constructions with which people have also operated in their study of the history of dogma. Gogarten says, for instance, that Luther places the man Jesus, the crucified Christ, and not the second person of the Godhead, in the center of his Christological thinking. (F. Gogarten, *Die Verkündigung Jesu Christi*, 1948, page 217.) And this in contrast to a theological tradition over a thousand years old, which had placed the heavenly Christ in his divine glory at the focal point of its interest. This characterization is the fruit of reaction and creates the impression that Luther had hardly any interest in the confession of Christ's deity, his resurrection, and his glorification. There is an undeniable contrast between Luther and scholastic Christology, but this contrast may certainly not be construed in the manner of Gogarten.

in that person and in the work.   Since, in the history of the
Christian church, people began to doubt that in Jesus Christ
God himself was present and operative among us, we notice
that conflicts, already early in history, ranged precisely around
the quality of this work of Christ.   It was not at all a warped
"ontological" interest in the being of Christ which prompted
the church, in the early centuries, to ward off every violation of
Christ's true deity and true humanity.   If anything stands out
in the early conflicts it is that the church in defending the person
of Christ was deeply concerned about keeping pure the message
of salvation and the quality of his work.

And so it remained in later times.   We are thinking of the
Reformation period when theologians had an unusually clear
eye for the unity of the person and work of Christ.   They spoke
of Christ, who came to us in his work.   And when they spoke
of his work and of the blessings implicit for us in that work,
they had in mind, as one with this salvation, him whose salvation it is.   For them the fruit of Christ's work was not an
impersonal blessedness, a peace and happiness which could also
be abstracted from his person, but they spoke of *his* blessing
and *his* nearness.   Calvin says somewhere "that the whole of
our salvation, and all the branches of it, are comprehended in
Christ," and since "blessings of every kind are deposited in
him, let us draw from his treasury, and from no other source,
till our desires are satisfied."[10]   There is a "mystica communicatio" of believers with Christ, a being planted in his
body, a being bound up with him — as this also comes to clear
expression in the Reformed confessions and liturgical formulas.
Particularly in the Reformed view of the Lord's Supper this
unity comes to lucid expression.   To Bavinck the most striking
aspect of Calvin's doctrine of the Lord's Supper was that there
is no participation in the benefits of Christ except after and
through communion with his person.[11]

10. Calvin, *Institutes* II, 16, 19.
11. H. Bavinck. *Calvijns leer over het avondmaal.* In: *Kennis en leven,*
1922, p. 177.

The Reformed formula for the celebration of the Lord's Supper teaches that as often as we receive the bread and the wine Christ nourishes and refreshes us with his crucified body and shed blood. There is a communion, not with impersonal gifts of Christ, conceivable also apart from him, but with himself, with his true body and blood, with him, truly God and truly man, through the power of the Holy Spirit. Bavinck points out that in Calvin the thought occurs that in the Lord's Supper we receive part in the *substance* of Christ's flesh and blood. The intent of this statement is obviously to guard against every separation between the person and work. It is Christ's work, qualified by his reality as truly God and man; and one who has not grasped this unity by faith can only grope for the salvation contained in him. Article 36 of the Confessio Gallicana also gives clear expression to this truth when it declares that in the Lord's Supper we have communion with Christ's body and blood, "so that we are one with him and share his life." We believe, the creed continues, that through the secret and incomprehensible strength of his Spirit he nourishes and vivifies us with the substance of his body and blood. When the synod of La Rochelle in 1571 further elucidated the word "substance" it stressed that we do not have part "in his merits and gifts, which he communicates to us through his Spirit, without having part in himself."

All this points to sharp opposition to the abstraction of Christ's work from his person. Just as little as one can speak of his person by itself without mentioning also his work, so one cannot understand and evaluate the work of Christ unless he know that it is *his* work.

*   *   *

When Korff speaks about the distinction between the person and work of Christ, he refers to the danger that "this work obtains, to our minds, a certain independence and is somewhat absolved from the person." This danger one can regard, as do

Calvin and Korff, as a terrible depersonalization of redemption. On the other hand one can abstract the person of Christ from his work and so get lost in a speculative Christology which bears the marks of impoverishment on its forehead. Either danger can be overcome, but only by the continual reference to Scripture of a Scripture-oriented faith. In concerning ourselves, in this book, with the confession touching the person of Christ we are convinced this work can be faithfully carried out only if we continually remember that the aim is not to gather abstract data about the person of Christ but rather to gain an insight into what the Scriptures tell us about the person of him whose name is Jesus and who, as the Christ, exercised his office in the completion of the work God the Father had assigned to him.

Many and various are the givens of Scripture about the person and work of Christ, about his identity and work. Not every subdivision of theology treats of each aspect with the same elaborateness. But dogmatic reflection is, at bottom, one. Hence it is possible first to discuss the person of Christ and then to speak about his work, without slipping into the abyss of abstraction.

Promise and Fulfillment

CHAPTER VII

Promise and Fulfillment

A STUDY of the Scriptural message regarding Jesus Christ leads one almost automatically to the subject, currently a center of interest, of the significance of the Old Testament. The cause of this renewed interest, spurting up as it does in numerous theologies of the Old Testament appearing in our day, lies undoubtedly in a reaction to the flood of anti-Semitism which characterizes our time. Under the influence of anti-Semitic propaganda many began to depreciate the significance and value of the Old Testament because they increasingly viewed it as representing a specifically *Jewish* religion. And, to be sure, anti-Semitism is not solely responsible for this far-reaching devaluation of the Old Testament, for it has a long history which begins already with Marcion and continues through Harnack who declared with emphasis that the Old Testament is of no value to the Christian church; but it cannot be denied that anti-Semitism played an important role in the characterization of the Old Testament as a purely Jewish book. In our day, out of a strong and sometimes passionate reaction against this depreciation, an intensified interest in the Old Testament can be observed. With increasing emphasis it was denied that the Old Testament is a mere document of the Jewish religion. The church, it was said, correctly saw it as the record of God's revelation also for the church of Jesus Christ, as the church, in confessing that the Old and New Testament are a harmonious unity, had viewed it from ancient times. The Old Testament, too, was again regarded as a book of testimony concerning Jesus Christ and, by this route, the problem of the

Christological exegesis of the Old Testament came again to the fore. A strong stimulus to the discussion of this exegesis has been the work of Wilhelm Vischer about "Das Christuszeugnis des Alten Testamentes," in which he tried to carry out his program for a Christological exegesis.[1] Some enthusiastically accepted Vischer's program and began to work it out in detail, while others regarded it with growing misgivings and saw in it a new allegorical exegesis which would in the end evoke new reactions and thus contribute to a fresh aversion to the Christological exegesis of the Old Testament.[2] In Vischer's program they thought they saw a complete absence of historical-critical research, because while he thought he could, at every point, cause "the testimony" to be heard he failed to do justice to a genuine historical approach to the text.[3]

The result is that today we are caught in new tensions surrounding the Old Testament. In any case, the assurance with which Harnack and many others after him spoke of the Old Testament is quite gone. We now encounter, at the opposite pole, the most vigorous statements about the surpassing significance of the Old Testament. Van Ruler says, for instance, that the Old Testament is the real Bible; the apostles, says he, in no sense wrote a new Bible; in fact, they did not even add a new piece to the Old Testament, but merely gave the only interpretation of the only Bible: the Old Testament. The books of the New Testament are intended only as "the list of explanatory notes in the back. That the list should contain something different from the book itself would have sounded

---

1. Wilhelm Vischer, *Das Christuszeugnis des Alten Testamentes*, Volume I (Das Gesetz) 1935, and Volume II, *Die früheren Profeten*, 1942.

2. Squarely opposed to Vischer is E. Hirsch, *Das alte Testament und das Evangelium*, 1936. To him the Old Testament is a document of a legalistic religion displaced by the Christian faith, page 26.

3. Apart from several contributions on this subject published in the *Theologische Blätter* of 1935 and 1936, see W. J. de Wilde, *Het probleem van het O.T.*, 1938, and H. W. Obbink *Theologische Bezinning op het O.T.*, 1937.

blasphemous in the ears of the New Testament writers."[4]
Against this position came the reaction that the unique significance of the New Testament, in which the message of the fulfillment of the promise revealed the fulness of Redemption much
more plainly and lucidly than the Old Testament, threatened,
in Van Ruler's extravagant statement, to be eclipsed. Thus
the relationship between the Old and the New Testament re-
appeared on the program of theology. It is plain that from
a certain point of view we must deal with these questions, especially since the conflict pivotally concerns the Messianic
prophecies in the Old Testament.

*   *   *

These questions are the more important in view of the great
conflict between the synagogue and the church. In this conflict the church believingly testifies to the progress of redemptive history and to the promise-fulfillment relationship between
the Old Testament and the New, while, with equal emphasis,
the synagogue declares the opposite.

It is important to note that in this debate the church appealed
to the New Testament itself. There, in numerous and varied
statements, the interconnection and harmony between the two
Testaments are pointed out and expressed. We are referring
to the wealth of quotations in the gospels and epistles which
indicate fulfillment.

Christ himself declares that the Old Testament scriptures
"are they which bear witness of me" (John 5:39). The Old
Testament to him was not a book of significance to the Jews
only but a book having direct bearing on him and his work.
This point of view he applied concretely when, after the Resurrection, he was in conversation with the two men on the road
to Emmaus about the central cause of their extreme depression.
He ascribed it not to a misunderstanding of, but to their unbelief toward, the Old Testament prophecies: O foolish men,

---

4. A. A. van Ruler, *Religie en Politiek,* 1945, pages 123 and 125.

and slow of heart to believe in all that the prophets have spoken!
Behooved it not the Christ to suffer these things, and to enter
into his glory?   (Luke 24:25-27)   And although we do not
know the details of the instruction which then followed, we do
hear of a program: "And beginning from Moses and from all
the prophets he interpreted to them in all the scriptures the
things concerning himself."

The evangelists and the apostles, on numerous occasions,
point out the same connection.   They view Christ's coming
into the flesh as the fulfillment of Old Testament prophecy.
They perceived the deep and wonderful unity in virtue of which
the Old Testament, far from being merely a Jewish book, is
full of Jesus Christ.   They do not provide systematic elucida-
tions of this unity but in their thinking and preaching and acting they proceed from it.   Any number of historical events are
illuminated by reference to the prophets.   The unbelief of the
Jews toward Christ is viewed in connection with Isaiah, "because he saw his glory; and he spake of him."   In Peter's
speech on Pentecost these same connections are indicated when
he introduces the quotation of Psalm 16 with the words: "For
David says concerning him. . ." (Acts 2:25).   He points out
too that David, as prophet, foresaw the Resurrection of Christ,
and says "that neither was he left unto Hades, nor did his
flesh see corruption" (v. 31).   Seeing these connections, the
apostles never worked them out in a systematic whole but they
referred to them in concrete and lively fashion.   Here and
there, however, we note a more general characterization.   In
discussing the relationship between the Old and the New Testament and the transition from the Old to the New Covenant,
Paul declares that the Jews who read the Old Testament have
a covering over their hearts which will disappear only in Christ
(II Cor. 3:14 ff).   Hence there can hardly be a difference of
opinion about the proposition that the New Testament never
assumes a breach between itself and the Old Testament.   It is
rather the meaningfully fulfilling continuation of the Old; a

fact to which the Church's acceptance of the whole canon —
Old and New — corresponds.   When the church or theology
spoke of promise and fulfillment it was this undeniable interconnection they were referring to; one can also say: they were
referring to the Christian character of the Old Testament. One
can boil down the church's credo regarding the Scriptures into
the statement that it is no anachronism to say that the Old
Testament is Christian.

The more one studies the New Testament the more he discovers these varied connections.   We hear of a connection between the birth of Christ and the Immanuel prophecy (Matt.
1:23; Isaiah 7:14); between the flight to Egypt and the
prophecy of Hosea: "Out of Egypt did I call my son" (Matt.
2:15; Hosea 11:1); between Christ's being left alone by his
disciples on the night of his passion and the prophecy of the
smitten shepherd (Matt. 26:31; Zech. 13:7); between the
Man of Sorrows, Jesus Christ, and the prophecy of Isaiah 53
(Compare Acts 8:32 ff. with I Peter 2:23-24; also Isaiah 53:9
with Matt. 27:56-60; Isaiah 53:12 with Mark 15:27).   Christ
is viewed as the fulfillment of the entire Old Testament.   When
John points out a connection between Christ and the sacrificial
lamb (John 1:29), and manna (John 6:22 ff), and the serpent
in the wilderness (John 3:14), then by that token he views the
Old Testament as the great, historical, preparatory illumination
of the coming redemption.   It is evident from all the data that
we face, not a few incidental and arbitrary illustrations, but a
comprehensive testimony pointing to and converging on the
coming Redeemer Jesus Christ. Even personages surrounding
Jesus Christ share in these prophetic unities, as is evident when
a relation is pointed out between the prophecy of Malachi and
John the Baptist (Mal. 3:1 and Matt. 11:10), and even for
Judas' betrayal and death we are referred to the Psalms (Compare John 13:18, "He that eateth my bread lifted his heel
against me," with Ps. 41:9; see also Acts 1:20, Ps. 69:25,
and Ps. 109:8).   Sometimes the relationships pointed out are

strikingly concrete; as, for instance, the prophecy of the birth
of Christ at Bethlehem (Micah 5:2; Matt. 2:5-6) and the
reference to the Old Testament in connection with the crucifixion: "For these things came to pass, that the scripture
might be fulfilled, A bone of him shall not be broken" (John
19:36; Ps. 34:20; Ex. 12:46).

These few examples, picked from the many which could be
added, are sufficient to make plain how the church came to point
out, with such great emphasis, the indissoluble connection
between the Old Testament and the New. It did not, to be
sure, deny the distinction, and it tried in every period to arrive
at a definition of the unity and the remaining distinction, but
it maintained both the Old and the New as the canon of its
faith and practice.[5]

The conflict about the meaning of the Old Testament was
serious precisely because the confession of the church is directly based upon the incontrovertible testimony of the New
Testament itself. In this discussion the New Testament illumination of the Old particularly became a target of
criticism. The church, it was said, did not have the right,
from the use which the New Testament makes of the
Old, to derive a rule by which to point out and prove the unity
of the two Testaments.

We can summarize this discussion as follows: the objectors frequently regard the Christological exegesis of the Old
Testament as an act of violence, a forced interpretation which

5. Compare Calvin's view of the relation between the Old Testament
and the New, when he speaks of "their similarity or rather unity" (Inst.
II, X, 2). When Hibert speaks of a "certain antinomy running through
the Christian acceptance of the Old Testament," and then points to what
Paul says about keeping the law and circumcision as means toward finding
peace with God, and about unbelieving Jews who, because they do not
recognize Jesus, are not true sons of Abraham, we sense in these examples that the concept "antinomy" is plainly unserviceable. This is the
more apparent when we note what follows: Yet, though the Jewish system
is thus declared to be superseded, appeal is invariably made, for the
justification of this, to the Old Testament itself." Old Testament and
"Jewish system" are not identical. See A. G. Hibert, The Authority of
the Old Testament, 1947, page 200.

proceeds a priori from a given view of the text and takes little
or no notice of what the Old Testament itself says or intends to say. They regard the Christological interpretation
as edifying but untrue. Thus arose a sharp conflict between
the historical-critical exegesis and the Messianic exegesis of the
Old Testament. Although the decision to be made in this
conflict is ultimately a decision of faith, we must not forget
that the issue has been frequently obscured by an arbitrary
search for and indication of connections and parallels. Facile
conclusions were then often made with regard to Christ in the
Old Covenant on the basis of striking parallels. While we
note that even the New Testament was considered arbitrary
by critics, we may not underestimate the danger of arbitrariness lest it should in the end contribute to a devaluation of
the Old Testament. People have too often believed themselves safe because they witnessed the criticism to which the
New Testament in its approach to the Old was subjected. Von
Rad, to mention one critic, directed sharp accusations against
Vischer for this reason. With the assurance of historical criticism he observes that Vischer's exegesis is irresponsible. One
can no longer assume a connection between Christ and Genesis
3:15, "after Old Testament scholars have, for a long time and
unanimously, regarded that interpretation of Genesis 3:15 as
faulty."[6] Nor should we give a Messianic interpretation to the
songs about the suffering servant of the Lord or see in Psalm
22 anything more than "the lament of a devout man in a deep
crisis."[7] Von Rad does believe that Christ is in the Old Testament but . . . it is not our power to say how and where; we
must begin by approaching the documents of the Old Testament
in their temporal uniqueness and historical conditioning.

We are facing a profound question — this much is plain —
surrounded from various directions by danger. On the one
hand, there is the influence of historical criticism which often

---

6. G. von Rad, *Das Christuszeugnis des A.T.*, Theol. Blätter, 1935, page
253.
7. *Ibid.*, page 253.

rejects with vigor the interpretation of the Old Testament in light of the New and tries to get from under the grip of the New Testament point of view. On the other hand, there is the danger, by no means imaginary, of interpreting the Old Testament arbitrarily.

In this connection we note especially the allegorical exegesis which has been such a powerful influence in the church and in theology. Most characteristic of this exegesis is that it always dissociates itself more or less from the text and probes beyond the so-called "sensus litteralis" for a deeper meaning, a deeper truth, in which the reader, if he wishes to have a truly spiritual understanding of the text, should be primarily interested. This allegorical exegesis is applied not only to the Old Testament but also to other literature, to Homer, for instance; in more enlightened times the reader stumbles over various "discrepancies" in the text which are then removed with the aid of allegorical exegesis.[8] In the allegorical method there is often a concealed apologetic intent: the exegete wishes to vindicate the text by pointing out that the reader must not fall over the offensive literal text, but penetrate into its deeper meaning. Hence the exegete does not eliminate part of the text but offers a given interpretation.[9] Philo already applied the allegorical approach to the Old Testament in order to show that the Old Testament teaches the wisdom of the Greeks. For this purpose he tries to get beyond the literal text by finding the "deeper" meaning. This hidden meaning can be found only by those who permit the spiritual to dominate the sensuous. By means of this approach one discovers that the kings mentioned in Genesis 14 are psychological conditions and thus this passage gets significance for our day. The literal sense evaporates at the approach of allegorical exegesis. But this exegesis

---

8. Compare R. H. Woltjer, *Allegorie en allegorische verklaring in de Oudheid*, 1941.

9. Stein says: "Allegory issues from distress of the conscience and is intended to adjust the conflict between religion and the maturing critical mind" (in Torm, *Hermeneutik*, p. 213ff.).

is not limited to Philo; we find it also in the Christian church when it had to endure numerous attacks, among others in connection with certain difficulties in the Old Testament.   We already find it in Barnabas and in the Alexandrine school of Clement and Origen; in him we repeatedly run across the idea that the Bible actually conceals its real meaning behind a facade of literalness in order that we would search the more diligently for it.[10] Origen distinguished between the literal, the psychic, and the pneumatic meaning of a given passage, while in the Middle Ages theologians distinguished between four levels of meaning.[11]

The allegorical approach, it is clear, was an open gateway to arbitrariness in the interpretation of Scripture.[12]   Its great influence is certainly due to the striking new perspectives which seemed to open up and also to the idea that, rather in this manner than by the literal exegesis, the Christ would become visible to the eye of faith also in the Old Testament.   There has nevertheless been persistent opposition to allegorical exegesis.   The Antiochian school already demanded a return to the literal text. In its strong reaction it showed a tendency at times to give an "ordinary" interpretation to various prophecies which plainly speak of Christ.

In the Middle Ages, too, a few people became aware of the dangers of arbitrariness attending the allegorical approach. It was Thomas Aquinas to a certain extent, and especially Nicolaus of Lyra, who began to break with the tradition of the fourfold meaning of Scripture and wanted to get back to the literal sense of the text.   But the real revolution in hermeneutics came about in the Reformation period.   Not Erasmus, but

---

10. See W. dem Boer, *De allegorese in het werk van Clemens Alexandrinus,* 1940.

11. E. von Dobschutz, *Vom vierfachen Schriftsinn. Die Geschichte einer Theorie.* In: *Harnack-Ehrung,* 1921, pages 1-13. Also G. Ebeling, *Evangelische Schriftauslegung. Eine Untersuchung zu Luthers Hermeneutik,* 1942.

12. Compare: F. W. Grosheide, *Hermeneutiek,* page 187ff.; B. J. Alfrink, *Over "typologische" exegese van het O.T.,* 1945; J. Ridderbos, *Over de uitlegging van het O.T.,* Bijbles Handboek I.

Luther, and especially Calvin, wanted to hear again what the text itself said, and they became increasingly aware of the dangers of arbitrary interpretation. According to Calvin, Origen robbed the Bible of its true meaning by asserting that the literal sense was too trifling and that under the surface much deeper truths lay hidden — truths which could be displayed only by allegorical exegesis. This opinion Calvin regards as a fiction of Satan who wishes to avert our attention from the real meaning of Scripture by pointing out the "fertility" of the text.[13]

He refuses to distinguish between the literal and the spiritual meaning of Scripture and again combats, in his exegesis of II Cor. 3:6, the view of Origen as a pernicious error.[14] Calvin's opposition has been of great significance in keeping at bay the obscuration of Scripture as well as arbitrariness in exegesis. The fertility and depth of Scripture do not consist in what caprice can disinter from it, no matter with what sweet homiletic effect such exegesis would speak of Christ in the Old Testament. But they consist in that which God has really put in the text. For this reason Calvin wrestles with so much *élan* for a sound treatment of the literal meaning. To him there is no tension between the text of Scripture and Divine truth and to him the depth of the Word of God is in the text. In allegorical exegesis the text functions only, really, as "Hinweis," as a springboard for a dangerous exegetical leap. The text, as starting point, is swiftly left behind in order that the exegete may hasten to his remote destination.

In our day the problem of allegorical exegesis again became important because there was a renewed dissociation from the simple meaning of Scripture. We no longer, to be sure, have the facile exegesis of earlier times when people, by inventively musing over the parable of the good Samaritan, believed that

13. See Calvin's commentary on Gal. 4:22: "hoc procul dubio Satanae commentum fuit ad elevandum Scripturae auctoritatem." Calvin denies that the fertility of the Scriptures is to be found in "variis sensibus."
14. perniciousus error; fons multorum malorum; see further *Inst.* II, V, 19.

Jericho was the world, that the man who fell among robbers was Adam, and that Jerusalem was Paradise. Blind men immediately became spiritually blind and lepers were heretics. We no longer face allegorizing in this coarse form. The allegorical exegesis of our day originated in a vehement movement of reaction to a technical, literary-critical, exegesis. Amid a multiplicity of kinds of exegesis, as the psychological, pneumatic, theological, and existential, there was a return to the Christological exegesis, which was to do justice to the Old Testament witness to Christ. People were no longer content with a historical exegesis which, though it offered the preacher a great deal of contextual and literary materials, did not enable him to preach the Christ on the basis of a given passage. They emphasized that the heart of the Old Testament was "testimony," not any human morality or religion, or examples to be followed, or histories having intrinsic interest. The book of Vischer was called a "judgment" upon Old Testament scholarship which had lost itself in archeology and the history of religion. Again the search was on for connections and analogies which would make plain to the entire church that the Old Testament was basically a "witness to Christ."

*   *   *

This places us before a peculiar dilemma. On the one hand we witness a continuation of the attitude which rejects all Christological exegesis and recognizes only historical-critical exegesis. And on the other we face a Christological exegesis which leaves the impression, in many ways, of being forced and arbitrary. Between the two of them lies the cardinal question: In what manner do you point out the Christ in the Old Testament? Representatives of current Christological exegesis often impress us with the idea that what is needed is a special charismatic ingenuity which enables a person to track down all sorts of parallels and to point out associations which make a startling impression. But who will guarantee us that we are given the true meaning and intent of Scripture and that we are not treated to the startling discoveries of an exegete? Vischer is certainly right in saying: "The Christian Church stands or falls with the recognition of the unity of the two Testaments."[15] And Vischer is right, too, when he defends the value of the light shed by the New Testament on the Old. But at the same time we observe clearly the threat of arbitrariness in the concrete application of his theses. It has been said of Pascal that he understood the entire Old Testament Christocentrically and, for that reason, made various transformations and omissions in his translation of the Bible. Here lies the danger — for which every exegete must be on his guard — of allowing his imagination to dominate the text. In this manner one arrives at a devaluation of Scripture in the interest of a system. Vischer is a good example. At every point his ear itches to detect the "testimony" and thus he finds himself construing a discrepancy between the "testimony" and history. His exegesis of the history of Joshua is a case in point. In it, he says, we do not have a historical record but a "joint history," in which elements from different periods play a role — also elements from the past. This is plain to Vischer because there is, according to him, an incongruency between historical fact and the biblical record, since in Joshua's day it was eight centuries before that Ai had been reduced to rubble, while the Bible presents the destruction of Ai as a real conquest. The Bible story ascribes to Joshua events which took place before or after his lifetime. One must therefore be able to see through the record in order to get a glimpse of the true witness with which all these chronicles are concerned. To Vischer the whole historical-critical problem is swept away in this manner. The historical aspect of the text and of the actual events is no longer important, since the aim of the Old Testament is not reportorial accuracy but "testimony" and "by this presentation the actual facts of history

---

15. Vischer, *Ibid.*, I. page 32.

become much more apparent." It is the true history of the people of God which is here recorded.

The result of this view is a consistent elimination of the perspectives of redemptive history: everything is adjusted to a historically unimportant witness. In Hellbardt the results are even plainer, for he even goes beyond Vischer in excessive formulations. To him there can be no actual redemptive-historical difference between the Old Testament and the New; to him a genuine progression in redemptive history is non-existent.[16] The only difference is that the Old Testament testifies to the reality of the Gospel as truth whereas the New Testament testifies to the *reality* of salvation. Truth and reality: with these two words Hellbardt wants to indicate the relation between the two Testaments. It is not a matter of promise and fulfillment, or of a contrast between law and gospel, but in both the message is the Gospel. The message of the Old Testament is already that God has compassion on us through the sacrifice of his Son and that this act of God must necessarily issue into the Son's becoming a sacrifice and into the Lord's becoming a servant. "But that this has therefore happened the Old Testament does not say." The truth is present only in word, not in historical fact. The New Testament then proclaims to us the reality.

Under the Old Covenant there can be no question of a redemptive history. The witness is the thing, as in Vischer, who, on the basis of the witness-concept, declares that the Old Testament tells us "what the Christ is and the New, who he is." These men do not hesitate to speak of the Old and New Testament as *identical*. For the idea is not progression on a single historical line, but a circle drawn about a center; in this circle, to the left and to the right, are two arcs equidistant

---

16. Hellbardt, *Das A.T. und das Evangelium*, 1933, and *Der verheiszene Konig. Das Christuszeugnis des Hosea,* 1935. See further N. W. Porteous, *Towards a Theology of the Old Testament*: "In fact, he (Hellbardt) seems to think that the dignity of exegesis depends on the extent to which we do exclude the concept of time" (Scottish Journal of Theology, 1948, page 142).

from the center. Thus the entire concept of promise and fulfillment is altered. On this point Hellbardt does not leave us
in doubt: "The futurity of the fulfilling events is not, as far
as the Old Testament is concerned, the historical futurity of
the birth of Jesus and of the course of his life. The fact that
Jesus appeared in the world subsequent in time to the Old
Testament is, theologically speaking, of secondary importance."
Now it is perfectly clear why he has no headaches over historical criticism; his concern is limited to·the "Zeugnis" which,
though it takes place in history, nonetheless transcends history.
On this view the idea is to have one's eyes and ears open for
"the witness to Christ." One can also say that, not historical
progression, but an epistemological principle, is the crux of this
view. The history of the people of God in the Old Testament
evaporates. One cannot really posit any essential difference
between the Old Testament and the New since in both the same
witness is operative. It is not hard to point out that the Zeug-
nis-view does less than justice to the total witness of Scripture
which does not cease to point out to us God's progressive
action in history — and does not merely refer to the knowledge
of the Messiah. Here, correctly says Eichrodt, lies the "cardinal point" of Christological exegesis. The revelation of God
enters into history. God's path through the world and through
the history of his elect people is eschatologically directed. The
knowledge of the salvation prepared and to be realized by God
is, to be sure, of supreme interest to that people but, wrapped
up in it, is the action of God, which is fully directed to its
realization. Excessive and incorrect is Hellbardt's statement
that the Torah and the prophets culminate in the testimony
that God "has redeemed," not, "is going to redeem," his people
from all their sins. No one will deny that God saved his
people out of Egypt but this act is immediately related to the
promise concerning Canaan and, in this promise, to a still
bigger future. "All of Israel's historiography is sustained by
the conscious knowledge of a grand meaningful unity in God's

guidance of and control over Israel — a unity in which everything, from the beginning of the historical process to the end,
has as its final goal that God's kingdom shall shed its light
upon all nations."[17] The witness of the Old Testament is re-
plete with this action of God and must never be isolated from
it. This witness is conditioned by history and must, therefor,
be viewed as something different from what Vischer and Hellbardt make of it. On the basis of their essentially unhistorical
Zeugnis-concept there can be no variation and progress as determined by the acts of God. Hellbardt is completely consistent when he says: "Into this revelation one cannot introduce
the category of 'more or less.' "[18]

This seems to give the highest possible honor to the authority
of Scripture, specifically to that of the Old Testament, but the
consequence is that on this view one should find in every text
an equally explicit, testimony to the truth of Jesus Christ. The
sign of Cain, for instance, is interpreted as the mark of God's
inviolable property in such a way "that the sign of
the cross in its deepest meaning renews and confirms the
symbolic content of the sign of Cain."[19] In other exegetes this
perspective is completely missing but in Vischer the sign of
Cain becomes a summary of the *locus de justificatione*. It is
caprice which dictates meanings here. The interpretation does
not arise from the text itself but is based upon ingenious parallels and fantastic combinations. Vischer cannot be blamed if,
when he discusses the sacrifice of Abraham, he searches in
all of Scripture for passages which have a bearing on it. But
we do register our disapproval of the unhistorical "comparison"
he suddenly makes: "And do we not see, then, how the darkness of Good Friday enshrouds this sacrificial journey and how
the dark cloud is fringed with the brightness of the Easter
sun?" When the story mentions that God himself will provide
the lamb for a burnt-offering, Vischer asks: "Can we read

---

17. Eichrodt, *Theol. Blätter,* 1938, page 79.
18. Hellbardt, *Das A.T. und das Evangelium,* page 136.
19. Vischer, *Ibid.,* I, page 95.

this without looking through a window into the distance and seeing the Only-begotten Son treading the road of his passion from the Mount of Olives through Gethsemane as the lamb which bears the sin of the world?" Vischer presents parallels without making plain the redemptive-historical perspective and, for that reason, his exegesis strikes us as arbitrary. He proceeds on the assumption that every text *must* explicitly deal with Jesus Christ and on this a priori basis he is driven to his Zeugnis-concept. He is not sufficiently aware that the Old Testament witness to Christ is imbedded in a long history in which the witness concerning redemption is related to God's guidance of Israel. Thus the single-pitched "Zeugnis," as we find it in Vischer, disappears and makes way for an extremely vital and lively revelation of God which, though it has its center in the promise touching Jesus Christ, is woven together with all the acts of God which, in this history, are directed to the Christ. Hence a study which points out these organic interconnections makes a stronger impression and is of greater help than the often far-fetched parallels of Vischer.[20] And the witness of the Old Testament will not, then, have to be limited to a given part of the Old Testament — as Vischer, though inconsistently, limits it.

No one may say that a given part of the Old Testament is without bearing on Jesus Christ, even though certain parts do not belong to what are generally called Messianic prophecies. The prophecy touching Christ is historical in nature and is integrally one with all the works of God. It is focussed on the coming of the Messiah but, in connection with him, it reaches out to the completion of the work of God, to the kingdom of God, to the new heaven and the new earth. A person may call the Old Testament Christocentric, provided this is not placed in opposition to the trinitarian view, for we know that

---

20. I am thinking now of books as that of Martin Schmidt, *Prophet und Tempel, Eine Studie zum Problem der Gottesnähe im A.T.*, 1948, and Norman H. Snaith, *The Distinctive Ideas of the O. T.*, 1947.

Christ himself referred to the Father and will one day return the kingdom into his hands. These perspectives can in the nature of the case mean nothing to one who hears only "testimonies" in the Old Testament — testimonies lying on the periphery but referring to the center: the incarnation of the Word. Such an exegete must remain within the boundaries of a narrow Messianism in order, at last, to relapse into allegory. Such a method may seem fruitful to the church of Christ and to open new homiletic perspectives but, after a while, such preaching will be noticeably characterized by a peculiar monotony which contrasts sharply with the vitality of the redemptive-historical drama found in Scripture. Anyone who views the circle of the Messianic testimony to the exclusion of the line of redemptive history must, in the end, regard as unimportant all historical data and specific circumstances, and thus lose the possibility of thinking in truly historical fashion of the works of God. We are conscious, too, of the possibility that, in reaction to the Zeugnis-approach, people may lapse into the opposite error of a superficial fear of any integrated point of view. Then too the Christological perspective of the Old Testament is lost. Against this error one can arm himself only when he penetrates deeply into the fullness of Scripture. Christ's disclosure to the men of Emmaus serves as a sharp warning against any superficial exegesis which fails to recognize the depths of Scripture after it has first been opposed to the "deeper meaning" of allegorical exegesis. But there is still another possibility: the view that seeking the truth *behind* the truth is an escape from what God has really said, and the effort to understand the unity of redemptive history, and the conception of the New Testament which sees in Christ the fulfillment of the Old. *Tertium non datur*: either the Old Testament is truly full of Christ or the writers of the New Testament have simply, on the basis of their Christian faith, read Christ into the Old Testament — an undeniable falsification of history.

At this point lies the ultimate decision as to the truth of the testimony and the canon of the Christian church and of the Old Testament as a "Christian" book. Without bias and with complete honesty the church and its theologians will have to study the entire Scriptures in order that they may, in the way of caution, begin to understand something of the riches of God's historical course through the world and of his dealings with his people. In this manner one will see continuities which emerge from Scripture itself and thus lose the hallmarks of arbitrary exegesis.

We are often struck by the fact that Protestant exegetes are more conscious of the dangers of allegorical exegesis than their Roman Catholic colleagues. This is especially evident in the evalution of certain forms of exegesis current among the church fathers. When C. J. De Vogel speaks about the opposition of Athanasius to Arius,[21] she points among other things to Athanasius' polemic against the Arian heresy that Christ is merely a perfect man. In reply Athanasius quotes a text from Deuteronomy: ". . . and thy life shall hang in doubt before thee" (28:66). These words clearly remind the church father of the crucified one, who is our life; a conception which was certainly not implied in the text since it describes the curse of God upon the infidelity of his people. This is so plain that De Vogel herself says: "The text is made to say something not intended by the author." Still she does not reject the exegesis of Athanasius. She says this is no exegesis in the common sense of the term but meditation. "The words are understood in their prophetic import, quite apart from the historical context." According to her we could speak here of a pneumatic exegesis, a spiritual interpretation to be placed alongside of the historical interpretation. In principle we have here a weakening of resistance to allegorical exegesis and a denial of the revelational character of the words of the Old Testament.

---

21. C. J. de Vogel, *Redevoeringen van Athanasius tegen de Arianen* (Monumenta Christiana II, 1949, par. XXIV, XXXVI, and XXXVIII).

For the purpose of mystical interpretation is not to explain the Word of God but to provide a "Zeugnis," even while the claims of historical exegesis are admitted.

We face the same charitable attitude in the instructive book of Danielou who gives a fascinating picture of patristic exegesis and shows how the patres pointed out various analogies and parallels in the Old Testament.[22] He mentions, for example, the parallels between the sleep of Adam and the birth of the church,[23] the mystical exodus, the fall of Jericho, and the end of the world. He arrives at the conclusion that in spite of the differences there is extensive unanimity in the patres and this exegesis therefore belongs to the traditional deposit of the church. But in patristic exegesis there appears a glaring weakening of critical insight over against arbitrary exegesis.

It is only when we are deeply convinced of the calling of exegesis truly and exclusively to understand the Word of God and that in all its depth, that we may be preserved from the confusion of allegorical exegesis which, after all, loses sight of history in the interest of the "testimony" and forgets that the testimony can no longer be heard when it is lifted out of its historical context.[24]

All this is integrally connected with the central problem of the relation between promise and fulfillment. This relation can be understood only in the light of the biblical-historical point of view. Van Ruler, in defending the thesis that the Old Testament is the true Bible, vigorously rejects the idea of continuing revelation. Various aberrations, according to him,

---

22. Jean Danielou, *Saeramentum futuri. Etudes sur les origines de la typologie biblique,* 1950. To Danielou's conclusions belongs also the following: Patristic exegesis continues the messianic typology of the Old Testament prophets who described the Kingdom to come as a new paradise, a new Exodus, or as a new Deluge," page 257.
23. Compare K. Barth in his *Kirchliche Dogmatik,* III, 1, 367, where Barth explains the deep sleep of Adam during the creation of Eve as follows: "As the church of Jesus has its origin in his death sleep, so it shall stand before him completed in his Resurrection."
24. Compare the arbitrary allegorical exegesis with the epistle to the Hebrews to relish the contrast. See also Goppelt, *Typos,* page 193ff.

are concealed in this idea. First of all: a wrong concept of history.[25] The idea of a progressive revelation presupposes a linear view of history, while the Biblical view of history is cyclical: it reveals a circle of prophetic and apostolic witness around the real history, in the fullness of time, of an ingressive revelation. Further, the idea of a continuing revelation presupposes an intellectualistic concept of revelation: revelation is viewed as communication of doctrine. The biblical notion of revelation is however that of an *encounter* in the reality which takes place in Jesus Christ. "The once-for-all fact of the forgiveness of our sins by the Son of God in human flesh excludes every notion of a continuing revelation." In the third place, Van Ruler points to the pattern of promise and fulfillment by which people like to indicate the relation between the Old Testament and the New but then in such a way that the fulfillment invalidates the promise, because a realized salvation takes the place of the promise. According to Van Ruler, this is "one of the most fatal confusions of all Christian categories."

For the fulfillment of the promise in the New Testament does not mean that "the promise has passed over into reality and has laid aside its character as promise but it means that the promise has now come to its culminating potency and concentration."

To us it is clear that in this manner one cannot formulate the relation between promise and fulfillment and that Van Ruler's theses are too much conditioned by reaction. In the last few years there has been a change of mind on the biblical concept of history, especially through the influence of Cullmann who militated against a cyclical concept of history and defended a linear concept which, says he, is the biblical view.[26] As a result there was in many people a growing appreciation for the

25. A. A. Van Ruler, *De waarde van het Oude Testament,* in: *Religie en Politiek,* 1945, page 127.
26. O. Cullmann *Christus und die Zeit,* 1946, page 44, "the ascending line versus the circle." On the cyclical concept of history see K. Schilder, *Heid. Catech.* II, page 270ff.

relationship between promise and fulfillment and especially in connection with the idea of continuing revelation. Van Ruler's objections against this idea do not convince us, and proceed from untenable premises.[27] In the first place, it is not true that the idea of progressive or continuing revelation is necessarily intertwined with an intellectualistic concept of revelation. On the contrary, one should rather say that the idea of continuing revelation is charged with the thought of God's actions in the encounter with his people. Integral with God's active concern with his people is communication, but this has nothing to do with intellectualism. The most important point of Van Ruler's view touches the relation between promise and fulfillment itself. The New Testament concept of fulfillment is improperly characterized, in my opinion, when it is simply described — in the article referred to — as a concentration of the promise. For in the coming of Christ into the reality of history there is a fulfillment of the promise; there is a new situation which Christ himself indicates as "now," and this situation is new compared with what people earlier desired to see but did not see. This fulfillment in the reality of the body does not in the least exclude, however, a living out of the promise in the present. This fulfillment — and this makes it unique — points simultaneously to the eschatological perspectives of salvation and that on the basis of the present of fulfillment. The promise in the Old Testament was Christological, surely, but in virtue of this, and not in addition to this, it was trinitarian and eschatological. For this reason the actual fulfillment is charged with the perspective of the ultimate fulfillment in the kingdom of God. Van Ruler is right in opposing the idea that the fulfillment should rule out a living out of the promise but he may not base this opposition on, and combine it with, a polemic against the idea

---

27. It is plain that Van Ruler does not in the least deny the significance of the categories: promise and fulfillment. See his dissertation on *De vervulling der wet*, 1947.

of continuing revelation. It is precisely the New Testament
which is full of the unique character of fulfillment, a fulfillment
which is not identical with a *coming-true* of a given event once
predicted. If that were the case, the fulfillment would suspend
the prediction, but in the fulfillment of the promise in the Messiah is contained the perspective of the salvation of God in the
future. The New Testament speaks of the fulfillment of
prophecy in the words of Christ himself: "Today hath this
scripture been fulfilled in your ears" (Luke 4:21), and Paul
says strikingly: "And we bring you good tidings of the
promise made unto the fathers, that God hath fulfilled the same
unto our children, in that he raised up Jesus" (Acts 13:32, 33).
Here is a fulfillment on the basis of atonement. In the fulfillment is contained an extremely well-grounded promise, already caught sight of in the Old Testament; and therefore Paul,
who sees the fulfillment of the promise in the Resurrection of
Christ, can write that the grace of God has appeared in order
that we should live God-fearingly in this present world, *"looking for* the blessed hope and appearing of the glory of the great
God and our Saviour Jesus Christ" (Titus 2:15). One cannot
really object to the term "continuing revelation," for the entire
Old Testament testifies to us of the dynamic and purposeful
action of God as He proceeds to the reality of the mystery of
the Word become flesh. In the epistle to the Hebrews we encounter the same thing, namely, that God spoke "by divers
portions and in divers manners" to the fathers and at the end
of these days spoke to us in his Son (Heb. 1:1). There is
progress in redemptive history. There is progress in God's
action. The epistle to the Hebrews fully stresses the uniqueness
of the appearance of Christ and the universal significance of the
"once for all." But this is the transition to which the Old
Testament points — from its beginning and fully. It is the
transition from the old to the new covenant, to the elimination

of the numerous typological sacrifices now that the great sacrifice has come.[28] All this does not by any means imply a devaluation of God's dealings under the Old Covenant, or a devaluation of the significance of the Old Testament. The value
of the revelation which took place in the Old Covenant lay
precisely in its sign-post character and called for the transition
included from the beginning in God's purposes. One cannot
indicate the relationship between the Old Testament and the
New by saying that the New is primary and the Old secondary;
for the aim of the Old Testament revelation is directed completely to the reality of the fulfillment and found its full depth
and meaning there. In line with this fact is the vehement
prophetic criticism which strikes all who — with Judaism —
try to find the meaning of the Old Testament in something
other than the redemption which God promises and will provide. In opposition to every nomistic interpretation of the
Old Testament stands the preaching of grace and of faith, of
election, covenant, the circumcision of the heart, and of the
sacrifice to come.

And therefore the Old Testament has not, now that the fulfillment has come, lost its meaning to the Christian Church.
For a person who looks at the relationship between the two
Testaments in the light of the categories of promise and fulfillment as in themselves transparent and universally valid categories it may seem a logical conclusion to eliminate the Old
Testament. But this conclusion will not satisfy the man who
sees in the Old Testament the history of God's coming to the
world in his coming to his people; and not some abstract

---

28. Compare Art. XXV of the Belgic Confession: "We believe that the
ceremonies and symbols of the Law ceased at the coming of Christ, and
that all the shadows are accomplished; so that the use of them must be
abolished among Christians; yet the truth and substance of them remain
with us in Jesus Christ, in whom they have their completion."

"truth" about a coming Redeemer.[29]   The significance of the
Old Testament to the Christian church is to be understood precisely in the light of the *historical* character of the Old Testament.   The Old Testament is more than the mere prediction
of the "advent" of Christ.   Prophecy concerning Christ in the
Old Testament is not exhausted by a few striking Messianic
prophecies but is to be found in the entire history of God's
coming to the world.[30]   For that reason the Old Testament
bears the hallmarks everywhere of revelation about God in his
majesty and his holiness, in his mercy and his justice.   In it is
revealed the same God who is the Father of Jesus Christ.   In
all the Scriptures, Old Testament and New, resounds the message of the salvation of God, which can be understood only in
these interrelationships.   This salvation is not one which stands
out sharply, and visible to all, against the background of a
general cosmic emergency, but one which can be understood
only after one learns of God, his holiness and wrath, his grace
and mercy. Hence the message of the Old Testament still reson-
ates throughout the church of Christ, not as reaching back to
a bygone age but as witnessing to the Christ in all the interrelationships of the great trinitarian work of God in the world.
Thus the Old Testament enables us the better to understand
the depths of the salvation proclaimed to us in the New Testament, just as the New Testament enables us the better to under-

---

29. Korff believes (*Christologie*, II, page 49) that the scheme. "promise
and fulfillment," though indicating an important characteristic, does not
exhaust the value of the Old Testament.   He refers to Romans 9:4
where "the promises" are but a part of the treasures of the Dispensation.
To us this does not seem an argument against these categories, because
promise does not mean prediction but concerns the period of the preparatory speech (*making promises in history*) and action of God.   Article 17
of the Belgic Confession, referring to this historical revelation, says God
was pleased to *seek* and to comfort man with the promise that he would
give his Son.   The word "promise" in this sense does not clash with Rom.
9:4 but is designed rather to characterize the Old Testament dispensation in view of Christ's fulfillment.   A different matter is the characterization "law and gospel" for the relation between the two Testaments.
Against this certain obvious objections are to be registered (See Korff.
Ibid., II, page 38).
30. K. Schilder, *Heidelbergsche Catechismus,* II, page 309.

stand the meaning of the Old. Were it merely a matter of a prediction which came true, then after its fulfillment the prediction would have only historical value and no longer continue to be fruitful for our lives. But now that the fulfillment is preached to us as consisting in the grace of Jesus Christ and this grace proves to be the knowledge of God which is life eternal, now the church of Christ still loves the Old Testament as the Word of God, just as it was the book of prayer and practice to the Son of man. In the rich message of progression and transition the church, if all is well, will hear the voices of salvation and see, also in the Old Testament, the traces of him who was Man of Sorrows, Servant of the Lord, Son of man, of the house of David, and at the same time truly God.

And so the New Testament is full of the Old, not merely as a historical recollection, but as the fullness of the revelation which casts its light upon the reality which now arouses the astonishment of all the angels.

*   *   *

All this is implied in the historical character of Old Testament revelation. It does not follow, however, that it is possible for us to offer a detailed systematization of the course of redemptive history. The history of revelation does try to trace the path which God has trodden in dealing with Israel and with the nations of the world, but, just as we cannot write the biography of Jesus, so we cannot offer a comprehensive description of the course of God's redemptive acts under the Old Covenant. There is no doubt that the Old Testament designs to give us history; for God's redemption enters into history, finds, and will find, its consummation in history. But we are not offered a complete description of all God does in the history of the world. The revelation of God comes to us in the Old Testament in what we might call lucid fragments. We note that these fragments form parts of a mighty whole culminating in the advent of Christ. Here and there, in relation to Assyrians, Philistines, and Babylonians, who play a role in God's actions, certain relationships light up in full view of God's mercy or wrath.   In all this God's action is not dependent on the historical situation but it does come to various expressions in different situations.   Some introduced the idea of the clock at this point and pointed out with emphasis that we should be concerned, in the *historia revelationis,* to note *into what stage* God's action has advanced in a given text.   Only on this condition, it was said, can we understand the meaning of God's Word in the Old Testament.   A vigorous polemic was then carried on against the so-called exemplary exegesis which, so ran the charge, neglects the dates on which the redemptive events took place.   We must realize, however, that we are in no position to pursue by the minute the hands of this revelational clock, since the dates of the history of redemption are not always known to us.   A complete systematization of redemptive history is not possible, if only because it is historical and follows, in the divine pedagogy, the course of numerous concrete happenings.   Suddenly the light shines in a special way and the mountain-tops of God's revelation become visible.   Without direct preparation or information as to why a given revelation was necessary at a given moment, and came at a given moment, we encounter concrete indications about the Messiah, about his birthplace, name, suffering, loneliness and dishonor.   God's action is concentrated in response to apostasy and with a view to the renewed humility of his people, with its apostatizing kings, its misunderstanding of the ceremonial laws, its going into exile and crying for redemption.   Of this course of God's dealings we read in the "fragments," which God has preserved for us, in order that in our knowledge of salvation they may be related to the fullness of his gracious doings in Jesus Christ. Therefore, too, people who lived in different periods occur together in the New Testament gallery of those who lived and died by faith (Heb. 11).   Their lives were, in various ways, involved in these acts of God by which he reveals himself in the tabernacle, the temple, the royal line, the exile, the new temple, prophecy, and the Exodus.

In this revelation God points out the sins of his people, and the sin and misery of the entire human race, which is incapable of self-redemption and digs its own grave. But simultaneously he discloses the plan of redemption by which he brings back his people which had wandered to the precipice of complete annihilation — a sudden revelation of his faithfulness in the context of the most passionate prophecy of doom. It is the revelation of his faithfulness and his mercy, the disclosure of his covenant which is eternally sure and of the holy remnant saved by grace alone. Hence we must not limit ourselves to a few specifically Messianic texts. These Messianic utterances will be meaningful to us only against the background of the entire Old Testament which witnesses to the Christ. It is true of the Old Testament, no less than of the New, that the person and work of the Redeemer are inseparably united. And page after page witnesses to the fact that salvation cannot arise from human flesh and blood but only by an opening of the heavens and the descent of God. It is he who must act to save and salvation will be his work alone. Salvation is not from man, not even the Israelitish man, but from the mercy of God. In that message the contours of the absolute salvation become visible — a salvation coming to the fore squarely centered in the message of God's spotless sanctity; it is the message that his people, once saved, will live in his presence, and that he will remove their sins as a vapor and make their scarlet sins as white as snow (Isaiah 1:18). The contours of this salvation become visible as from afar and are shadows of what shall one day be full historical reality. To say, as does Obbink, that in Israel it was not yet known in what form God will reveal that salvation,[31] is putting it too strongly. There is in this statement an element of truth which corresponds to Romans 16:25, but one can never separate the

---

31. H. W. Obbink, *Theologische Bezinning op het O. T.,* among others, in pages 23 and 29.

reality from its *form*. This is clear from the Old Testament designations of Christ as the Messiah-king and at the same time as priest. Before us rises the image of the Man of Sorrows and the Servant of the Lord, and he is called Immanuel. The fact of salvation cannot be separated from its form. Here, too, the extent of the disclosure of the mystery is determined only by God's sovereignty and his pedagogical intent. Still this revelation points to what, when it appears, will arouse the amazement over this historical mystery. The New Testament describes the mystery as having "been kept in silence." And Paul writes concerning the revelation of the mystery that it has "been kept in silence through times eternal, but now is manifested" (Rom. 16:25). This "silence" does not mean in an absolute sense that there was no disclosure concerning the Christ under the Old Covenant at all. But this expression indicates how overwhelming the mystery of Christ coming into the reality of our flesh was; this mystery is great: God revealed in the flesh. These words can be understood only on the basis of the New Testament evaluation of the mystery. The shadows have fled before the coming day. The New Covenant has become a reality. The meaning of Israel's history has been fully revealed in Christ, for salvation was intended for the world. Paul speaks in the epistle to the Ephesians about the mystery of Christ as that "which in other generations was not made known unto the sons of men, as it hath now been revealed unto his holy apostles and prophets in the Spirit; *to wit,* that the Gentiles are fellow-heirs, and fellow-members of the body, and fellow-partakers of the promise in Christ Jesus. . ." (Eph. 3:5, 6). The contrast with the Old Testament is not absolute as becomes quite apparent when Paul writes that in other generations it was not made known *as* it has now been revealed. The promise of salvation, according to the Old Testament also, was extended to the nations of the world which would be blessed in Abraham; but as concretely and clearly as the Spirit has now revealed it, in relation to the salvation which has come, so it was not made known to earlier generations. The uniqueness of the historically concretized salvation of God is repeatedly placed in the limelight in the New Testament, possibly never more clearly than by Christ himself: "But blessed are your eyes, for they see; and your ears, for they hear. For verily I say unto you, that many prophets and righteous men desired to see the things which ye see, and saw them not; and to hear the things which ye hear, and heard them not" (Matt. 13:16, 17).

This is what is meant by progress and fulfillment. The grace of God has appeared. Yet this incomparable and insurpassable reality does not place the Old Testament in the shadows; for, owing to the numerous coherences in which the Old Testament witnesses to the coming Christ, it still illumines the reality of salvation in Jesus Christ.

*   *   *

Since the Old Testament is the book of God's promise, of his gospel, the church cannot but listen with reverence to its voice. Precisely because the Old Testament is void of a monotonously repeated promise of the Messiah in the form of a prediction and is filled with the comprehensive dealings of God which include the advent of the Messiah, we can say that neither Testament makes sense apart from the other. The acceptance of this interrelationship is not a product of scholarly thinking but the fruit, rather, of faith in the unity of the Word of God. It is possible even to appreciate the Old Testament as the book of promise and still, as do the Jews, look for a coming Messiah. It is possible to read the Old Testament without believing that Jesus is the Messiah. This is the decisive issue between church and synagogue.[32] The synagogue says of the church that it reads its own faith into the text of

---

32. Compare W. H. Gispen, *Oud Testament en Christendom,* and A. R. Hubst, *Oud Testament en Jodendom;* both of them in *Vox Theologica,* 1941.

the Old Testament while the church speaks with Paul about the veil before the Jewish face on account of which the Old Testament is not read as it should be, and intends itself to be, read.[33] Here the story of Philip and the eunuch suggests itself. The eunuch, who is reading Isaiah 53, wonders "of whom speaketh the prophet this? of himself, or of some other?" Philip's answer consists in preaching Jesus (Acts 8:35). This interpretation does not force the text its predetermined ways but is a believing interpretation of the text which teaches the secret of the Old Testament witness to Christ. This decision does not lie on a purely rational level. It cannot be made on the basis of self-evidence, as if the conflict between Christianity and Judaism could be resolved on a strict scholarly level. It is the confession of the church that God's revelation addresses us here and witnesses to the Man of Sorrows. The acceptance of this testimony is not the result of logical considerations, but it does issue into the salutary fact that a light shines in a darkened soul and that the beneficiary goes on his way rejoicing (Acts 8:39).

*   *   *

The most incisive point discussed in this connection is perhaps the origin of the Messianic expectations of God's people under the Old Covenant. The neutral, historical-critical approach to the Old Testament throws up the conflicts in bold relief when it views Messianic hopes as arising, not out of a divine revelation, but out of historical or psychological motives. The "national" explanation is one which points out in particular certain parallels in other nations,[34] in which national expecta-

---

33. The relation between the church and the synagogue is discussed vigorously by H. J. Schoeps, who says that the faith of the Jew can only protest against the idea that Christ is the fulfillment of the Old Testament. The antithesis is one which excludes every rapprochement. See the *Jüdischer Glaube in dieser Zeit. Prolegomena zur Grundlegung einer syst. Theol. des Judentums*, 1932, page 25. For the idea of a rapprochement, see Lev. Gillet, *Communion in the Messiah. Studies in the relationship between Judaism and Christianity*, 1942.
34. H. Greszmann, *Der Messias*, 1929, page 445.

tions had given shape to the hope for a hero who would realize the ideals of the people.[35] The study of the origin of the Messianic hope achieves color and form especially when psychological motives are taken into account and it is explained from a people's wishes in time of need, in the spirit of: the wish is mother of the thought. We find here a striking parallel to the explanation of religion which sees it as arising from the depths of the human heart. At stake here is all of Israel's religion as well as its rootage in divine revelation.[36] The Messianic expectation then becomes basically a psychologically understandable cry for redemption in which the expectation is projected on the screen of Israel's nostalgia. The danger of this theory lies in its bearing on the fact that there is indeed a close connection, in the course of God's redemptive dealings, between Israel's need and God's redemption. Just as in the Christian religion there is an apparent correspondence between the disease and the remedy, so there is often an immediately demonstrable connection between Israel's need and the revelation of redemption. This connection appears throughout the history of the people from its earliest times. When the children of Israel sigh and cry in Egypt "by reason of their bondage" and their cry comes up into heaven, then we read that God hears their groaning and remembers his covenant (Ex. 2:23-25). In this awareness of their need the people then catch sight of their hope and sole redemption. And when in the bitter period of the Judges the children of Israel again begin to cry out to the Lord, confessing their sins and apostasy, then there is first of all the answer that God refuses to redeem Israel, but when they persist in their humble confession, the light of redemption again shines over Israel (Judges 10:10-18). The psychological theory about the connection between the need and its satisfaction, as well as that about the origin of Messianic expectations,

35. G. Holscher, *Die Ursprünge der jüdischen Eschatologie*, 1925, pages 12 ff.
36. Edelkoort, *Christusverwachting*, page 125.

makes the relation between misery and salvation a *causal* connection; the misery is believed to be the origin of the idea of salvation while any real connection between human need and divine redemption is denied. The connection is a causal one within the limits of the human heart. The other possibility — the biblical one — consists in the fact that the divine revelation itself repeatedly arouses human expectation and springs from a background of grace: God calling his covenant to mind. In virtue of God's redemptive concern, the cry for redemption and for the opening of the heavens repeatedly arises in time of need. This cry cannot be explained in terms of the human heart; in times of selfrighteousness the Messianic expectations grow feeble.[37] Nostalgia for God's grace and redemption is but the response to the divine promise, the fruit of the Spirit of God who stirs up hope for him who would sooner cause mountain and hills to shake than bid his work and his people adieu. In addition, it is only by a forced construction that one can maintain that Messianic expectations arise only in time of need and misery. Here too the systematization in this theory of origin clashes with the real data of the Old Testament and with the course of God's salvation in the world.[38]   God the Lord is sovereign also in his revelation concerning the salvation he has prepared in times of joy and prosperity also God aroused and stimulated the expectation of redemption and warns against the obscuration of the insight of faith as in times of prosperity this eclipse can become a genuine menace. Just as with the pyschologizing of religion, so here too the issue is decided by faith in God's revelation. There are basically but these two possibilities: either the religion of Israel and

---

37. Bavinck, *Geref. Dogmatiek,* III. page 223: "In general the selfrighteousness of Judaism did not favor the expectation of a Messiah; for Israel had the law, was righteous in keeping it, and therefore felt no need of a Redeemer."

38. Edelkoort, *Christusverwachting,* page 126: "The Messianic hope flourished greatly, in people and prophet, in times of prosperity and political glory." Edelkoort mentions as such the time of David and that of the prophets Amos and Hosea.

its concomitant Messianic hopes arose from Israel itself under the weight of adverse circumstances, or they arose in response to the divine revelation which brought new hope in the midst of misery.

For this reason the conflict over the origin of Israel's hope is so important and decisive. All depends on whether we believe the Scriptures or whether we try "without prejudice" to trace the course of Israel's history without proceeding from the a priori basis of its entire existence as a nation: its election and the divine revelation. Without the light of this divine revelation we would remain in the dark and have to resort to a merely historical or psychological analysis of the strange history of this people. Its history is full of attempts at self-redemption, of a nomistic interpretation of its religion, which are in direct opposition to the Messianic hope. But God himself repeatedly interrupted these attempts by his judgment, preserved a remnant throughout the tumultuous history of his people, and kept the fire of expectation burning in the hearts of that remnant.[39] This remnant is the people who have learned once again to look for divine redemption and to trust the Name of the Lord. Whenever it ceased to live in expectation, it was cast into the crisis of God's judgment up to the edge of its national existence, but in this judgment the light of the divine prophetic revelation again breaks through and the way to the expectant life is once more made possible.[40]

The choice between the psychological and the revelational point of view as to the origin of Messianic expectations comes into open view in David's mighty Messianic prediction as it is recorded in II Samuel 23:1-7. The period in which it occurs

39. This remnant shall lean upon Jahwe the Holy One of Israel, and return to the mighty God (Isaiah 10:20-21). See Kittel, *Theol. Wörterb.* under "leimma," Vol. IV, page 215; also J. C. Campbell, *God's People and the Remnant,* Scottish Journal of Theology 1950, pages 78ff.

40. One thinks here of the theory that the prophecy of redemption does not really belong in prophecy but is a concession to popular eschatology. See on this L. H. K. Bleeker, *Over inhoud en oorsprong van Israels heilsverwachting,* 1921, page 16.

is not one of calamity and of precariousness for the nation. We are told of the gratitude of Israel's king for deliverance, for lovingkindness to the Lord's anointed, to David and his seed.

Then comes the prophecy of David — his last words — about the righteous Ruler, a Ruler in the fear of God. But this prophecy is introduced with the words that the Spirit of the Lord is speaking through David and that his word was on David's tongue. It was the Rock of Israel who spoke to David. His expectation is based upon a gift out of God's hand, and is the fruit of divine revelation.[41]

One denying this relationship and detaching Messianic expectations from a true divine revelation is forced in various other ways to look for the origin of this expectation. The upshot is that it is explained in terms of various tensions and disparate elements. A clear example of this is Schmidt who believes he can point out in the Old Testament three levels of viewing the Messiah: the mythical view in which the coming of the Messiah is accompanied by a change in nature reaching even into the animal world; the historical-patriotic view which expects David to return as king in the end of time (later it was toned down to a king of the house of David); and finally a synthesis and elaboration of both motifs by the great prophets.[42] Once the basic idea of Messianic revelation has been laid aside — a position which does not countenance a facile disqualification of the idea of the Messiah-king, Immanuel, and his birth as mythical — one comes automatically to a many-layered view full of inner tension.[43] Sight is lost of the unity of revela-

---

41. Edelkoort, *Christusverwachting,* page 165 ff. and O. Procksch, *Theologie des Alten Testament,* 1950, page 583, about the clear reference to the Messiah and its background in the Word and Spirit of Jahwe.
42. Hans Schmidt, Messias in R. G. G., III, page 2143.
43. Note the grounds for the mythical motif: the rising of the sun (Isaiah 41:2; cf. II Samuel 23:4); "whose goings forth are from of old" (Micah 5:2); his mother, "who is mentioned in an unusually concealed, mysterious manner" (Isaiah 7:14); and the origin of the Messiah is wrapped in mystery. Witness the total eclipse of insight into God's revelation of the Messiah resulting from the introduction of the mythical motif.

tion; and the interconnection between the Old Testament and the New, which leads one to see in the promised Messiah-king the prophecy of Jesus Christ, is reduced to a theory. But on the basis of belief in this unity it is precisely the disparateness of these motifs — which emerge from Israel's national or religious life itself — which stamps the theory as an obvious construction choking off admittance to the secret of Israel's religion.

One is then compelled to search for the underlying reason for these different motifs and then discovers the idea of the royal ruler and, at the same time, the peculiarity of this ruler. But that which in any number of views touching the Old Testament expectation of the Messiah is consumed by inner tensions and contradictions achieves its deep divine meaning in the fulfillment of this prophecy, in which the idea of the king proves to be fulfilled in *this* ruler, who cannot be compared with ancient, oriental despots, but who will be ruler in the fear of the Lord and whose royal government is described, not in conflict with, but in full, gracious harmony with the *suffering* servant of the Lord. All prophecy of the coming Messiah-king finds its only, final, and legitimate disclosure in the kingship of Jesus Christ. In this fulfillment his humiliation is the way to his exaltation without doing violence to his true kingship. In these reflections on the Messiah, more than anywhere else, we understand that the Old Testament cannot be read or grasped without the New. Only in the conversion to this true kingship, which shows us the unity, the unique and incomparable harmony between this rulership and this humiliation, is the veil taken away in reading the Old Testament.

In connection with the maternal promise of Gen. 3:15 Schilder spoke about the "first intentional riddle"[44] with which we are concerned and which is serviceable "to God's pedagogical exercise of authority"; a bit further, referring to the well-known Shiloh-text, he takes account of the possibility that here

---

44. K. Schilder, *Heidelbergsche Catechismus*, II, 1949, page 289.

too there is the intentional use of a "mysterious expression."[45]
When in this connection he discusses the Old and New Testament "mashal" (similitude, parable, proverb — Gesenius) in
its divisive effects, one can also call to mind the conflict between church and the synagogue.[46] Undoubtedly this is related
to the fragmentary, partial, and penumbral[47] character of Old
Testament prophecy, which is in turn related to God's progressive action in history. The Old Testament nowhere presents
a systematic and completely transparent analysis of the figure
of the Messiah, but the various characteristics of the coming
Messiah appear now here, now there, now in this, now in that
historical situation and context. The idea of the royal ruler is
associated with the fear of God; the Messiah, who is to realize
God's coming to the world, is at the same time the Son of man
in the night-vision of Daniel.[48] The powerful Messiah, in

45. K. Schilder, *Ibid.*, page 297, with reference to Aalders, *Korte Verklaring,* on Gen. 49:10 — about the mysterious names used to indicate the
wonderful person of the Messiah.
46. *Ibid.* page 289, "a mashal which gives to this first of redemptive
prophecies the same character as to all others, as long as it pleases God
to speak in parables."
47. By "fragmentary" we mean that in a given context the prophetic
picture of the Christ is presented without completeness. In Daniel, for
instance, the Son of Man appears as having dominion while no mention
is made of his suffering and humiliation (compare Ridderbos, *Matthew,*
I, page 172). Suffering is central in the prophecy of the suffering servant of the Lord. The total picture of the Messiah appears only in the
reality of the fulfillment. For the suffering servant of the Lord see:
J. Schelhaas, *De lijdende knecht· des Heren,* 1933, and Chr. R. North,
The Suffering Servant in Deutero-Isaiah, 1948, with its conclusion (page
218): "May we not, then, in the light of the principle of the unity of
Scripture, believe that in the purpose of God the Servant songs were
primarily intended to afford Him guidance?"
48. See Daniel 7:13, 14: the being "like unto a son of man" is associated
with dominion, glory, and a kingdom which shall not be destroyed. When
Christ is asked about his Messianic pretensions (Matt. 26:63), he replies
in direct reference to Daniel 7: "Henceforth ye shall see the Son of
man sitting at the right hand of Power, and coming on the clouds of
heaven," an utterance followed by the charge of blasphemy. Compare
Aalders on Daniel in *Korte Verklaring,* page 134, and H. N. Ridderbos
on Matthew, page 210. Ridderbos points out that, whereas in an earlier
stage (Matt. 8:20) the designation "Son of Man" was serviceable in
concealing Christ's glory (*Matt.*, I, page 170 ff., II, page 7), in the final
critical stage he applies Daniel's prophecy directly to himself.

whom God reconciles himself to the world, is simultaneously a
royal scion of the house of David and the suffering servant of
the Lord. Here we find, not an excerpt from the doctrine of
the two natures, but the divine revelation about the Messiah
who is not known until the New Testament shows him to be
the Son of God and the Son of Man.

*   *   *

In conclusion we must still discuss briefly a point closely
connected with the preceeding. It is a fact that people have
more than once, in view of the redemptive-historical progression and the transition from the Old to the New Covenant,
posed the question whether the believers under the Old Covenant shared in the riches of redemption. In the answer to this
question one can often detect a certain hesitation. Coccejus,
namely, came to make an essential distinction between believers
under the Old and believers under the New Covenant. His
views culminated in the opinion that Old Testament believers
only enjoyed a divine "passing by" of their sins without having
shared in the true forgiveness of sins received by New Testament believers. The reason given was the forgiveness of sin
could not antedate Christ's historical act of shedding his blood.
And with an appeal of Romans 3:25 and Hebrews 10:18 he
believed he could put a Scriptural basis under this view.[49] The

---

49. Romans 3:25 reads: ". . . whom God set forth to be a propitiation,
through faith, in his blood, to show his righteousness because of the
passing over of the sins done aforetime," and Heb. 10:18 reads: "Now
where remission of these is, there is no more offering for sin." Coccejus
appealed to the fact that Rom. 3:25 has "aphesis" while Heb. 10 reads
"paresis." According to him, these words contained the typical difference
between salvation under the Old Covenant and that under the New.
"Paresis" would indicate the fact of temporarily overlooking sin in view
of the coming propitiation and could not be genuine forgiveness. A sound
exegesis of Rom. 3:25, however, points in another direction. Paul indicates here how it was possible for God to "pass over." It was possible
"pros," in view of, the coming reconciliation. Though it seemed a "passing
over" in the sense of not taking seriously, it was something else, because
God would provide reconciliation in Jesus Christ, so that — this is the
leitmotif of Paul's argument — not a shadow falls upon the righteousness

background of this view was Coccejus' desire to think historically — not on the basis of the idea of redemption in general, since then the historicity of Christ's reconciliation on the cross would no longer be absolutely determinative. Sins must first be atoned before there can be forgiveness. It is clear that Coccejus, in his antispeculative tendencies, falls into the other extreme and, with an incorrect appeal to Scripture, historicizes redemption in Christ. His anti-speculative and anti-scholastic views made him deny the fact that God's saving work for all times is contained precisely in the historical reality of atonement, so that a person need not be religiously estranged from salvation because he was not a contemporary of Christ. Thus the eternal significance of atonement is recognized. The rejection of this view of Coccejus actually rests upon the same basis as does the rejection of the Roman Catholic idea of the Mass, although these two views are inherently dissimilar. For the Roman Catholic Mass is based on the idea that the cross of Christ can have no significance unless the sacrifice of Christ is repeated in onward-rushing time. The church expressed in its confession, however, that this view of Mass was at bottom nothing other than a denial of the suffering of Jesus Christ in its universal power and significance. In Coccejus we find the same historicizing tendency, be it in another context, which forced a break between believers living in different periods. But the Old Testament itself points out how we must understand the life of its believers when they put their trust in life and death on God and live out of the forgiveness of sins. Here the believers who truly live out of the Word of God's promise

---

of God. Hence Paul did not speak of a total forgiveness in distinction from "paresis," but about God's righteousness in relation to human guilt. As to Coccejus' view, "solido caret fundamento." Turrentinus, *Inst. Theol. Elenct.* II, page 274.

For the O. T. view of forgiveness see Bavinck, *Geref. Dogm.* IV, page 163; A. Kuyper, *E. Voto* II, page 351 and Joh. à Marck, *Het Merck der Chr. Godts-geleerdheit*, XXIV, 7. On Coccejus see G. Vos, *De verbondsleer in de Geref. Theologie*, 1891, and O. Ritschl, *Dogmengeschichte des Prot.*, III, 1925.

confront his wrath and holiness and, at the same time, they
may hide in faith beneath his wings. Here they sing that there
are clouds and darkness about God's throne but, at the same
time, they see the light of grace radiating from that throne.
Here they pray for a fullness of joy all the days of their lives
because they know a God who hears prayer and who in his
wrath remembers his mercy. Anyone who would deny the
existence of this joy under the Old Covenant on the ground
that there is a rupture between the two Covenants, confuses the
progression of redemptive history with a progression from relative alienation to communion, a progression quite unlike that
from promise to fulfillment. Diametrically opposed stands the
message of the two Testaments, both of them full of the beneficent power of the one Messiah, once promised and now come.[50]

*   *   *

We began this chapter by pointing out the disdain the Old
Testament suffered from the propaganda of anti-Semitism;
this was after many had relativized it, for a considerable period,
with an appeal to the fulfillment of the New Testament. The
remark has been made that one who begins by devaluating the
Old Testament will, by some inner logic, end up depriving the
New Testament of its value. History is there to prove the
correctness of this remark. One who tosses out the Old Testament, though he still speak with appreciation about the New,

---

50. To accept this is not in the least to shift from a biblical view of history
to the cyclical idea of a circle about a center. We can fully understand
the objections which Korff and others have against those who speak about
the Christ under the Old Covenant in such a manner that the uniqueness
of the Incarnation is hardly recognized. These objections can be understood, that is, when people go so far as to say that the incarnate Christ
was already operative under the Old Covenant, not properly distinguishing between theophany anl incarnation, however much they stress the distinction later on. In this sort of theologizing, it seems to me, there is a
peculiar use of the expression "Incarnation of the Word," so that there is
reason to ask, "Does not the Old Testament know only the logos asarkos?"
(W. J. de Wilde, *Het problem van het Oude Testament*, 1938, page 34).
See also Korff's remarks on Barth, in *Christologie*, II, pages 40 ff.

is bound, like Harnack, to have an improverished view of it
too. Progression in the history of redemption from the Old
Covenant to the New does not imply an elimination of the witness of the Old. The elimination of this source can only result
in impoverishment. Reject the Old Testament and one will
have left a Christ who is detached from the broad background
of human misery and of divine redemptive action, the background of God's righteousness and his wrath, his love and his
holiness. Nothing but impoverishment and error can result;
but what else could we expect, since Christ himself appealed
with emphasis to the Old Testament when it was fulfilled and
realized in his blessed, beneficent life and in his final humiliation. Even on the cross the words of the Old Testament re-
sounded, as they arose, in Christ's forsakenness, out of the
heart that had pondered the written word of his Father from
his youth on. Here the church can but follow him lest, neglect-
ing the Old Testament, it should get lost in the New. The
New Testament is perspicuous, to be sure, and anything but
confusing. But the human heart is deceitful, and nowhere
more than in interpreting Scripture. Let the man, who believes he can live in terms of the fulfillment amidst all these
perils in understanding the Scriptures, look up his whole Bible,
so that he may rightly understand this fulfillment and honor
God in the incomprehensibility of his counsel and his election.
Let him honor his God in the long road he "travelled" to reveal
the way of faith in contrast to the way of works, in the witness
of his word which speaks to us of guilt and grace, and of his
servant in whom he himself opened the heavens in such a way
that one can say that eye has not seen, nor ear heard, nor has
it entered into the heart of man, the great mystery of God revealed in the flesh.

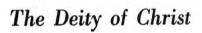

The Deity of Christ

CHAPTER VIII

The Deity of Christ

I T WOULD be onesided to assert that the conflict over the
person of Christ was concentrated almost exclusively upon
the confession of his deity. Such an assertion would neglect the fact that a vehement conflict also raged around the
reality of his *human* nature. The fact that the church also defended with vigor the doctrine of "vere homo" proves that it
did not lapse, in its confession of Christ, into a onesided reaction but permitted itself to be guided by the testimony of
Scripture. A striking illustration of this refusal to be one-
sided is that in the same century in which a passionate struggle with Arius took place there was also a struggle with Apollinaris who, though he stood side by side with Athanasius in
opposition to Arius, nonetheless failed to do justice to the
truly human nature of Christ.

The danger was far from imaginary that the church should
have been satisfied with an attestation of agreement with the
confession of Christ's deity and that it should have been less
attentive to the purity of the confession of his humanity. It
would not have been surprising if it had been content to establish that it was God himself who came to redeem us in
Jesus Christ. The church has resisted this threat, however,
and, as we shall see later, opposed docetism in whatever form,
refined of unrefined, it appeared.

This is not to deny, however, that in different phases of the
history of the church the battle over the divine nature of
Christ was of deep and far-reaching significance. It was not
only the ancient church which conducted, with deeply religious

earnestness, a battle for the phrase "co-essential with the Father," but later centuries too saw a resumption of the high-points of this conflict, as is clear in the controversy with the Socinians in the sixteenth and in that with Modernism in the nineteenth and twentieth century.

Repeatedly the confession of Jesus Christ as being truly God was subject to denial from various directions. With reference to Christ, people did not wish to deny at all that there was every reason to think and speak with high respect about the great and noble qualities of Jesus of Nazareth. They even spoke at times of the uniqueness of his appearance, ascribed to him a divinity of some sort, and acknowledged that God had revealed himself in Christ in a special manner. But at the same time it was evident from the restrictions made that this admiration and respect was operative within definite limits and did not, at bottom, transcend an appreciation for the *man* Jesus of Nazareth, in whom God's revelation came to us. In his moral and religious qualities he was elevated above many others, indeed, sometimes above all others; but despite God's revelation in his person there was no question of Christ's transcending his humanity. At this point we confront the violent clash between the church and Arianism or Modernism. This conflict was difficult precisely because heretical opinion continued to assert with emphasis that in its own Christology it did take account of the *essence* of the New Testament revelation and hence it continued to value being called Christian. The church, on the other hand, recognized on decisive points that the issue was not one of minor differences in interpretation, not a matter of theoretical and ingenious distinction, but one in which the church could and had to use the word "intolerable," regardless of the disgrace which it would and, in fact, did have to endure because of this intolerance. It asserted that the heart of the Christian religion pulsates in the confession that in Jesus Christ, in

THE DEITY OF CHRIST

the Incarnation of the Word, God truly came down to us.[1]
The church continually sensed and understood that the pivotal
difference could not and might not be reduced to a variation
or nuance in formulation, but that it concerned a confession
of which it is as true as of the confession of *sola-fide* that the
church stands or falls with it.

This conflict would not have been so difficult if the front-
lines could always have been drawn with clarity and if there
had been clarity from the side of heresy in its speaking about
the humanity of Christ. The opponents of the deity of Christ
used various terms, in this struggle, which could and, in fact,
did create misunderstanding. They spoke with emphasis
about the revelation of God in Jesus Christ and even came to
call him "the Son of God" in a certain sense; indeed, some of
them had no objection to describing him as "God." At the
same time they stressed that these terms were not intended
in the sense current in church dogma; but this modern terminology nonetheless penetrated into modern preaching and
made it extremely difficult to pinpoint the issue for the benefit
of the whole church. The differences sometimes seem to be
trivial and the same terms which the church used are in dispute. I am thinking of Van Holk's thesis: I am a liberal
Christian because I believe that Christ is the way of truth
through life.[2] But he immediately adds that he does *not* wish
to proceed from "the mystery of the Son of God, the second
person of the trinity."[3] He wishes to approach Christ in his
human aspects. He emphatically maintains the "God with
us" but as the "redemptive intent of the gospel as it proceeds
from God." Christ is not just an "ordinary human being"

---

1. Compare H. Bavinck: "Simple was the faith with which the church
appeared in the world. But one thing it knew: that in Christ God himself had appeared to it and taken it up into communion with him. This
was certain, this it refused to be deprived of, this it defended against odds
of all sorts, and this it formulatel, clearly and unequivocally, in its creed,"
Geref. Dogmatiek, III, page 265.
2. L. J. Van Holk, *De boodschap van het vrijzinnig Christendom*, 1939,
page 42.
3. *Ibid.*, page 44.

but a highly unusual man, "bearer of spiritual power par excellence." Christ is the possessor of superior dignity but orthodoxy misinterprets it by speaking of an incarnation. Van Holk would prefer to speak of a transfiguration: there and then the flesh became Word, man became God.[4] Here, of a sudden, everything is clear, but the terminology is rarely transparent. This is also the case in Van Holk when, forgetting for the moment this sidelight, we hear him say that Jesus of Nazareth "is truly God's anointed."· Any number of words current in the treasury of the church occur also in the mouth of those who emphatically oppose the confession of the church. This became especially clear in the speculative Christology of the nineteenth century; there we find the unperturbed use of the phrase "God becoming man." For this reason it continues to be necessary to check the meaning of words by their contexts. These litmus-tests of words are necessary, because the vocabulary of the church is more and more absorbed into a context which is foreign to the Gospel. We encounter Christ, as the center of world-history; as the power of God's love, which preserves through judgment; Christ as *kurios;* Christ as God's decisive act.[5] But, lest one do the author an injustice, one must read on and let the total context resonate: "God becoming man is an event taking place not only in the historical figure Jesus of Nazareth but in everyone who repents to obedience."[6]

There is even a more advanced accommodation of language when the non-orthodox talk of Christ as the Son of God and mention his divinity. Such use of language greatly aggravates the church's battle for the defense of its confession.

Thus we already heard Heering speak of his faith in "the Son" and "the divinity of Jesus," while these designations are

---

4. *Ibid.*, page 53.
5. W. Banning, *Het vrijzinnig Protestantisme op de tweesprong,* 1945, pages 75 ff.
6. *Ibid.*, page 76.

detached from the confession of the Incarnation. In this connection he emphatically states that "the word 'deity' is too
reminiscent of the second person of the Trinity." But in
isolation from church dogma there appear some very positive
statements: "Though the realism of the Incarnation be foreign to us, Jesus Christ to us is real, a sacred Reality; in him
God approached us. In him God is near to us. Christ is with
us all our days, even to the end of this world. He is our
Kurios."[7] Here the words of Scripture are fitted into the context of liberal Christology which claims to be the Scriptural
one in distinction from the theological-mythical interpretation
which came to be dominant in church dogma. The conflict
comes most sharply to expression in the qualification of Christ
as "divine." In this word there is an ascription to Christ of
very special qualities but it stands nonetheless in conscious
antithesis to the confession of "vere Deus."

The issue in this conflict — a serious one to the church —
must be settled in terms solely of the Scriptural testimony to
the Christ. In the conflict with Liberalism, of earlier or later
vintage, the fronts were drawn up at that point. The question
has of late become particularly relevant in view of the confessional formula adopted by the World Council of Churches.
It speaks of Christ as follows: "The World Council of
Churches is a fellowship of churches which accept Jesus Christ
as God and Saviour." As a result the question arose whether
the Liberals could agree to this formula and since then there
has been again a general debate about "Jesus Christ as God."
Did this formula refer to the "divinity" of Jesus or was it
an expression of agreement with the "vere Deus" of the
church, an expression of the church's doxological praise to
Jesus Christ? One can understand, upon serious consideration, that the World Council formula in a sense produced a
crisis in liberal thinking. The one rejected it because he
heard in it the language of the ancient church and of the

---

7. G. J. Heering, *Geloof en Openbaring,* II, page 157.

creeds; the other thought he could accept it if interpreted so that the phrase "as God" no longer has the full weight it has in the creeds. Mönnich believed one should note the significance which the confession of "Christ as God" had in the ancient church. In many an early writer he believed he found rather the "divinity" of Jesus than the Sonship of the later confessions. Still, if one distinguishes between the "Deity" and the "divinity" of Christ, he must face the question whether Christ has not been deified here. The divinity ascribed to Jesus of Nazareth may indicate the reverence in which he is held but it throws up, as the ancient church well knew, the problem of polytheism. Mönnich believes that early gentile Christianity could call Christ God without having a feeling "that an injustice was done the essential core of Christian monotheism."[8] In the liturgical and hymnological tradition of the church, according to Mönnich, "this simple — and, for later dogmatic purposes, too simple — mode of expression, namely, that Christ is God, has been preserved. For there where the element of prayer predominated one could, in this formula, indicate the nature of Christ as it were impressionistically, rather than exactly, but neither was such exactness necessary in this sphere." It appears to us that this is strange talk about the doxologies and the hymns of the church. There are any number of indications that precisely in the selection of church hymns there was a serious effort to act with care; and that the simplicity of the language used by the church was owing to another fact, namely, its subjection to the Scriptures. This subjection led the church, amid the problems of monotheism and polytheistic paganism, to its confession of the Deity of Christ. Hence, also for the history of dogma, as regards the right view of the development of the creeds, the essential question will remain whether the testimony of Scripture can

8. C. W. Mönnich, *Jezus Christus God en Heiland. Proeve ener vrijzinnige beschouwing over de basis-formule van de Wereldraad der Kerken,* 1948, page 43; compare his *Het geloof der oude Kerk,* 1948.

in fact be the foundation of the confession of "vere deus" —
an offense in creed and hymn in many a period.

*   *   *

Various motifs are operative in the conflict over the confession of the deity of Christ.   Still it is not hard to discover
that one motif has been, in one polemic and another, predominant.   We can call it the projection-motif.   We are referring
to the opinion that the idea of the deity of Christ at bottom
originates in a projection of the church.   In response to this
idea we must decide between the alternatives: we either confront, in the confession of Christ's deity, the reality of the
mystery of Christ, or we face, as a projection of the church,
a deification of the man Jesus of Nazareth.   It is this question
which must, in this chapter, be of special concern to us: is
the confession of Christ as God the product of a pious projection or is it, through the means of the prophetic and apostolic
witness, a fruit of revelation?

*   *   *

To anyone who explains the Scriptural witness concerning the deity of Christ as a projection of the church to which
no reality, at least not the reality of Christ's deity, corresponds,
it cannot remain a secret that there is great unanimity in this
designation of the Christ.   Those also who reject the confession of the church have more than once acknowledged that
there is no mistaking the witness of the entire New Testament to the Christ.   The Christ of the New Testament is truly
human and nothing human is foreign to him who has become
like us in all things, sin excepted; still he cannot be understood
in terms of human categories, as if they could explain his
miraculous life.   The Scriptures, certainly, never provide us
with a theoretical picture of the deity of Christ.   The practice

of the ancient church, to speak of Christ "as of God,"[9] goes directly back to the New Testament itself where we hear adoring voices addressing Christ as truly God and not as quasi-God. A person has only to reflect upon the large number of Scriptural utterances which occur in various contexts. John speaks of the Logos who became flesh, that Logos who was eternally with God and was himself God,[10] whose glory could be beheld by faith, the glory as of the only-begotten from the Father. It is this Christ his companions adore. Songs of praise are raised around his cradle and they accompany the Son of Man as he proceeds to his goal. Eyes illumined by divine revelation see in this disgraced and humiliated Son of Man the Son of the Father. Peter confesses him as the Son of the living God (Matt. 16:16). And Thomas, delivered now from his doubts, expresses his final certainty in the adoring exclamation: "My Lord and my God" (John 20:28). Paul speaks of Christ as "God blessed for ever" (Rom. 9:5). The words in which the growing church witnessed to the glory of Christ are doxological in tone and express humble amazement.

There is jubilation over the Name of Jesus, the only Name, and over the grace of our God and the Lord Jesus Christ (II Thess. 1:12). Believers expect "the blessed hope and appearing of the glory of the great God and our Saviour Jesus Christ" (Titus 2:13). The incomparable exaltedness and glory of Christ are celebrated whenever use is made of expressions indicating, and hence not depreciating, the humanity of Christ but also by far transcending this humanity. He is the Son, the eternal Logos, the Holy One of God, the Light of the world, he that is sent of the Father, the fulfillment of the prophecy regarding Immanuel whom Isaiah calls mighty God (Isaiah 9:6). All these names, far from being abstrac-

---

9. See II Clement 1, 1: "Brethren, we must think of Jesus Christ just as we do of God."
10. For a more elaborate discussion of the prologue of John's Gospel, see my *De Algemene Openbaring*, 1951.

tions are indissolubly related to his incarnation, his humiliation and exaltation; related to his work, through which God
himself acts to redeem. He knows the Father as the Father
knows him (John 10:15). The Father loves the Son and
shows him what he is doing (John 5:20) and has given all
things into his hand (John 3:35). As the Father raises the
dead and gives them life, so the Son also gives life to whom
he will (John 5:21); all this, "that all may honor the Son,
even as they honor the Father" (John 5:23). The relation
between Father and Son is so close that Jesus lays down the
rule: "He that honoreth not the Son honoreth not the Father
that sent him" (John 5:23).

There is a discussion in several places about the Son's being
subject to the Father, and about his being sent and given by
the Father, but at the same time, lest any notion of Subordinationism should arise, there occurs the truly mysterious assertion: "For as the Father hath life in himself, even so gave
he to the Son also to have life in himself" (John 5:26). The
mystery of the Son does not consist only in his *being sent* but
no less in his *having come* (John 5:36, 37, 38; 6:29). At
this point we encounter the confession of Christ's pre-existence, one of the most embattled parts of Holy Scripture, and
no wonder since the pre-existence of Christ is bound up closely
with his trinitarian life. Christ's own references to his pre-
existence repeatedly came up for discussion. We are thinking
of the highpriestly prayer: "And now, Father, glorify thou me
with thine own self with the glory which I had with thee
before the world was" (John 17:5). This unmistakable utterance forced many to make a decision. One can hardly dis-
miss the difficulty by saying that Jesus says "little" in this
gospel about his pre-existence.[11] For this petition in John's
gospel is surely not an isolated one. Heering too is compelled
to admit that the idea of pre-existence is clearly expressed in
John 3:13: "And no one hath ascended into heaven but he

11. Heering, *Geloof en Openbaring*, II, page 149.

that descended out of heaven, even the Son of man, who is in heaven." But any number of other texts point in the same direction. Repeatedly Christ asserted that his existence was not exhausted by his being a man on earth. We call attention to Christ's saying that he is the bread out of heaven (John 6); and when the Jews refer to manna as bread out of heaven, Christ points, with an emphatic and solemn "Amen, amen," to the unique bread out of heaven which is he himself. "Verily, verily, I say unto you, It was not Moses that gave you the bread out of heaven; but my Father giveth you the true bread out of heaven. For the bread of God is that which cometh down out of heaven" (John 6:32, 33). Precisely these words called forth the opposition of the Jews who saw him in the limited frame of his temporal human existence. "Is not this Jesus, the son of Joseph, whose father and mother we know? how doth he now say, I am come down out of heaven?" (John 6:42). But in response to this groping for the limits of his existence Christ then refers to the mystery of his person and work which no one can or will understand unless the Father draw him (John 6:44). And so his descent out of heaven is related to the message of salvation (the life-giving bread) which places man before a decision to believe or to be offended. Later too, when Christ's opponents say they *know* whence he is, their effort at enclosing Christ's life within the temporal, humanly comprehensible frame of history comes sharply to the fore. It is this knowledge of his historical origin which leads them to criticize his high pretensions. These pretensions by far exceed their "interpretation" of his existence and confirm from day to day their inner vexaation. But Christ then speaks of this "acquaintance" with him. "Ye both know me, and know whence I am" (John 7:28). But this knowledge circumvents the mystery and is not the true knowledge of Christ. It is a knowledge of the historical context into which they, in their unbelief, have put him: the man Jesus of Nazareth without secrets and without mystery. For the mystery they have closed their eyes. But Christ suddenly breaks through this neatly delimited frame and reaches out beyond the relations they have discovered: "I am not come of myself, but he that sent me is true, whom ye know not. I know him; because I am from him, and he sent me" (John 7:28, 29).

In all such utterances Christ points to the mystery of his origin; and certainly theology is in bad form when, in discussing them, it reaches for such depreciatory words as "speculation" and "ontology." For in order to eclipse *this* origin, *this* miraculous being, *this* gracious reality, it has to set aside the whole gospel. What this reality means is indicated by another statement of Christ, an utterance which again elicits the opposition of the Jews because this too upsets their historical delimitation. To the Jews it was a mysterious and unacceptable statement: "Before Abraham was born, I am" (John 8:58). It was in absolute conflict with their scheme of evaluation.[12] Christ mentions "his day" as one which Abraham saw from afar and rejoiced over. The Jews will have nothing of any connection between Abraham and the day of Christ and oppose it with a query about his age. In response to this question Christ says: "Before Abraham was born, I am." Hearing this the Jews attempt to stone Christ: they understood that Jesus ascribed divine existence to himself and made himself equal with God. Implied in Christ's dictum is no denial of the correctness of their "knowledge" touching his earthly ties, nor of his historically dated birth. The gospels operate within the same historical context when they mention the twelve-year old Jesus and his public appearance at the age of thirty. In his debate with the Jews, Christ is concerned with another dimension of his life. To one who is ignorant of the mystery of Christ's ultimate origin, his statement about his relation to Abraham must have seemed

12. Bultmann, in his *Commentary on John,* page 247, speaks of "the inadequacy of Jewish standards."

senseless, indeed, Christ was not *born* before Abraham. But
Christ's temporal existence does not coincide with his total
existence.   There is in his life something more than this
existence which makes him comparable with others on the
horizontal level of history.   Grosheide speaks in this connection, of a summit of revelation in Christ.[13]   He "is," and
this being is not subject to calendar dates but reaches infinitely
higher, reaches into the depths of eternity.   This utterance,
too, is a part of his message.   The idea is not to build up an
independent ontology but rather to bring the message of *this*
Christ, *this* subject, who can and may so speak.   Bultmann
emasculates this text by counting it among speculative theories
of pre-existence, because, says he, Christ is here viewed under
"the category of time."   But the contrary is true: the statement "Before Abraham was born, I am" rather breaks through
the categories of time-bound thinking which imagines it can
interpret Christ in terms of our existence and that *without
mystery*.   This is the kind of thinking which is critical of
Christ, because it measures him by the norms of days and
years, of being born and dying.

But these norms are crushed by the reality of his divine
existence.[14]

* * *

In the course of time people have made several attempts to
escape the force of the witness to Christ's pre-existence by
assuming that pre-existence is practically taught only in the
gospel of John.   It, more than the synoptic gospels, wished
to express the glory of Christ and to touch up the picture of
his life *in terms of* the idea of his exaltation and hence has

13. Grosheide, Commentary on John 8:58.
14. See J. Ridderbos, K. V., *De kleine profeten,* II, page 92, on Micah
5:2.   "Whose goings forth are from of old, from everlasting . . ." — "a
vague indication," says Ridderbos, which nonetheless, in view of the total
witness of Scripture, relates to Christ's Deity.   Compare Edelkoort,
Christusverwachting, pages 273ff, and D. Deden, *De Messiaanse profetieën,*
1947, page 91.

but little historical value. Bousset said, for instance, that in the Synoptics there can be found "barely a trace" of Christ's pre-existence.[15] According to Heering, too, the Synoptics do not yet know of the Incarnation: Jesus' "coming" merely indicates his "being sent."[16] This divorce between John and the Synoptics on this point has been disputed by Sevenster, who is of the opinion that pre-existence occurs repeatedly in the Synoptics. He refers, among other things, to the texts which speak of Christ's "having come," which cannot be interpreted in the fashion of Heering. It is not correct, says Sevenster, to see in this phrase merely a prophetic term which indicates the divine commission, the calling which he received and must fulfill.[17] Only when a person isolates the "I-have-come" texts from the whole of the Scriptural message, can he deny their deep meaning. But whoever listens without bias to the entire testimony of Scripture will discover in many utterances of the Synoptics the same background which appears so clearly in the gospel of John when he speaks of the great mystery of Christ: He has descended out of heaven.

* * *

It need not surprise us that there is an intimate connection between the fact that many theologians are not interested in the pre-existence of Christ and the fact that they oppose his true deity. Both prove to be aspects of the same negation. In Scripture, on the other hand, one can detect a positive conjunction of the two: in knowing Christ as pre-existent it knows him as the true Son of God, co-essential with the Father, and Light of Light. This is a matter of revelation, not of dis-

---

15. W. Bousset, *Kurios Christus. Geschichte des Christus-glaubens von den Anfängen des Christentums bis Irenaeus*, 1913, page 19; 4. *Aufl.* 1935.

16. Heering, *Geloof en Openbaring*, II, page 148; compare Van Holk (*De Boodschap van het Vrijzinnig Christendom*, 1939, pages 50, 51) who says that orthodoxy in its theological thinking is really always Johannine while the Liberal thinks "Synoptically."

17. G. Sevenster, *De Christologie van het N. T.*, pages 102 ff.

torted ontology. For this reason, too, there was such a profound relationship between the Christological and the Trinitarian conflict in the ancient church. The two cannot for a moment be separated, as also the testimony of Christ can be understood only in Trinitarian light. To violate the confession of Christ's pre-existence is to violate the mystery of Christ and to lose the background of his entire self-testimony. Here lies the origin of Christ's words — the word he uses with absolutely unusual authority among the multitudes.

We are now thinking of the manner in which Christ speaks of himself in the currently much-discussed "I am" texts.

In the gospel Christ not only says in various ways what and who he is, as for instance the shepherd, the vine, the light, the way, the truth, the life and the door, but he also says of himself: I am. Thus we read in John 8:24: ". . . Except ye believe that I am (he), ye shall die in your sins." In this unusual "I am" we have, says Grosheide, a self-disclosure such as had not, till now, been given us. "*I am*: with these words any living man can indicate his earthly existence but the *I am* of Christ transcends this by far and can become an object of decisive belief. The use of these words is reminiscent of the divine utterances occurring in the Old Testament; for instance, "I am that I am" (Ex. 3:14); or "See now that I, even I, am he, and there is no God with me" (Deut. 32:39).[18] For Christ, no less than for God, the *I am* without a predicate is valid; and upon this extraordinary reality, also here, faith is focussed.[19] Christ repeats these words of the Father, taking them from the Old Testament, as having unique knowledge of his being, a being which places man before the decision of life and death. He has come; but we can also say, He has come, he who *is* as God is and reveals himself in grace. He has not merely been commissioned as

18. Compare the rendering of the Septuagint; and E. Schweizer, *Ego Eimi*, 1939; Staufer in Kittel, *Theol. W. Buch z. N. T.*, II, pages 350 ff; Grosheide, *Comm. op Johannes,* on John 8:24.
19. Compare Ps. 90:2; Isaiah 43:11, 15, 25; 44:6, 8, 24; 45:5, 18, 22.

a prophet or a man whose "being" can be regarded as self-evident, but he *is* in a very special sense. "He that hath seen me, hath seen the Father" (John 14:9; cf. verse 7).

There is in these self-disclosures none of the ostentation, none of the self-display, of men who are so self-absorbed that from others too they demand attention. One can even say that Christ not seldom silenced his self-testimony; as in harmony with his mission as Messiah he concealed himself in his Messianic glory.[20]

But the temporary concealment is aimed at final, full recognition of his secret: a secret not lightly thrown on the streets, in order that it be publicly preached in increasing volume for the redemption of the world. The church understood this witness of and concerning the Christ. In the light of the entire gospel it understood the commission to baptize, in which Christ is placed alongside of the Father and the Holy Spirit (Matt. 28:19). This unique equivalence is the background of many expressions found in the introduction to the epistles, expressions pointing to Christ's existence as transcending the human, the created level. Only in view of this reality, attested of and by Christ, can the faith of the church be understood. This faith is anything but creative, anything but a projection from its own bosom. The true deity of Christ radiates from the entire gospel, from his sacred names and from his self-testimony. But this irradiation is not intelligible if one thinks merely of divine majesty or surprising theophanies. The miracle of his appearance does not make sense apart from the "vere homo" but it surely does not eliminate the "vere deus." The man Jesus of Nazareth so spoke and could by rights so speak in the midst of his humiliation. Only when people accept his deity in faith do they see the New Testament in its true light. Only thus can a person understand the unheard-of call to come to him and to learn of him (Matt. 11:28, 29). Only thus one understands the authority with which he speaks

---

20. H. N. Ridderbos, *Zelfopenbaring en zelfverberging.*

about the law: I say unto you (Matt. 5). Thus one understands the manifold use of "my Father" and of "We" in the highpriestly prayer: "Holy Father, keep them in thy Name which thou hast given me, that they may be one, even as we are" (John 17:11, 22). The Father is in him and he is in the Father (21) and the Father loves him (23; compare John 10:38).

It was only a deep alienation from the testimony of Scripture which could bring men to speak, not of the deity of Christ, but only of his divinity. Increasingly it is dawning on the unbiassed thinker that the word "divinity" is not a way out but a subterfuge. *Not* by confessing the deity of Christ, but by speaking of his "divinity," people are escaping into ontology or into a deification of man. The pretensions of Christ are radically misunderstood when explained as an accumulation of creaturely phenomena and qualities. Stauffer correctly says of the "we" in the highpriestly prayer that "in the mouth of anyone else it would have been blasphemy."[21] The "I" of Christ confronts us with "a unique, authoritative self-proclamation of Christ." He reveals himself "as the fully-empowered representative of God in the absolute formula used by God: *Ego eimi,* the purest expression of his unique and still quite immeasurable significance." Christ witnesses of himself but in this witness he seeks, not his own honor, but God's (John 7:18), while the Father witnesses of Christ (John 8:18). And the faith of the church has heard both witnesses, understands and knows of the witness called up in human hearts in order that it may sound forth over the length and breadth of the earth: the witness of the incarnate Word and his glory, *also* and *precisely* in his humiliation.

* * *

The self-proclamation of Christ has been so unmistakable and clear that it aroused, already during his sojourn on earth,

---

21. In Kittel, *Th. W. B.,* II, page 347.

the most vehement opposition. In the gospels there is not the slightest attempt to transvalue the self-witness of Christ or to rob it of its content, as happened many a time in later ages.[22] On the contrary, it was this witness about the mystery of his person which aroused opposition and even proved a decisive factor on the way of the cross. This appears plainly from the gospels. When Jesus declared: My Father works even until now and I work (John 5:17), the Jews sought to kill him, not only because he broke the Sabbath, but also because he called God his own Father, *making himself equal with God.* This opposition arose not from a misunderstanding but from Jewish, "unitarian," resistance to a genuine claim.

When Christ speaks with emphasis about his Father and his unity with him, and about what the Father has given him, the Jews are about to stone him, not because of his works but for blasphemy and "because that thou, being a man, makest thyself God" (John 10:29-33).

Christ's answers to this criticism is surprising. His appeal is to Psalm 82:6, where judges, government-officials, are called "gods." One may not infer, certainly, that Christ puts his equality with God on a level with that of the "gods" of this psalm. That Psalm 82 does not allow for a deification of human dignitaries appears clearly from the fact that these judges are *criticized* (verses 2 and 7). Christ's design is plain. He wants to break the certainty of Jewish conviction, to undermine their reasoning. If judges, to whom the Word of God has come, are called "gods" because of the splendor of God's majesty which cloaks them as office-bearers, must not the Jews stop and take notice now that Christ speaks to them of *his* communion and union with the Father? But there is much more food for reflection, much greater reason to stop and consider *here,* for Christ, unlike the judges in the Psalm, has been sanctified and sent into the world by the

-----
22. "The Jews understand what the Arians cannot grasp," as Augustine has it. See Kittel, *Ibid.,* under *isos,* page 353.

Father (John 10:36). Having made this disturbing reference
to Scripture, and the Scripture cannot be broken, Christ re-
acts as follows: Do you then say . . . "Thou blasphemest;
because I said, I am the Son of God?" At the end of his defense he again emphatically states that the Father is in him
and he in the Father.

Hence the charge of the Jews is not based upon a misunderstanding of Christ's claims. He is the Son of God. No interpretation is attempted to take the edge off this claim or to
make it humanly intelligible. No, this charge, this accusation
of blasphemy, drives Christ to his cross. The worst thing conceivable to a Jew is ascribed to him. How seriously the Old
Testament takes blasphemy is plain and well-known. Blasphemy violates the glory of God; it is "the speech and action,
particularly of the heathen, which as a rule oppose God"; a
"human presumption which always means discredit to God,"[23]
and therefore blasphemy was punished by stoning.

In the charge of the Jews Christ is said to be in the last
stage of alienation from God; as in the apocalyptic vision of
John (Rev. 13:5, 6) there is mention of the beast who speaks
"great things and blasphemies" against God, and now only
judgment can follow.

The charge of blasphemy pursued Christ to the end, and
provided the decisive motivation for his ultimate condemnation. In the encounter between Christ and Caiaphas, the
high priest adjures him to tell the council whether he is the
Christ, the Son of God. The answer is affirmative: "Thou
hast said," but he adds: "nevertheless I say unto you, Henceforth ye shall see the Son of man sitting at the right hand
of Power, and coming on the clouds of heaven" (Matt. 26:64).
This speech of exalted self-proclamation is qualified as evident
blasphemy and becomes the immediate occasion of his final
verdict. For having heard this speech, the highpriest tore up
his clothes and said: "He hath spoken blasphemy: what fur-

---

23. Compare Kittel, *Ibid.*, under *blasphemia*.

ther need have we of witnesses? behold, now ye have heard
the blasphemy: what think ye? They answered and said, He
is worthy of death." The charge pursues him even on the
cross: "If thou art the Son of God, come down from the
cross" (Matt. 27:40). "For he said, I am the Son of God"
(Matt. 27:43).

* * *

From the preceeding it is plain that the question of Christ as
the Son of God, indeed, as himself truly God, is charged, already in Jesus' lifetime, with the awful seriousness of final
decisions; and that Christ has been mocked and tempted on
account of his claim. This is all the more striking because
later on this seriousness was quite lost at times. Christ's
deity is then interpreted as a creation of the infant church
which more and more endowed Jesus of Nazareth with divine
attributes. The Jews took another direction. They accused
Christ himself of this creation, of this deification. "He made
himself the Son of God" (John 19:7).[24] Their testimony,
annoyance, criticism, and opposition, with all its consequences,
point to the clarity with which Christ made his claim. Theirs
was not a misunderstanding which Christ, to avoid the worst,
could have eliminated, but theirs was the seriousness of an
ultimate decision, the decision regarding life and death. How
plain is here the inseparable union of the person with the work
of Christ! In the self-testimony of Christ, he who died outside the gates of Jerusalem for blasphemy, the two confront
us as a unity.

* * *

The issue of the deity of Christ came up for discussion also
in the special context of the forgiveness of sins. Not the least
because of Christ's supreme deed of acquittal, ("Son, thy sins
are forgiven"), was Christ accused of blasphemy. Hence this
charge was not only based on his self-testimony but also on his

---

24. See Grosheide on John 19:7.

work. "Why doth this man thus speak? he blasphemeth: who can forgive sins but one, even God?" (Mark 2:7).[25] His accusers saw in the act of forgiveness an intolerable arrogation. Did they not know the words of the Old Testament which declared the forgiveness of sins to be a divine privilege? "I, even I, am he that blotteth out thy transgressions for mine own sake; and I will not remember thy sins" (Is. 43:25). "I have blotted out, as a thick cloud, thy transgressions, and as a cloud, thy sins: return unto me; for I have redeemed thee" (Is. 44:22). In response to their accusation Christ speaks about his authority, his power, to forgive sins on earth. Then he performed a miracle "that ye may know that the Son of man hath authority on earth to forgive sins" (Mark 2:10). The healing is a sign of the authority of Christ.[26] Christ's act of forgiveness points to the reality of the Messianic period now begun. When John, after his imprisonment, sends his disciples to Christ to ask whether he is truly the Messiah, then too Christ replies by referring to the salvation which has come: Go and tell John, "the blind receive their sight, and the lame walk, the lepers are cleansed, and the deaf hear, and the dead are raised up, and the poor have good tidings preached to them" (Matt. 11:5). That which in the Old Testament has been predicted concerning the Messianic period[27] has become reality in him, in his divine authority. Here is the unity of God's act of forgiveness with Christ's act of authority. Forgiveness is something purely divine and now it proceeds from the mouth of the man Jesus of Nazareth. He is not the neutral messenger of forgiveness, but its origin and its content, now that God himself brings about forgiveness in him. Although the secret of God acting in Jesus Christ may still be hidden for those present, so that they marvel over the fact that God has given such power "to men" (Matt. 9:8), the fact of this authority is inseparably bound up with his person and

---

25. Compare Matt. 9:3; Luke 5:21.
26. Schniewind, *Das Evang. nach Markus,* page 58.
27. Isaiah 55.

work. It is the authority of the Son of man, of the Son of God, which has now become the content of the gospel.

Although the entire testimony of Scripture is the basis for the confession of the deity of Christ, there are places in Scripture which in a special way point to the mystery of Christ as the Son of God. The most striking is probably the designation of Christ as the "only-begotten" of the Father. This is how John 1:18 has it. It is an expression which does not occur in the Synoptic Gospels and in which is indicated, in a special manner, that which is unique and incomparable in Christ. We already learned that the Jews took it very ill of Christ that he called God his *own* Father (John 5:18). This expression "his *own* Father" is closely related to John's designation of Christ as the "only-begotten" of the Father. The words of John 1:18 represented a high pitch in John's thought. "No man hath seen God at any time; the only begotten Son, who is in the bosom of the Father, he hath declared him." In this translation we read of the only begotten *Son*. According to Grosheide and others it is admissible, however, that we should follow another reading, namely, as the best manuscripts have it: the only begotten God. He regards it as more likely that in certain manuscripts the word "God" has been replaced by "Son" than vice versa. In that case we have here an expression which indicates in a unique sense the deity of Christ. The expression "only-begotten" occurs also in the Old Testament and then refers to an only and, therefore, greatly beloved child,[28] and for this reason the Septuagint reproduces it by means of "beloved."[29] Christ is the only begotten, not only in the sense of being a beloved child, but in the unique sense expressible by the words "only-begotten God." This Beloved is the beloved of the Father, again not in an Adoptionistic sense by which he is put on the same level with others who share the special affection of God, but in the full

---

28. The daughter of Jephthah, for instance, Judges 11:34.
29. Compare: Matt. 3:17; 17:5; Mark 1:11; 9:7; Luke 3:22.

trinitarian sense. He is in the bosom of the Father.[30]

* * *

In comparison with the total Scriptural presentation of Jesus Christ, both as he declared himself to be and as others, who were illumined by divine revelation, knew him and declared him to be, all efforts at detracting from this witness, at levelling it down, make a poor impression. We are thinking of the argument which depreciates the Sonship of Christ by referring to the use of the expression "son of God" in a less stringent sense. As one sees this argument emerge from a context of alienation from the entire testimony of Scripture, it is hard to ascribe any value to it. It is becoming increasingly apparent that one does the New Testament a distinct disservice if from it one infers an Adoptionist Christology.[31] The Adoptionist danger has been a real temptation in the history of the church and more than once the Adoptionist Christology was regarded as representing at least one motif of New Testament thought. But it is plain that this Adoptionism has isolated the Scriptural witness to Christ as truly man from the total context of Scripture. However intelligible Adoptionism may be as a reaction to various monophysite tendencies which allow the humanity of Christ to be absorbed by the predominance of his deity, it remains true that, in order to find Adoptionism in the New Testament, one must make a radical selection in Scripture — a selection which obscures the mystery of the person and work of Christ. The Gospel does not present Jesus Christ as a man whose secret is that, as a reward for his faithful fulfillment of a task, he is *adopted* as Son of God; it rather speaks to us of the divine quality of this work which he, the man Jesus Christ, has performed.

---

30. Compare John 1:18; 3:16, 18; I John 4:9. In this connection there is frequent reference to the parable of the landlord who sent his servants to collect the landlord's share and, last of all, also his son, a beloved son (Mark 12:6).

31. Compare G. Sevenster, *Christologie*, pages 106-108.

Christ struggled all his earthly life to maintain this distinction. We are thinking particularly of the passage about Christ as David's *Son* and as David's *Lord*.[32] The question broached here, though seemingly very theoretical because it concerns the "Messiah," is essentially a question about the reality of Jesus Christ. The Jewish idea was that the Messiah would be a Son of David. Hence the problem brought up for discussion was: "Whose son is he?" (Matt. 22:46). With reference to this Messianic expectation Christ then confronts the Pharisees with an incisive question. He quotes Psalm 110 where David calls the Messiah his Lord. In this Psalm we read: "Jehovah saith unto my Lord, Sit thou at my right hand, until I make thine enemies thy footstool." This is the riddle Christ brings to the attention of the Pharisees.

People have wrongly inferred from this passage that Jesus protested against the doctrine that the Messiah would be the son of David. That Christ had no objection to the idea as such is evident from his reply to the repeated call of the blind Bartimaeus who appeals to him as son of David (Mark 10:47, 48). But in the passage itself there is not a single ground for this opinion either. The riddle of the passage is contained, not in a protest against the Davidic descendance of the Messiah, but in the reality of Christ's own person, visible, as it is, only by the eye of faith in line with Psalm 110. Christ presents the question how it is possible that David can call his son also his Lord. One may call to mind the discussion of John 8 concerning the relationship between Christ and Abraham where Christ also speaks in such a way as to undercut the thinking of the Jews. Here the contrary line of thought presented is taken from the Old Testament. It is noteworthy that Christ's question was not provided with an answer. Human thought, refusing to be enlightened by divine revelation, had reached its limits in interpreting the Scripture. No one could answer him; no one could solve this exegetical

---

32. Matt. 22:41-46; Mark 12:35-37; Luke 20:41-44.

problem. Suddenly there appears a vacuum in the Jewish interpretation of Messianic passages. Billerbeck has called attention to the fact that the Messianic interpretation of Psalm 110 has later been temporarily abandoned by the Rabbinic interpreters out of hostility to Christianity.[33] This is completely in line with the impasse of the Jewish leaders who were unable to answer Jesus' question. To Christ himself there is no insoluble problem in the twofold witness: David's Son and David's Lord. This duality is quite intelligible in terms of the mystery of his person. He not only applies the Messianic psalm to himself but is fully conscious that he, who is the son of David, is also David's Lord to whom Jehovah speaks of his Messianic glory and of his divine dominion at the right hand of God.[34] It may be correct to say that Christ is not speaking directly and explicitly about his own person and one can agree with Ridderbos who says that Christ posits the question "objectively" without expressing his own relationship to it,[35] but it remains true that in this indirectness Christ does bring up for discussion the mystery of his person in a most challenging manner.

* * *

The faith of the church is therefore a response to a revelation of Christ, and not a projection of its own consciousness. This is expressed in the fact that Jesus Christ is the object of *faith* in the New Testament. He is not known merely in his historical appearance, and it is not just his lineage, his parents, brothers and sisters that are known; but to those who have

33. Strack Billerbeck, *Kommentar zum N. T. aus Talmud und Midrasch*, IV, 1928, pages 453-460. His opinion is contradicted by A. Vis, *Is Psalm CX een Messiaanse Psalm?* Vox Theologica, 1944, page 93.
34. According to Th. C. Vriezen (*Psalm* 110, Vox Theologicia, 1944, page 85) the Messianic character of this psalm is not original, but it does indicate the dignity of Israel's king. Edelkoort, however, points out that the exalted language of this psalm is never used of an ordinary king but only of the Messiah (*Ibid.*, page 89). He calls this psalm "a compendium of Messianic expectations." Compare Acts 2:34; I Cor. 15:25, and the Epistle to the Hebrews.
35. H. N. Ridderbos, *Zelfopenbaring en zelfverberging*, 1946, pages 58, 59..

been enlightened, he is the object of faith. This faith does not originate itself in the depths of the human heart but results from a call to believe and is generated by the Holy Spirit. Believers are those whom the Father has "drawn." To believe in Christ means to have eternal life and not to perish (John 3:16). "This is the work of God, that ye believe on him, whom he has sent" (John 6:29), while the sin of the world consists in not believing on him (John 16:9). Not to believe that he "is" results in one's dying in his sins (John 8:24). In his highpriestly prayer Christ says: "Neither for these only do I pray, but for them also that believe on me through their word" (John 17:20). "Let not your heart be troubled: believe in God, believe also in me" (John 14:1).

Associated with this faith is the possibility, not only of taking offense at his *message,* as something isolable from himself, as an abstract truth, but of taking offense at *him*; for "blessed is he, whosoever shall find no occasion of stumbling in me" (Matt. 11:6). This possibility of personal offense is completely in harmony with the question put to his disciples "Who say ye that I am?" and with the blessedness flowing from the right answer (Matt. 16:17).

* * *

If one gives free course to the powerful witness of the gospels and thus learns about the "secret" of Christ, he can understand too the homage paid him in the epistles. It is not necessary to treat all the passages in the New Testament in which Christ is honored and salvation in him is celebrated. It is sufficient for us to consider now the force of the apostolic witness. It turns out then that here as in the gospels there is an emphatic witness to Christ as the Redeemer in whom God himself, compassionately, came to us. We note several utterances in which occurs an unmistakable witness to Christ's pre-existence. The striking thing is here that there is not a trace of abstract interest in this subject, something one could brand as "speculative ontology," but that the witness to Christ's pre-existence occurs in a patently *doxological context,* as it does also in the creeds. And again the issue is not the person considered apart from his work. One can apply again what Elert says: "In the nature of the case, the person and work of Christ refuse to be separated in any respect."[36]

These utterances are so lucid that many who for themselves do not believe in pre-existence nonetheless acknowledge that these texts teach it. We are now referring to the passages in Phil. 2 and II Cor. 8:9.[37]

In Philippians 2 Paul exhorts the church to be of one mind, having the same love, doing nothing from motives of rivalry or personal vanity, and to be humble and to promote the interest of others. In this context of exhortation he points to Jesus Christ and admonishes his readers to "have this mind in you, which was also in Christ Jesus: who, existing in the form of God, counted not the being on an equality with God a thing to be grasped, but emptied himself taking the form of a servant, being made in the likeness of man." Paul speaks of Christ as one who was in the form of God and who did not regard his glory as something to cling to for his own benefit.[38] He did not apply his glory, which he had with the Father before the world was, to himself, but did the opposite and assumed the form of a *servant.* "Existing in the form of God" is all the more pronounced by its association with "being on an equality with God."

The second epistle to the Corinthians (8:9) points in the same direction: "For ye know the grace of our Lord Jesus Christ, that, though he was rich, yet for your sakes he became poor, that ye through his poverty might become rich." As in the epistle to the Philippians, there is here a "before" and

---

36. Elert, *Der Chr. Glaube,* page 358.
37. See Sevenster, *Ibid.,* 146 ff. and B. B. Warfield, *The Person of Christ* in *Biblical Doctrines,* 1929, page 176 ff.
38. S. Greydanus, *Commentaar;* also Kittel, I, under *"harpagmos"*: "he did not regard it as profit to be equal with God."

"after": the form of God, then the form of a servant; riches, then poverty. In various ways people have tried to escape the force of these words in order to eliminate the witness concerning Christ's pre-existence. But the bias in such efforts is completely transparent. Many had to acknowledge the correctness of an exegesis as that of Bachmann who says that the riches of Christ consist of "the situation from which Christ emerged when he entered into poverty," and that Paul's statement in II Corinthians must be understood "in terms of the contrast between the pre-existent and the historical 'Sein' of Christ."[39] We can observe clearly the irrefragable linkage between what is said of Christ's person and what is said of his redemptive work and this is always the case in the New Testament. Thus Paul speaks in his epistle to the Colossians about the creation of all things *in Christ*: all things "in the heavens and upon the earth, things visible and things invisible, whether thrones or dominions or principalities or powers; all things have been created through him, and unto him; and he is before all things, and in him all things consist" (Col. 1:16, 17). This concern of Paul with Christ is not a matter of neutral ontological interest but rather of the knowledge of Christ which enables believers to rest in his greatness and unconquerable power. No other power can dethrone him. All the fulness of the Godhead dwells in him bodily,[40] says Paul; therefore, why should they still be afraid? To have in full view the reality of the Son of God is at the same time to have the rest which is announced to all who share in him and whose lives can therefore no longer be critically endangered by powers or dominions.

We find the same ideas in the epistle to the Hebrews in which the author refers to the incomparable greatness of the

---

39. Bachmann (Zahn), *Comm.*, page 314. Compare Meyer's Commentary on II Cor. 8:9 (1882), page 239, which stresses the real relinquishment of previous possessions. Poverty is not contrasted with contemporaneous riches but with abandoned riches which Christ had in his previous existence.

40. Col. 2:9 and 1:19.

Son of God. He is the effulgence of his glory and the very
image of his substance and upholds all things by the word of
his power (1:3). He far exceeds the angels in glory, for to
him words have been spoken which were never addressed to
angels. It is at such points that issues are settled, as is evident
when we listen to what Windisch says about such passages; he
speaks of "terms and views of Jewish-hellenistic speculation."[41]
According to Windisch, the original tradition has been changed
into the "myth of the heavenly Son of God." In such statements one detects the attitude of radical criticism which makes
impossible an open perspective toward the reality of Christ and
reduces the whole Bible to one grand projection full of confusion — making it completely meaningless to modern man.
To one who understands the unity of the New Testament witness to Christ it is plain that the Scriptures here tell us of the
person of Christ and his work, the work is eternally lifted out
beyond the vicissitudes of earthly life because it was God
himself who came to us in Christ. This is not a deification of
the creature but the revelation of the mystery which was hidden for ages and generations, but now it has been manifested
(Col. 1:26).

In the confession of Christ's pre-existence, so far from being
a theological construct, the die is cast for the redemption of
God, as is attested by the whole New Testament. All the out-
lines of the apostolic witness become vague if one does not
silence forever the criticism of the proud mind. Sidetrack the
confession of pre-existence and the whole message becomes
meaningless. A century ago Scholten tried to explain pre-
existence in the sense of an ideal foreknowledge of God which
from eternity enclosed the Messiah. When Scholten bade adieu
to the confession of the church his rationalism led him to say:
"Herewith collapses the unreformed conception of a Son of

---

41. Windisch, *Der Hebräerbrief.*

God who left heaven and laid aside his glory."[42]   The pre-
existence of Christ is changed over into a pre-existence of the
Messiah in the mind of God, in order thus to evade the divine
event of which the apostles spoke in prayerful adoration: *God
revealed in the flesh.   The Word became flesh.*   Scholten's
attempt seems to be to safeguard the sheltered rest of self-
elevated human thinking and protect it from the disturbing influence of a Christology which speaks at this point of divine
realities.

The Scriptures, however, repeatedly disturb the protected
poise of human thinking.   It is the clarity of Scripture which
again and again upsets the schematisms of man in the history
of exegesis and brings unrest into the equanimity of speculative thinking which is unwilling, in fact, that God, the living
God, *should perform something real on earth,* that he should
come and has come for the redemption of the world.

The confusion to which this exegesis frequently fell a prey
often led to an admission of the fact that one *cannot,* in this
modern way, interpret Paul.   Along this route people came to
acknowledge that the idea of pre-existence really occurs in
Scripture and then tried to trace the origin of this idea.   In
Bultmann, for instance, this acknowledgement is roundly asserted.   He regards as integral with Paul's theology that it interpreted the gospel of Christ with the aid of a gnostic Redeemer-myth: "he is a divine figure from the heavenly
Light-world, the son of the highest, who is sent down by the
Father, clothed in human form, and who through his work
brings redemption,"[43]   an idea which, in his opinion, had penetrated the church before Paul's day.   This myth Bultmann finds
for instance in the epistle to the Philippians where Paul mentions that "Christ, a pre-existent divine being, left the heavenly

42. Scholten, *Leer der Herv. Kerk,* II, page 343.   The Roman Catholic
Deodat de Basly seems to have given a similar explanation.   See H. Diepen,
De assumptus-homo-theologie, 1948, page 85.
43. R. Bultmann, *Das Urchristentum im Rahmen der antiken Religionen,*
1949, page 219; see also pages 198, 199; and Bultmann's *Theol. des N. T.,*
1948, pages 163ff.

world and appeared on earth in the form of a servant and was
exalted as Lord after his death."[44] In John too Bultmann finds
many utterances which "speak of Christ in mythological form
as the pre-existent Son of God."[45] He descended from heaven
— as this mythology has it — and will be glorified with the
glory which he had in his pre-existence with the Father. But
Bultmann — this much is plain — does not for a moment intend, on this basis, to express his approval of church dogma.
Bultmann is interested in the eternal value of the atonement
made on the cross of Christ but he does not believe this has
anything to do with a real pre-existence. In the final analysis,
the reliability of the New Testament, the veracity of Christ's
self-witness, and that of the apostolic witness, is at stake here,
and, in this veracity, the mystery of the ages, the act of God
in Jesus Christ, the revelation of God in the flesh.

Behind all opposition to Christ's pre-existence lies the rejection of the historical salvation of God, the incarnation of the
Word, not in a speculative or Hegelian sense but in the Scriptural sense of the words, which form the foundation of the faith
of the church and of its dogma.

* * *

From the polemics conducted about the pre-existence of
Christ it is plain how closely this doctrine and that of the
Trinity are interrelated. Those who reject the one as speculation reject also the other. Pre-existence is said to be a ration-
alization of the mystery of Christ but people fail to see it rest
upon the revelation of the Father, the Son, and the Holy Spirit,
a revelation which excludes speculation.[46]

Of greater significance than these charges of speculation
against the pre-existence and deity of Christ are the attempts to

44. Bultmann, *Theol. des N. T.,* page 163.
45. *Ibid.,* pages 380 ff.; The Son comes and goes "as it were as a guest"
(381).
46. Compare W. Elert, *Der Chr. Glaube,* page 373; and P. Althaus,
Die Chr. Wahrheit, 1948, page 212.

show from the Scriptures that, despite all the honors accorded
to Christ in the New Testament, the confession of Christ's true
deity conflicts with as many passages of Scripture in which
Christ is described as being inferior to the Father. From this
it would appear that the church committed an overstatement
when it said Christ was co-essential with the Father. Are there
not, so runs the question, indications in Christ's self-witness
that his own thinking tended rather to agree with what was
later called Subordinationism than with the confession of the
church? At issue especially was Christ's statement: ". . . the
Father is greater than I" (John 14:28). Christ may have
spoken repeatedly of his unity with the Father (John 10:30),
of his unique relationship to him; he may say that he is in the
Father and the Father in him (John 10:38) and that whoever has seen the Father has seen him (John 14:9); but in
addition to this we read that he has been sent, as Christ himself
attests (John 4:34) and as the gospels declare (John 3:17),
that he has a task to fulfill in all obedience, and that he actually
does fulfill it in complete dependence on the Father (John
5:30).

Does not the idea of pre-existence overstress Christ's *having
come* and neglect somewhat his *being sent*? Is not his meat to
do the will of the Father and to accomplish his work? Does
not Christ himself say that he can do nothing of himself but
only what he sees the Father doing (John 5:19, 20, 30)?
And does he not *receive* judgment from the Father (5:22, 27)?
In the same context, to be sure, we run into the words "even
as": "that all may honor the Son, even as they honor the
Father," but is not this offset by the announcement that the
Father *gave* the Son to have life in himself? Did not Christ
come in his Father's name and did not God press his seal upon
him? Think, too, of the prayer Christ addressed to God before
performing a miracle (11:42, 43) and of his thanking God for
powers received. Christ refers expressly to the Father when he
says: "He that believeth on me, believeth not on me, but on

him that sent me" (12:44). He says, moreover, that he does
not speak from himself but the Father gave him a commandment what to say and to speak (12:49). ". . .the things therefore which I speak, even as the Father hath said unto me, so
I speak" (12:50). And all these expressions of dependence
seem to converge on the statement that the Father is *greater*
than the Christ (14:28). There may seem to be almost a contradiction between the acknowledgement of complete dependence and the use of the mighty pronoun "We" in the highpriestly prayer. Must not we say that Christ's equality is in
any case limited by his dependence and subordination and perhaps question whether the church has taken sufficient account
of this limitation? In the conflict over the deity of Christ
those who opposed the church, again and again appealed to
that series of texts in which they seemed to see clearly the in-
feriority of the Son with respect to the Father. This appeal
formed a strong factor in the polemic against the confession
of the "homo-ousios." Athanasius already treated John 14:28
in his polemic with Arius, and denied that the Arians could
justifiably appeal to it.[47] In our day too Liberals have made
an appeal to this text and spoken of the "enormous danger
inherent in the virtual neglect of what John 14:28 says: the
Father is greater than I.[48] On the basis of this text people
have stressed the Messianic significance of the expression "Son
of God" and denied the so-called metaphysical significance;
they arrived at the conclusion that the expression "deity
of Christ" cannot, "on biblical grounds," be recommended.
One should have to accept then that Christ took back in John
14:28 what he elsewhere avers of himself. This view is obviously the offspring of an aversion to the confession of the deity
of Christ. These people do not allow this text to speak in
the totality of the biblical message concerning Christ but isolate

47. Athanasius, *Redevoeringen tegen de Arianen* (edited by C. J. de
Vogel), pages 86 and 228. See also Calvin on John 14:28.
48. P. Smits, *De Ned. Gel. Bel. critisch beschouwd,* 1948, page 73.

it from its total context and then interpret what is called the other series of texts in terms of accommodation or mythological scaffolding. In this manner the words which designate Christ as the "lesser" attain the status of a foundation for a humanitarian Christology. If a person believes he should object to this Christology as being out of accord with Scripture he will not, of course, neglect this text and thus fall into the same error from another motive. This text of John 14 is undoubtedly part and parcel of the entire message concerning Christ as being dependent on and obedient to the Father. In John 14 Christ speaks about the coming of the Comforter and about his going to the Father. To this he adds: "If ye loved me, ye would have rejoiced, because I go unto the Father: for the Father is greater than I." This superiority of the Father, therefore, is broached in a particular context. It is the Son of Man in his humiliation who now proceeds by way of suffering to the Father who will glorify him. It is noteworthy that in most modern criticism, when it is directed against the coessentiality of Christ with the Father and refers to this text, the historical setting is completely neglected. It points to the word "greater" and simply infers the impossibility of coessentiality. It ignores the humiliation of Christ which is contrasted with his impending exaltation. They should have rejoiced, we read, because of the glory to which Christ is going, namely, to the Father who is greater than he.[49] His going to the Father is related to the greater things which are to come, as he says elsewhere: "For the Father loveth the Son, and showeth him all things that himself doeth: and greater works than these will he show him, that ye may marvel" (John 5:20). To his disciples, too, Christ speaks of the greater things to come: "Verily, verily, I say unto you, He that believeth on me, the works that I do shall he do also; and greater works than these shall he do; *because I go unto the Father*" (John 14:12). In a sense one

---

49. See Grosheide, *Comm.*, and C. Bouma, *Korte Verklaring*, II, page 95: "For the Father to whom he is going is greater than the Mediator in his humiliation."

can agree with Grundmann when he says that John 14:28
makes plain that, "for all the utterances concerning the unity
between the Father and him, Jesus does not place himself on
a level with the Father," but this statement by no means implies a modern use of the text against the confession of the
deity of Christ. For thus the mystery of the incarnation is
denied as well as the act of *submission* to the Father implied
in it. In the ancient Christian church already there was a
refusal to try to make transparent the confession of Christ's
deity but it maintained simultaneously the deity and the Mediatorship of Christ — the Mediatorship in which he, though God,
had to show obedience to the Father. The Scriptures themselves posit this duality, which is inseparable from the fact
of the incarnation. The epistle to the Hebrews mentions it
when it says in a most remarkable passage: ". . . though he
was a Son, yet learned obedience" (Heb. 5:8). The conces-
sive clause does not imply a conflict between his deity and his
subordination but rather the acknowledgement of his true deity
and his ordination as Mediator: his having come and his being
sent. Kunze rightly rejected the appeal to John 14 and brought
in Luther on the text under discussion: "To go to the Father
means to receive the kingdom of God in which he will be equal
to the Father and acknowledge and honored in the same majesty. For this reason I go there, namely, to the Father, he says,
because I will be greater than I am now. Hence of his current
office, as he then carried on his work on earth, it was correctly
said: the Father is greater than I, since I am now a servant;
but when I return again to the Father, I shall be greater, namely, as great as the Father; that is: I shall rule with him in equal
power and majesty."[50]

---

50. J. Kunze, *Die ewige Gottheit Jesu Christi*, 1940, page 40. See also
B. B. Warfield, *The Person of Christ*, in *Biblical Doctrines*, 1929, page
199, on John 14:28: "Obviously this means, that there was a sense, in
which he had ceased to be equal with the Father, because of the humiliation of his present condition and in so far as this humiliation involved
entrance into a status lower than that which belonged to him by nature."

The text from John 14 refers to the glory which will be Christ's when he goes to the Father; the Father is now, while he is performing the mission of humiliation, superior to him. Nowhere in Scripture is this relationship regarded as a contradiction, although it does transcend human comprehension. Paul speaks in ecstatic adoration of the Christ but it does not prevent him from saying that the Son came *under the law* (Gal. 4:4). It is only the abstracting, superficial appeal to the passage mentioning Christ as the "lesser" which discovers tensions at this point and which is compelled to choose one series of texts to the exclusion of the other. Again we have encountered the impoverished insight into Scripture which is symptomatic of modern Christology.

*   *   *

Having discussed the witness of the New Testament to Jesus Christ as true God, we now wish to consider a question often asked in connection with the deity of Christ. It is the question whether the confession of the deity of Christ does not endanger the monotheism which the church from its infancy on had held dear. The question is more directly concerned with the doctrine of the trinity but there is one aspect we must discuss in this connection. Unitarians especially have repeatedly objected to the confession of Christ's deity with the charge that it violates the unity and simplicity of God. The sharp accusation of the Jews against Christ to the effect that he made himself God has later been revived by unitarians. It is of great importance, however, that in the New Testament we notice nothing of any threat to this monotheism. Also later, when the church's confession was attacked on the basis of monotheism, the church unconditionally resisted the attack. The church, to be sure, thought long and hard about these questions during the first centuries of reflection and defense, and in the Christological conflict the problem of monotheism was urgent indeed. This is particularly evident when in Monarchianism the unity of God is placed in the foreground in a sense which actually left no room for the deity of Christ, and thus led to the acceptance of an Adoptionistic Christology in which the "monarchia" of God could be maintained.[51] Opposed as they were to the Logos-Christology, they wished to protect the unity of God. It is important to note here that their opponents also used the term "monarchia" without admitting that their confession of the deity of Christ endangered this "monarchia." Jewish reasoning seemed so simple and the charge of polytheism so óbvious.

It is very important, therefore, to note that in Scripture the confession of the deity of Christ is not at all regarded as a threat to, or as competitive with, monotheism.

Stauffer once brought up for discussion the relationship between monotheism and Christology, pointing out that Christ himself strengthened monotheism by always and everywhere championing the glory and honor of the Father.[52] Christ was indeed conscious of his authority to forgive sin and Stauffer could write: "Jesus takes over the functions of God and takes his place in fullest scope"; nevertheless he immediately adds: "But he does not force him to one side." In everything Christ is concerned with the Kingdom of God. His eminent dignity does not limit that of the Father but proclaims and confirms it to the utmost. The church's adoration of Christ is well-founded, for it is the direct opposite of all blasphemy, which lies under the judgment of God. It is the confession of Father, the Son, and the Holy Spirit, a confession which is completely anti-polytheistic. All efforts to provide the witness of the New Testament with a "solution" by speaking of God's presence in Christ, or of a value-judgment in view of his significant work, end with open opposition to the confession of the Triune God.

---

51. At bottom we run into the problem of monotheism also in *patripassianism* and *modalism*. According to E. Kroyman (see his introduction to an edition of Tertullian, *Adv. Praxean*, page IX), patripassianism followed adoptionism as an attempt to preserve Christianity from the danger of Ditheism.

52. In Kittel's *Theol. Wörterbuch*, III, pages 103 ff.

To the faith which accepts the unity of Scripture there has
never been any conflict between the confession of Christ's
deity and the assertion of Jahwe in Isaiah: "I am Jehovah,
that is my name; and my glory will I not give to another"
(Isaiah 42:8). The church knew that in its confession it
honored the Father as it had been taught by the Son. And
the accusation that the confession of Christ's deity imperilled
monotheism the church laid aside, because it detected in this
criticism a mathematical type of thinking which barred its own
entrance into the fulness and riches of the life of God. And
when it is said that in this confession the language is hymnological and therefore impressionistic, it will always remind
itself that Thomas was delivered from his doubts by *these* im-
pressions "My Lord and my God" and that Christ pronounced
Peter blessed when, in confessing Christ as the Son of the
living God, the *Father* himself proved to have opened Peter's
heart, by a "revelation," for the glory of Christ.

*   *   *

At the end of this chapter we wish to stress again that, in
dogmatic reflection as well as in opposing heresy, it is possible
and meaningful to talk about the deity and humanity of Christ
in succession and not to combine them in an effort to say
all that can and must be said of Jesus Christ. But if we do
that in harmony, as we see it, with what Scripture also does,
when in a concrete situation it resists the emerging violation
of the glory of Christ, then this is possible only against the
background of the living faith of the church which knows
that any defense has meaning only when it is the effulgence
of the one, undivided light which has been lit in a dark world.
For this reason Scripture, and in obedience to it, the church,
speak of the fulness of salvation; hence the church never
speaks of the "vere deus" by itself as if it could be understood
or believed apart from the "vere homo." Nor is it possible
to speak of either without speaking of salvation. Only if the

church understands these interrelations can it win the vehement conflict over the ontology and speculation supposedly implicit in the two natures doctrine. And in this conflict it will be able to witness to the "vere Deus" only, and be a blessing to others only, when in its preaching and in its practice it demonstrates that it has transcended all abstractions in the living faith which addresses Christ in adoration — doxologically and hence indivisibly:

> Beautiful Savior!
> Lord of the nations!
> Son of God and Son of Man!
> Glory and honor,
> Praise, adoration,
> Now and forevermore be Thine!

Here lies the victory over the tension between ontology and salvation; and with this prayer agrees the witness which speaks, now here, now there, about the mystery, the *one* mystery of Christ in a world to which the warning of Christ still applies: "The Son of man, when he comes, will he find faith on earth?"

The Humanity of Christ

CHAPTER IX

The Humanity of Christ

I N THE beginning of the previous chapter we already pointed out that the danger was far from imaginary that the church should have been almost exclusively interested in the deity of Christ but that it escaped this danger and defended also the "vere homo" as part of its confession. Right now it is necessary for us to discuss this confession separately. First let us try to weigh its significance. How did the church come to stress the soteriological significance, not only of the deity of Christ, but also of his humanity? This question is the more important because it would have been conceivable if the church had regarded the confession of Christ's deity as primary and that of his humanity as secondary. For from the beginning of the history of the church it was certain that it was God alone who could redeem us from the guilt and corruption of sin. From men this redemption could not be expected — this it was that people had undeniably learned from the Scripture. Through man sin entered into the world, and death through sin, and so death passed unto all men, for that all sinned (Rom. 5:12).

Could one, after that, still really expect anything from man or from that which is human? Was it not the unceasing battle of the church to witness against every form of humanism which in some way or other still expected redemption from man or from the regenerating powers of man? This humanistic expectation runs like a scarlet thread through the thinking of man as the idea of self-redemption and self-liberation

—man as the redeemer of himself and of his neighbor. And over against this, was there not the confession of the church that all depended on whether God himself would redeem us, and whether he would eliminate the guilt of sin and death as the wages of sin?

Does not Scripture continually tell us that it is meaningless for us to lean on man, on that which is human? The Scriptures unceasingly present the following contrast: "Cursed is the man that trusteth in man, and maketh flesh his arm, and whose heart departeth from Jehovah . . . blessed is the man that trusteth in Jehovah and whose trust Jehovah is" (Jer. 17:5, 7).

Is there one, upon whom God looks down from heaven, who is wise and who seeks after God? "They are all gone aside; they are together become filthy; there is none that doeth good, no, not one" (Ps. 14:2, 3). The Scriptures warn against any trust in princes or "in the son of man, in whom there is no help. His breath goeth forth, he returneth to his earth; in that very day his thoughts perish" (Ps. 146:3, 4).

These and numberless other texts in Scripture confirmed in the mind of Israel and of the church the consciousness of the necessity of trusting only in the Lord, who saves from guilt and death. In view of all this one would expect that from the beginning the attention of the church would have been completely focussed upon the exclusive action of God, from which the human is barred and in which all honor from the beginning to end is due to God. *He* redeems from death and *he* performs his work, mightily, wonderfully, and mercifully, *he alone.*

If one asks by what sources the confession of the church was fed when with equal emphasis it defended both the deity of Christ and his humanity, the answer is not hard to give. The solution consists in its submission to the Holy Scriptures which proclaims to us the truly human Jesus Christ, like unto us in all things, sin excepted. Here lay its source of resistance against all constructions which in one perilous way or another reasoned logicistically, on the basis of the divine work of redemption, to the insignificance of the humanity of Jesus Christ. In virtue of this submission to Scripture the church was preserved from making the true humanity of Christ suspect, as if this confession was approximately on a level with placing one's trust in man rather than in God. The adoration of Jesus Christ, true God and true man, is certainly something other than a form of humanism which still somehow introduces man as a redemptive factor in the work of divine salvation. There too where reflection about the significance of the humanity of Christ has been scanty, one already discovers the Scripture-fed, sure conviction of faith that it amounts to a violation of the mystery of the Son of God to make him exclusively an ambassador of heaven who had nothing of the human in him. With great power and genuine love the church offered resistance also to those who, though they confessed the true deity of Christ, had no interest in his *true* humanity. It was not satisfied with their passionate rejection of the Arian heresy but it watched over what the Scriptures indicated as a pledge of faith. Here lay the strength of the church in the first centuries already — the power to resist the dangers of coming into conflict with the testimony of Scripture concerning Jesus Christ. These dangers early menaced the church in the form of Docetism.

*   *   *

A popular characterization of Docetism is generally that it teaches that Christ, during his sojourn on earth, had only a phantom body. This crude form of Docetism already occurs in the early centuries of the Christian church, namely, in Gnosticism, Marcion and others. But in thinking of Docetism one may not limit himself exclusively to this crude, easily recognizable, form. Various phenomena reside under the heading of Docetism; often they assume a much more refined form but they have in common that in one way or another they do less than justice to the reality and completeness of the human nature of Christ. One can be a Docetist by declaring that Christ's body was only a seeming body but also by speaking of a genuine human nature and still somehow detract from Christ's humanity. In the treatment of Docetism in various forms one could ask whether this is a transient danger which, though it was acute in the first centuries, can no longer be called relevant today. People sometimes compare this Docetism with the opposition to the deity of Christ which continues into our day. Does not everyone today accept —barring now a few radical exceptions — that there has been a real Jesus of Nazareth and must not we devote all our attention to those doctrines which deny that this man Jesus Christ is the Son of the Father? The question as it is thus formulated in the church tends to weaken the urgency of our warning against the Docetic danger. One must not think that the acknowledgement of the historicity of Jesus of Nazareth is identical with the confession of the church touching the human nature of Christ. The acknowledgement of his historicity is not *half* of the Christological dogma. The point of this dogma is not that there was a historical person, one of whom it is believed on historical grounds that he really lived, but the issue is the significance of the teaching that he was true God and true man in the unity of the person. For this reason, despite the practically general agreement on the historicity of Jesus, the confession of the church regarding the human nature of Christ remains of critical importance. Hence we invite the attention of the reader no less to the humanity of Christ than to his deity, the more since we meet Docetism, not only in a few bizarre Christological conceptions of the first centuries, but also in the later history of the church. The Reformers, for instance, had to fight hard against an undoubted Docetic Anabaptism and sometimes suddenly discovered it in a complex of conceptions

which were emphatically designed in terms of the true deity
and humanity of Christ.

*   *   *

The search for the essential core of Docetism is quickly rewarded. It was patent wherever it sought entrance in the
church. The central motif of Docetism, though it is not always
conscious, consists in the conviction that a tie-up, a genuine
union between God (or the divine) and the physical, material,
and terrestrial is basically impossible. Basic to all Docetism is
a dualism which in one way or another reveals itself as a
threat to the church. To put it simply, Docetism could never
yield to what John declared when he said that the Word became flesh. That God or the divine Logos should unite, really
unite, with the flesh, in some way, was deemed unthinkable.
Such a union was considered unworthy of the eternal, transcendent God. If it were a matter merely of a union with the
human spirit as the higher, more nearly divine part of man,
then the subjection would not be as great. In the affinity between God and the human spirit there lay, to the minds of
many, a point of contact for such a union. But in terms of a
dualism between the divine and the material such a union
seemed impossible. In Gnosticism especially this background
was operative when on the ground of incompatibility the inference was made that Christ only seemed to have a body, while
Marcion tried to find a synthesis between Paul and the Gnostic
contrast between spirit and matter, and so came to believe too
that Christ's body was apparent.

In the ancient church this idea soon arose, as one can tell
when the belief in Christ's apparent body is associated with
his birth or baptism — an idea accompanied by the belief that
this union will end on the cross. In this area of thought no
true incarnation could be admitted. In Gnosticism, for instance, man must be redeemed precisely from the earthly and
physical because therein lies his misery. It was the divine

Christ as one of the aeons emanating from God who brought about this redemption by liberating the light-particles from their being stuck in a material world, into which the fall had brought them. A redeemer with a real human nature would hardly be fit for a redemptive task of this sort. An apparent body is methodically and pedagogically conceivable but a true human nature, like us in all things, cannot be harmonized with the basic motif of Gnosticism.

Without simply dubbing Marcion a Gnostic, we nonetheless detect in him the Docetic motif. He made his appeal especially to Paul and his opposition to the law, in order to be able to eradicate the nomism he had signalized. But he was very selective in this appeal. In his selection he wanted to free the gospel from all the additions of Judaistic falsifiers who had imported foreign elements into Paul's epistles.[1] In Gal. 4:4 he also discovered such a falsification: there we read that in the fulness of time God sent his Son, born of a woman. This last phrase did not in the least fit Marcion's dualism which was basically a docetic dualism. In Christ God came to redeem the world, to be sure, but this God in Jesus is a strange God, strange to this creation, to the nature and order of this world. Jesus suddenly appeared and could not share in evil flesh; at best a temporary form of appearance, a phantom body, is possible and conceivable.[2] In Jesus God came "in human appearance and placed himself in a position to feel, act, and suffer as a man, although the identity with a humanly generated body of flesh is only apparent, since the substance of flesh is lacking."[3] Against this extreme form of Docetism there was op-

---

1. A. V. Harnack, *Marcion. Das Evangelium vom fremden Gott*, 1924, page 33.
2. Referring to Luke 4:30 ("passing through the midst of them") Marcion remarks that this text proves that Christ was a "phantasm," Harnack, *Ibid.*, page 119.
3. Marcion also appealed to Romans 8:3 ("God sending his own Son in the likeness of sinful flesh"), his "Grundstelle," according to Harnack, for the solution of the problem facing him, *Ibid.*, page 165.

position already in the early period of the church. People saw clearly the implicit threat to the Incarnation. They fought particularly against the idea of "appearance." Ignatius, who saw the danger sharply and soon, emphasized strongly the truth of the Incarnation, Christ's true body, and his *real* cross. "Some unbelievers," he says, "say that he suffered only seemingly." "Close your ears," he exclaims, "to one who denies the reality of it." If Christ only suffered seemingly, why do I still wear my chains and wish to fight with wild beasts? "Then I shall die in vain!" Ignatius is concerned about reality in Christ's entire life, for to deny his flesh means . . . blasphemy to him.[4] Not that he wishes to deny the deity of Christ, but the Logos became true man. To deny that is to do violence to the salvation of the Lord.

Tertullian, too, was sharply opposed to Docetism. Van Bakel rightly calls him the most passionate anti-Docetist. His objection to Marcion is particularly that he deems it unworthy of God to have come into the flesh and that he thus deprives the belief in the Incarnation of its "scandalous" nature. Tertullian's polemic is undoubtedly related to his view of materiality which pervades all that exists, also God, but this peculiar feature does not eliminate the fact that he sharply opposes Docetism as the idea that the Son of God cannot be united with the flesh. Irenaeus fights Docetism without this special feature. He emphasizes particularly that Christ overcame the act of disobedience committed by the man Adam, and in his elaborate doctrine of recapitulation he stresses the true humanity of Christ.[5] From everything it appears that resistance to Docetism was deemed necessary, because the humanity of Christ is not the neutral, ontological presupposition of

---

4. Ignatius, *Letter to Smyrna* V.
5. Irenaeus, *Adv. haer.*, 3, 18, 6.

his course of redemption on earth but concerns the central message of the Incarnate Word.

* * *

Later in the history of dogma Docetism appears again, but now in a more refined form. Then the issue shows up within the limits of the union of the two natures. Docetism then appeared in a form which was harder to recognize for the church but therefore all the more dangerous. Over against the idea of a phantom-body it was sufficient to use the apologetics of Ignatius and to refer to the gospel stories about Jesus Christ. Later on, however there was not an absolute denial of Christ's human nature but people still spoke about the human nature in such a way as to make it hard to believe in a *true* and *complete* human nature. Although they consented to the union, they so construed it that it was evident that the underlying bias was against the possibility of the unitability of the two natures. The classical form of this refined Docetism we find in the doctrine of Apollinaris and later in the influential Monophysitism which proved so powerful in the theology and church of the East.[6] In another connection we already saw that Apollinaris, though he assented to Nicea and registered dissent from the heresy of Arius, had trouble with the problem as to how the Logos can unite himself with a complete human nature. In monophysitism occurs a synthesis between the two natures into one theanthropic nature. With reference to this one theanthropic nature it was said unreservedly that it was the redeeming God; and, although Christ's humanity was not denied in view of his being God, it was a fact that the human nature was almost overpowered and absorbed by the divine, so that one could hardly speak of the reality and completeness of this nature. This became apparent later when monotheletism issued from monophysitism a doctrine which, in view of the

6. See Karl Adam, *Christus unser Bruder*, 1929, for a strong defense of the humanity of Christ.

one theanthropic nature, could find no room for the truly human will of Jesus Christ, an inference from the mono-physitism rejected by the church in 680.

* * *

People have believed that in the New Testament one can already detect something of Docetism. However surprising this may be, in Paul, too, this Docetic motif has been discovered. Even when people admitted that Paul certainly was no Docetist himself, and acknowledged the full humanity of Christ, they felt they detected in him a certain tendency in this direction. His utterances about the flesh seemed to carry a hint of it. Did not Paul also operate with the contrast between flesh and spirit which played such a large role in Docetism? Van Bakel discovers in Paul a dualism, worse, a contrast between the area of the supernatural pneuma and the area of the natural, of the world of the flesh.[7] This "flesh," acccording to Paul, is inseparably commingled with sin and the natural man must be made over into a spiritual man by baptism. In this context Van Bakel treats of the flesh of Christ. On the basis of Paul's view of the flesh, he cannot avoid regarding the flesh of Christ as something conflicting with the essence of this pneumatic man *par excellence.* "He would have prefered to be completely silent on it as it offends him to be continually reminded of his own *sarx.*" This aversion Van Bakel believes he also detects in what the apostle says about "being in the likeness of sinful flesh" (Rom. 8:3) and about the "likeness of men" (Phil. 2:7), and he then adds: "in any case he is approaching the boundary lines of Docetism." Van Bakel believes that Paul was still unconscious of the danger of heresy and unbiassed toward Docetism in contrast with John for whom this unbiassed attitude had already become impossible. This view of Paul is utterly at variance with his epistles. Indeed, everywhere in Paul, precisely

7. H. A. van Bakel, *De Carne Christi,* in *Circa Sacra,* 1935, page 5.

in the texts referred to in Van Bakel, namely Rom. 8:3 and Phil. 2:7, the true humanity of Christ appears. In these two texts the argument points to the true humanity, to the form of the servant. It was Paul who wrote the words — which had aroused the ire of Marcion — that Christ was "born of a woman" (Gal. 4:4). Paul's use of the word "flesh," too, does not express his sympathy for an anthropological dualism but his conviction that human life is destroyed by sin as the "imagining of the flesh," while over against this Paul refuses to find support in the qualities of the human spirit as something higher, more nearly akin to God, and hence not subject to the curse of the flesh. In the acknowledgment of the true humanity of Christ Paul is completely in line with the rest of the New Testament. His eye, as that of all the other apostles, is focussed upon the great mystery: God revealed *in the flesh* (I Tim. 3:16) and it is completely unrealistic to try to construe a somewhat credible contrast between John and Paul.

* * *

The New Testament not only does not contain a trace of Docetism but it already polemicizes against it. The epistle of John especially makes that very clear. He takes position against all who deny that Jesus Christ truly came into the flesh. At this point, according to John, one's whole faith in Jesus Christ is at stake. He takes position against false prophets. Here it is possible and necessary to test them: "Hereby know ye the Spirit of God: every spirit that confesseth that Jesus Christ is come in the flesh is of God: and every spirit that confesseth not Jesus is not of God: and this is the spirit of the antichrist" (I John 4:2,3). The belief that Jesus is the Christ is the victory that has overcome the world (I John 5:5). Everything is at stake in this confession. The issue is not merely the witness of man but the witness of God: "for the witness of God is this, that he hath borne witness concerning his Son" (I John 5:9).

The false teachers, against whom John takes position, first belonged to the church but later separated (I John 2:18, 19). John is apparently concerned in particular about their denial of the real Incarnation. In their doctrine there was undoubtedly a Docetic element, for they assume the impossibility of a union between God and the human. Probably in I John 5:6 ("This is he that came by water and blood") we encounter a polemic against the idea that a heavenly being temporarily united himself with the man Jesus from his baptism to the moment preceding his crucifixion.[8] Their Docetism lay in their opposition to "the scandalous idea that the Son of God, the Revealer, the Intermediary between the Divine and the human suffered the degradation of direct contact with matter, the embodiment of all evil."[9] Hence the New Testament already contains a strong polemic against a motif which will later become a many-faceted and dangerous Docetism.

* * *

The Gospels, no less than John's epistle, describe for us the genuine humanity of Christ and that with special emphases. Docetism is strongly at odds with the Gospels. To indicate the conflict we take our stance in the forty days between the Resurrection and the Ascension, the period in which Christ's glory is revealed. Anyone expecting that Christ's deity would completely overshadow his genuine humanity in this period is mistaken. The great change which took place in this period is his transition from the cross to glory; but he himself, the man Jesus Christ, remained unchanged. This is particularly evident in the kerygma concerning his appearances, everyone of which is a testimony against Docetism. Luke for instance describes an appearance of Christ to his disciples, who, in

---

8. "Since the Divine cannot suffer." C. H. Dodd. *The Johannine Epistles,* 1947, page 130. Greydanus, *Korte Verklaring,* page 116, says that the reference to the water *and the blood* imply a rejection of Cerinthus' idea that it was really not Jesus who shed his blood.
9. Dodd, *Ibid.,* XIX.

their terror, suppose they see a spirit (Luke 24:36-43). The Greek word we read here is the same word from which the word Docetism has been derived. Over against the wrong idea of the disciples, Christ utters the mighty declaration: "Why are ye troubled? and wherefore do questionings arise in your hearts? See my hands and my feet, that it is I myself: handle me, and see; for a spirit hath not flesh and bones, as ye behold me having" (Luke 24:38, 39). More realistically, concretely, or anti-Docetically Christ could hardly speak; and this revelation is confirmed when Christ, since the disciples are still not convinced, asks for something to eat and eats a piece of broiled fish before their eyes. All evangelists are unanimous in their anti-Docetic witness. None of them knows anything of phantom-bodies. The Lord is risen *indeed*. No sooner is the crucified Jesus risen than he resumes contact with this world. He goes before them into Galilee (Matt. 28:7). When Thomas doubts, he is told: "Reach hither thy finger, and see my hands; and reach hither thy hand, and put it into my side (John 20:27). Earlier it was said that Jesus showed his hands and his side (John 20:20) and that the women took hold of his feet and worshipped him (Matt. 28:9). Especially the reference to the crucifixion-wounds lifts the reality of his appearance beyond all doubt. Christ's statement to Mary: "Touch me not; for I am not yet ascended unto the Father" (John 20:17) certainly does not — Docetically — refer to the impossibility of touching Christ in his earthly appearance, but is designed to disabuse Mary of the idea that the old situation, which existed before Jesus' death, has returned to stay. In the new situation, which is qualified by the Resurrection, she is given her task: ". . . go unto my brethren, and say to them . . ." Markus Barth writes concerning touching Jesus — and correctly: "That the thought of this touching or the wish for it is not consonant with the Resurrection-body of Jesus or with the heavenly being of Jesus Christ, is nowhere indicated."[10]

10. M. Barth, *Der Augenzeuge,* 1946, page 257.

According to the Gospels there can therefore be no doubt about Christ's reality as genuinely human.[11] The apostles are just as certain of it as they were before the crucifixion. We read that Christ breathed on his disciples (John 20:22) and that he lifted up his hands in blessing (Luke 24:50). What John says is true in the full sense of the words: ". . . that which . . . .our hands handled, concerning the Word of life" (I John 1:1). This "handling" is not accidental but subservient to the fulfillment of the apostolic task: preaching the reality of the risen Christ. Accidental handling is something quite different from the touching which is consciously done in response to a command. "It was not till after the Resurrection that the 'handling' of the apostles gained normative and fundamental significance; for this reason special significance must be attributed to the presentation of the touching of the Risen one."[12] The idea is to prove "that the Lord is truly risen and that his appearance is not the apparition of a ghost." One almost involuntarily thinks of that earlier occasion when the disciples believed that Christ, who was walking on the sea, was a "phantasma" (Mark 6:49) and when Christ said, in words very similar to those used after the Resurrection, "it is I."

In everything the genuinely human reality of Christ, after the Resurrection, also, appears.[13] All these sensible encounters with the Risen Christ,[14] as taken up in the apostolic kerygma, point to the certainty of the salvation which appeared, victorious over death, in Christ. The Risen one is the same as the crucified one. Here one should not be faithless but believing (John 20:27). It is the reality attested by Paul when he says: "and if Christ hath not been raised, your faith is vain; ye are

11. It was already predicted (John 16:16) that "a little while, and ye behold me no more; and again a little while and ye shall see me." Compare R. Schippers, *Getuigen van Jezus Christus in het N. T.*, 1938, page 101, about the apostles as eye-witnesses.
12. M. Barth, *ibid.*, page 203.
13. Compare also Acts 1:4 ("being assembled together with them") and Acts 10:41 ("to us, who ate and drank with him after he rose from the dead").
14. Compare I Cor. 15 about Christ's appearing to many.

yet in your sins" (I Cor. 15:17). "But now hath Christ been raised" — this Christ, the human one, in whom existed none of the unreality inferred from the supposed impossibility of the Incarnation.

*   *   *

There can be no doubt either about the true humanity of Christ in the period prior to his crucifixion. Any number of texts point in some way to his genuine humanity. One can not detect any tendency to eliminate this humanity as something foreign or distasteful. One must register dissent from Van der Leeuw when he writes concerning John: "John's picture of Christ resembles the Byzantine figures of Christ: hard and impassive, speaking his divine words in unapproachable majesty." Dissent must be even louder when he adds that there is a certain inconsonance with the genuinely human: "The people in John's Gospel, too, are hardly human, at least insofar as they appear together.[15] For while the Gospel of John is a mighty testimony to the deity of Christ, it is precisely this Gospel which shows him to us as the Incarnate Word. Whatever the variations be in this Gospel, it never places the genuine humanity of Christ in the shadows. This appears strongly in the reality correctly ascribed in this Gospel to the crucifixion: "And he that hath seen hath borne witness, and his witness is true: and he knoweth that he said true, that ye also may believe" (John 19:35). This statement is immediately related to the piercing of Jesus' side and refers to the reality of Christ's death. Grosheide points out that this testimony concerning the truth (v. 35) precedes the mention of the fulfillment of prophecy (v. 36). One of John's purposes in writing the Gospel, says Grosheide, was the "polemic against Docetists."[16]

Van der Leeuw is much closer to the truth about these things when he says: "The mystery of the kenosis, the self-

---

15. G. v. d. Leeuw, *Bach's Johannes-Passion*, 1948, page 19.
16. F. W. Grosheide, *Commentary on John*, II, page 510. Compare I, page 52.

emptying of the Son of God, which was so dear to Bach and which we sense even in the background of the joyous and popular music of the Christmas Oratorio — the mystery of the Ruler who in bitter suffering assumes the form of a slave and was King precisely through and in his humiliation—that is the mystery proclaimed to us here."[17] In the Gospels the divine and the human characteristics never compete with each other. We are refered everywhere to the *man* Jesus Christ. He is presented to us in his birth, in his historical descent from Israel, in his development from child to man, and in all his human feelings and desires.[18] We hear of his hunger, thirst, sleep, anger, grief, fear, suffering and death. His public appearances do quite often make an overwhelming impression and we are told concerning him, "Never man so spake" (John 7:46). But in Scripture there is not a single instance of any denial of his true humanity. One can characterize his entire life with the words: "It behooved him in all things to be made like unto his brethren" (Heb. 2:17). This likeness is repeatedly emphasized: "Since then the children are sharers in flesh and blood, he also himself in like manner partook of the same" (Hebr. 2:14). He was made in the likeness of man (Phil. 2:7). He was even tempted and he suffered in his temptations. Because he himself was tempted, he can "succor them that are tempted" (Hebr. 2:18). He can sympathize with our infirmities as one "that hath been in all points tempted like as we are, yet without sin" (Hebr. 4:15). His sinlessness and holiness, according to Scripture, does not detract one whit from his true humanity. His humanity comes to the surface especially in the bitterness of his suffering, which was so intense in the garden of Gethsemane that, as we read, "there appeared unto him an angel from heaven strengthening him" (Luke 22:43). It was this gospel-text in particular which gave the greatest difficulty to those who had been influenced

17. G. v. d. Leeuw, *Ibid.,* pages 28 ff.
18. See Bavinck, *Geref. Dogmatiek,* page 259.

in one way or another by Docetic tendencies.[19] Still it forms only a part of the entire Gospel which ceases to be intelligible without the true humanity.

The true humanity stands in bold relief in the early part of the Gospel where we read of the ordinary human development of Jesus and not a word about the complete absorption of the human by the divine. We read of his development as a child who grew and became strong and was filled with wisdom; "and the grace of God was upon him." (Luke 2:40). "And Jesus advanced in wisdom and stature, and in favor with God and men" (Luke 2:52). All this is obviously written up analogously to the lives of other children: John the Baptist, for instance, who "grew, and waxed strong in spirit" (Luke 1:80) and Samuel who "grew on, and increased in favor both with Jehovah, and also with men" (I Sam. 2:26). Common expressions denoting human development are applied also to Christ. Whatever great things may and must be said of him, they never detract anything from the description of the maturation of his life. These "common" indications are all the more important because the rest of Scripture is almost completely silent about the first thirty years of Christ's life. This silence is broken only by the story of the twelve-year-old Jesus in the temple where he amazed the "teachers" (Luke 2:47).

This story is a far cry from all kinds of fantastic Christ-legends and apocryphal Christmas stories which introduce the miraculous already into his youth and attempt to avoid the fact that others *managed* Jesus.[20] The only thing we learn of Christ's own lips is addressed to his parents: "How is it that ye sought me? Knew ye not that I must be about my Father's business?" (Luke 2:49). Nowhere do we read of any

---

19. A striking example is Hilary of Portiers who uses various Docetic expressions. See his *De Trinitate* X, where he mentions the "corpus caeleste" of Christ (X, 18). On Hilary and Docetism in general see: Pohle, *Dogmatik* II, pages 41 ff; H. Vogel, *Christologie* I, page 349; Bruce, *The Humiliation of Christ*, pages 240 ff; and Relton, *A Study in Christology*, 1929, pages 3 ff.

20. Joseph, for instance, took the child (Matt. 2:14, 21).

miraculous deed or any unusual incident — just this one flash
of the growing consciousness that he must *unavoidably* be
busy in a completely self-consciously determined direction:
his Father's business. His life, also in his youth, was permanently bound up with the Father; but the same story tells us
of his childlike obedience to his parents: "And he went down
with them, and came to Nazareth; and he was subject unto
them." The Gospel tells us with the utmost simplicity of the
child Jesus on his way through the world a subject which
in later ages became the object of believing reflection and
increasing marvel and adoration.[21]

To one who tries without prejudice to follow the course of
people's lives this long silence and this sobriety are strange.
But the Gospel does not have this biographical interest and
holds its almost uninterrupted peace up to the moment of
Christ's assumption of his official work. It only mentions his
growth in the grace of God and describes but one moment of
his deepening insight into his absolute concern with the business of his Father. Thus the Gospel is oriented to the fuller
proclamation which will take place later. *This* life will be
characterized by its being concerned *solely* with the business of
the Father. The words "My Father" are the program of his
life and are repeated again and again during the toilsome
course of his life. In his youth these words form a true, childlike prelude to what will later fill his mouth and heart when
the zeal of his Father's house will consume him.

Every effort to disparage the humanity of Christ means a
disqualification of the Scriptural picture. Scripture never
permits the divine to threaten or relativize the human nature.

* * *

It can be understood that in later periods people asked
various questions, arising from the confession of the church,

---

21 Greydanus points out that Luke 2:12 and 16 have "brephos," verse
40 has "paidion," verse 43 "pais," and verse 52 "Iesous."

about this true human nature. If the unity of Christ's person, as it is founded on Scripture, must be confessed, is not the inference inevitable that the divine eliminates, or at least relativizes, the true, and therefore limited, human nature in Christ? In the history of the church we note that people repeatedly came to conclusions which, in effect, placed them in the Docetic camp — not, to be sure, from Docetic motives (the incompatibility of God and earthly reality), but in view of the union of the two natures. This led to the practice of reading the parts of Scriptures which most clearly bring out the humanity of Christ in such a way as to deprive them of their original force. As a striking example of this practice we mention the varying views held as to *knowledge* of Jesus Christ. Was not his knowledge purely divine just as his power was purely divine?

This question as to Christ's knowledge gained relief by an utterance of Christ concerning his knowledge of the coming day of the Lord. We are referring to Christ's much-discussed statement: "But of that day or that hour knoweth no one, not even the angels in heaven, *neither the Son,* but the Father" (Mark 13:32, Matt. 24:36). The first impression any reader would receive here is that Jesus Christ clearly puts a limit to his knowledge of the day of the Lord.[22]

In later conflicts over the meaning of this statement a certain amount of bias often began to play a role. In view of the union of the two natures people began to ask themselves how it was *possible* to put a limit, this or any other, to the knowledge of Christ since he was not only true man but also true God. Did not the union imply that he shared divine omniscience and was familiar therefore — *had* to be familiar — with the hour of the day of the Lord? Along this route various attempts were made to harmonize this text with a certain interpretation of Christological dogma. A lucid illus-

---

22. Van Leeuwen (*Markus* in *Korte Verklaring,* page 171) mentions Christ's candor in speaking of this human limitation involved in his incarnation.

tration of this particular complex of problems is the Roman Catholic exegesis of Mark 13:32.

This exegesis is largely conditioned by the interpretation which Thomas Aquinas provided. He believed that this text does not teach that Christ did not know the day of his return but that he did not tell his disciples. He himself knew it but not with a knowledge communicable to others, a knowledge intended for transmission. According to Thomas, this text runs parallel with Acts 1, where we read that Christ conceals from his disciples the day of the establishment of the Kingdom by asserting: "It is not for you to know times or seasons, which the Father hath set within his own authority" (Acts 1:7). Thomas reaches back at this point to the views of Gregory I (509-604), who offered the same exegesis.[23]

For this exegesis Gregory appealed to Genesis 22:12, where God says to Abraham: ". . . now I know that thou fearest God." According to Gregory and Thomas, this "knowledge" does not mean that the Lord only just now discovered that Abraham feared God but . . . he now *discloses* it to Abraham. In line with this is to be understood the Gospel-text about Christ's not knowing the day and hour.

In the year 1918 the Roman Catholic Church issued a decree[24] from the holy office and rejected the opinion that Christ meant here that as man he did not know the day of judgment. It also rejected the notion that it is uncertain that Christ's soul knew from the beginning all things in the past, present, and the future. The idea of any limitation to the knowledge of Christ cannot possibly be taught in view of the hypostatic union of the two natures.

---

23. See Thomas, *Summa* III, 10, 2. See also Grosheide, *Commentaar,* on Acts 1, page 18 where he says that the disclosure of a given time does not belong to the mediatorial work of Christ. In Thomas this interpretation is read back into the passages of Mark and Matthew.

24. *Circa quasdam propositiones de scientia animae Christi* (Denzinger 2183-2185).

It is not difficult to detect the dogmatic bias in this tradi-tional exegesis.[25] This bias is all the more evident because no account is taken of the fact that both Matthew and Mark mention, not only that the Son does not know, but also that the angels do not know. No one, says Christ, knows of that day or that hour, and then more specifically: not even the angels in heaven, neither the Son, but the Father. Of the communicability of this knowledge the text does not breathe a word; it rather contains a warning to be watchful and to pray, an exhortation all the more needed on account of the fact that the day and hour are not known.[26] Quite apart from the — to us untenable — appeal to Genesis 22, one still has to admit that the exegesis is controlled by a given dogma. Greitemann has pointed out that a Catholic exegete does indeed take account of the Catholic doctrine of Christ and that the doctrine illuminates the exegesis of this text. This is precisely why we demur: for by this dogmatic exegesis the text is robbed of its evident meaning. According to the Roman Catholic exegesis it is *a priori* impossible that the text should mean that Christ did not know. A limited knowledge of the future would dis-qualify his Godmanhood. This judgment of Roman Catholic theology has broad consequences for its evaluation of Christ's human nature. This employment of the word "impossible" conditions all of Rome's exegesis and compels it to look for parallels in order to escape the self-evident meaning of the words. To oppose this procedure does not imply that to the opponent the hypostatic union has become clear and trans-parent. Who can penetrate into the unfathomable mystery of this union? But the idea is not to penetrate that which simply passes our comprehension but to accept the message of Scrip-ture which distinguishes for us the power of Christ from the omnipotence of God (Matt. 28:19) and the knowledge of

---

25. Compare Calvin on the texts in Matthew and Mark. Calvin views this exegesis ("many believed this ignorance to be unworthy of Christ") as a reaction to Arian errors.
26. H. N. Ridderbos, *De Komst van het Koninkrijk*, 1950, page 435.

Christ from the omniscience of God. If anywhere, then here our thinking must be normatively conditioned by Scripture. The Roman Catholic exegesis of these words from Matthew and Mark is symptomatic of a conception which, operating as it does with dogmatic inferences, makes it hard truly to heed the witness of Scripture.

In view of the clarity of Scripture it is not surprising that Catholic theology itself at times senses the difficulty of this approach to the life of Jesus. If one reasons inferentially from the deity of Christ, he will not encounter these difficulties but will simply dissociate himself further from the Scriptures which speak of the true humanity of Christ. But off and on we observe the pressure of the words of Scripture which remind us of the limited human character of Christ's earthly life.

Pohle, one such Catholic, continues, to be sure, to exclude all ignorance from Christ's mind as to past, present, and future, and operates with the "blessed knowledge" of Christ, but nonetheless ascribes to the soul of Christ, on the ground of its union with the Logos, a *"relative* omniscience."[27] The problem obviously lurks in the word "relative." By this means he can still admit to a certain development in Christ and in his knowledge. "The soul of Christ also possessed . . . a developing experiential knowledge or the so-called acquired knowledge." That is the knowledge which distinguishes the man who is on a pilgrimage. As man Christ already knew everything experience could teach him but still there was room in him for a "genuine learning-process," in the sense, namely, that he learned to know by experience the things with whose content he was already familiar. Pohle then tries to demonstrate that this knowledge was not meaningless or superfluous. The impasse into which Pohle has gotten is evident from what he says about this experiential knowledge. Pohle says that to what is already known it adds "valuable, new, unknown, and enriching elements of knowledge" — a thesis

---

27. Pohle, *Lehrbuch der Dogmatik*, II, page 149, 150.

which can hardly be squared with the position already taken to the effect that Christ's knowledge is complete.[28]

This discussion nonetheless shows us that something of the unsatisfactoriness of dogma-conditioned exegesis is still felt when the dogmatic view is confronted with the course of Jesus' human life.

In this same context we must stop to consider still another problem. It is closely related to the fore-going discussion and also concerns the true reality of Christ's human nature. It is the problem of the relationship between the knowledge of Christ and his suffering. And again we encounter Roman Catholic theology on our way. We confront here the question of the reality of the suffering of Christ. In line with Chalcedon it is Rome's design to combat monophysitism and to maintain the distinction between the two natures. But this does not prevent Rome, in view of the conjunction of the human nature with the Logos, to elevate the human nature to unknown heights. As a result there arose in Roman Catholic theology the problem of the reality of Christ's suffering, the problem of his experiencing suffering in connection with his uninterrupted vision of God.[29] Striking in all this is that the course of Catholic thought is generally determined, not by the data of Scripture, but, as with the exegesis of Mark 13:32, by the doctrine of the hypostatic union. The problem centers particularly at the point where people proceed from the idea of the human nature in its vision of God. Thomas taught, for instance, that Christ, as man, was from the first moment of his conception the true and perfect possessor of blessedness.[30] In this he is distinguished from earthly pilgrims. For men the vision of God is an absolutely supernatural and eschatological gift. For a created spirit intuitive knowledge of God

---

28. Compare Schmaus, *Kath. Dogmatik* II, 1949, page 643.
29. Compare my: *Conflict met Rome*, page 270.
30. "quia Christus, secundum quod homo, a primo instanti suae conceptionis fuit verus et plenus comprehensor." *Summa,* III, Question VI, IX-XII.

is in itself impossible. Over against Beghynen and Begharden the Council of Vienna posited in 1311 that it is incorrect to say that the soul needs no special light of glory to arrive at the blessed vision of God. There are no exceptions here, *apart from the person of Jesus.*[31] Only the blessed can, by the reception of the light of glory, intuitively see the being of God. But Christ shares this blessed knowledge *already on earth.* The soul of Christ "like the blessed in glory, immediately viewed the being of God." Bartmann, for all this, fully acknowledges: "As ground one again introduces the hypostatic union first, hence a theological and not a revealed ground." Indeed, he even says that we find in Scripture any number of statements "which seem to be at odds with perfect knowledge such as the full vision of God yields." It is not surprising that especially exegetical theologians demurred against this "blessed" knowledge of Christ on earth. But also for Bartmann all counter-arguments disappear in the light of the hypostatic union which makes this vision self-evident because the union is absolutely the highest grace, incapable of increase. Hence arises the problem whether this "blessed" knowledge is compatible with the reality of the suffering of Christ. Roman Catholic theology of course assumes this reality and wants to maintain both: "blessed" knowledge and true suffering.[32] But it still tries to find a transparent solution. In the theology of the Scholastics the problem was solved by a division of the soul into a higher and a lower part: the *visio Dei* corresponding to the higher and the experience of suffering to the lower part of the soul. Thus a synthesis was attempted by way of an anthropology; but it is plain, even on immanent grounds, that this solution cannot be correct, because the *entire* human nature was taken up into the hypo-

31. Bartmann, *Dogmatik* I, page 92.
32. See J. Braun, *Handlexicon der Katholischen Dogmatik*: "The vision of God, which the soul of Christ already possessed during the entire course of his life, eliminated neither the capacity to suffer nor the actual suffering of Christ."

static union. Still this is the direction in which many look for a possibility of uniting the *visio* and *passio*. The position of Thomas is noteworthy. He treats of those who say that Christ's vision of God carries beatitude with it and that also his body shares in this glory, and suggests as a solution that it was fitting for the Son of God to assume frail human flesh so that in it he could suffer as well as be tempted and thus help us. Here the witness of Scripture counteracts dogmatic premises as is confirmed by the quotation from Isaiah 53: "He was wounded for our transgressions" and that from Philippians 2 about his being made in the likeness of men. In answer to those who say that the absolute and permanent vision of divine things prevents the feeling of fear and sorrow, Thomas refers again to Isaiah 53.[33] Dogmatically his solution is that the pleasure of contemplation was confined to the spirit so that it did not spread to the senses and hence did not make physical pain impossible. By these means Thomas tries to show them that one can still speak of the genuine sorrow of Christ. Christ was both one that had, and one that did not have, beatitude: both "comprehensor" and "viator."

Hence also Thomas solves the problem anthropologically. The problem of *visio and passio* is laid out in an anthropological division and subsumed under various levels of Christ's human existence. The soul is given its due on the basis of the hypostatic union and the suffering, somewhat more under pressure of Scripture, is explained in terms of an anthropological split. There is a recognition of the suffering of Christ but it is not plain how room can be reserved for it since it is all taken up by the beatitudinous vision of God.

How differently the Scriptures speak about the suffering of Christ! The person of Christ in Scripture is viewed in the light of his office and humiliation and, since the person and the work are never abstracted one from the other, one is not permitted to draw conclusions from the person as such. The

---

33. *Summa*, III, 15, 5.

Scriptures speak to us of the suffering Son of man, the Man of sorrows, who suffers, is grieved, and fearful, who prays, weeps, and is amazed, who yearns, believes, hopes, and trusts. Who could make all this transparent by means of a distinction between a higher and a lower soul, by means of "the assumption of levels in his human nature"? When everything is viewed in terms of the vision-passion schematism it is easily understood why those who concern themselves with the Gospels are deeply moved by the passion and give its full due, while the *systematic* thelogians, without denying that passion, still so strongly view the passion in the light of the vision that they take serious exception to the way in which the Reformation spoke about the depth and terror of Christ's agony and about his being truly *forsaken* by God.

*   *   *

Similar questions arise when Roman Catholic thought is concerned with the fear, faith, and hope of Christ. Thomas for instance treats the question: Did Christ have fear?[34] In this chapter he quotes the gospel passage about the fear of Christ in Gethsemane (Mark 14:33); but he does not get beyond saying that fear is excluded in the case of Christ: to prove that he had a genuine human nature he voluntarily took fear and sorrow upon himself. Thomas further discusses the question whether faith and hope were, and could be, present in Christ. As far as faith is concerned, Thomas appeals to Hebrews 11:1, where we read that faith is the conviction of things not seen, but, says Thomas, "there was nothing Christ did not see."[35] From the first moment of his conception Christ saw God perfectly as to his essence; hence in his case there could be no faith.

---

34. *Ibid.,* III, 15, 7.
35. *Ibid.,* III, 7, 3.

As concerning hope, Thomas refers to Romans 8:24: ". . . who hopeth for that which he seeth?" Hence what applies to faith applies to hope: there can have been no hope in Christ. It is admitted, of course, that Christ while on earth did not possess everything belonging to his perfection, as for example, the glorification of his body. In a sense Christ could hope for this perfection, but such hope is not the genuine virtue of hope, for genuine hope does not concern the bliss of the body, but that of the soul which consists in the enjoyment of God.

The entire argumentation, it is clear, is conditioned by the "visio beata." Here and there the influence of Scripture does play a role but the peculiar formulation of the problem remains evident. In this there is an obvious failure to do justice to the true human nature of Christ. In the hypostatic union, the divine nature thus forms a real threat to the human nature. That is the indubitable element of Docetism which must be signalized here. Thanks to the undeniable perspicuity of Scripture there is still a counter-weight to the danger of having the reality of the human nature eclipsed by the divine.

In the theology of the Reformation one does not encounter, at least not in the same measure, the coercive restraints of a given conception of the union upon Christological thought. It did heartily confess this union of the two natures but in this confession it maintained rapport with the Scriptures precisely because, in acknowledging this mystery, it wished to be guided by revelation. For this reason one does not find, in the theology of the Reformation, any elaborate arguments about the problem as to the possibility of the suffering of Christ in view of the union of the two natures. The Reformation did not need the crutch of one anthropological distinction or another in order to make the possibility of the suffering at least somewhat transparent. The lack of bias, which characterizes Calvin in his exegesis of the text about Christ's not knowing the day of judgment, is visible everywhere also in his reflection on

the suffering of Christ.[36] The Reformers know of the divine
nature and of the human as well as of their union in the unity
of the person but, in fidelity to Chalcedon which refused to
eliminate the several properties, they respected the mystery of
it. Roman Catholic theologians often believe they detect, in
the Christology of the Reformation, a devaluation of Christ's
human nature because, say they, the Reformation does not take
seriously enough the union of the human with the divine nature. They cannot and will not, like Kuyper, accept that in
Christ, too, one must distinguish between faith and vision and
that, on that basis, Christ too believed and hoped in clinging
to the Word of God.[37] With reference to his suffering the
Catholic bias appears clearly when Brom charges both Calvin
and the Heidelberg Catechism with the error of viewing Christ
on the cross as plunged in "hellish agony." Reformed theology
has rightly asked itself how one could then explain the fourth
statement from the cross, an utterance of anguish in which
even the word "Father," though Christ used it in his first and
in his last declaration, is missing. One could probably shed
light on the whole mass of problems surrounding the *visio-
passio* distinction simply by means of an exegesis of the utterance "My God, why hast thou forsaken me?" It would then
become apparent that the *visio-passio* dilemma prevents one
from fully acknowledging the reality of Christ's being forsaken
and that the way is barred ultimately by a certain view of the
hypostatic union. We are confronting a way of thought which
practically conforms to a question once expressed in the
Middle Ages: "How can God be forsaken by God?" In this
type of thinking we observe that the person of Christ is abstracted from his work and office, from his work of substitu-

36. See *Institutes*, II, XVI, 5, where Calvin says concerning Christ's
suffering that ". . . it was no mean specimen of his incomparable love to
us, to contend with horrible fear, and amid those dreadful torments to
neglect all care of himself, that he might promote our benefit." See also
his beautiful defense against the "subterfuges." II, XVI, 12.
37. A. Kuyper, *De Vleeschwording des Woords*, page 153. Compare my
Conflict met Rome, page 271.

tion.[38] Here, it is likely, lies the deepest root of the controversy on this point. In Roman Catholic thought there is continually observable a strong tendency to think inferentially from the personal union, viewed apart from the humiliation and work of Christ. One guilty of this abstraction is compelled later, in view of the reality of the Gospels, to posit various restrictions. The paradoxicalness between *visio* and *passio* must then be solved in a sort of synthesis while justice must nonetheless be done to the testimony of Scripture concerning Christ's being forsaken and the suffering of him "who in the days of his flesh, having offered up prayers and supplications with strong crying and tears unto him that was able to save him from death" (Hebr. 2:7). We even run into some who appeal to miracle for a solution: "God miraculously prevented the origination of the joy resulting from the vision of God."[39] Thus people try to pave the way back to the Gospels. In devotional literature the Gospels come to their own more than one would often expect in view of the theological literature. We are thinking of Van der Meer's meditations about the bitter suffering of the Lord. He does not contradict the church in regard to its doctrine of the "beatific vision" but his *emphases* are important and derived from Scripture. "Was he not able to crowd into the background the enjoyment of his experience of the divine in his humanity, to endure genuine despair, and to scoop out ravines of windowless desolation in his humanity, depths surpassing all common capacity for suffering?"[40] Thus room is made for the acknowledgment that Christ threatened to succumb and needed the presence of the angel to strengthen him. We discover the same thing in the work of Romano Guardini, who — averse as he is to anthropological illumination of the possibility of true suffering — exclaims in meditating on Gethsemane: "Psychology no longer has anything to look for

38. See Calvin's title of *Institutes* II, XII: The Necessity of Christ Becoming Man in Order to Fulfill the Office of Mediator.
39. M. Scheeben, *Dogmatik* II, page 276.
40. F. Van der Meer, *Catechismus*, 1941, page 193.

here." It is at this juncture that he refers to guilt-bearing as the cause of the desolation now beginning: "We may say perhaps that in the hour of Gethsemane the knowledge of the guilt and misery of men came to its most cutting climax before the face of the Father, who began to forsake him."[41] Thus Guardini attains to deep awareness of the cross and speaks, with reference to the fourth word of the cross, of, the "awful reality" of Christ's being forsaken. He even reminds us of the somberness which Brom sensed in Calvin and the Heidelberg Catechism, when he says in reflecting on the fourth word of the cross: "Thus, in an inconceivable sense, he descended into hell."

He views the person and work of Christ under the single aspect of the love of God in Jesus Christ. If that had always been done, people would have been open to Christ's own anguished assertion that he had been forsaken. No compensating meditation would have been needed for that which theological dilemmas tended to exclude. And then Rome would not continually have left the impression that, though it formally held to the Chalcedonian creed, it did not fully honor this creed in practice. Then, too, Rome would have again caught sight of the incomprehensibility of this humiliation in which Christ, in the deep crisis of his being forsaken by the Father and in great agony, placed his belief and hope upon the Father. Scripture itself points out that the Christ, who is not ashamed to call us brethren, declares: "I will put my trust in him" (Hebr. 2:11); those who stood about the cross, despite their hostile heart and misuse of words, witnessed to this trust: "He trusteth on God" (Matt. 27:43).

*   *   *

Inseparable, in dogmatics, from the work of Christ is the significance of the true humanity of Christ. The confessions

41. R. Guardini, *Der Herr. Betrachtungen über die Person und das Leben Jesu Christi,* 1944, page 483.

also make explicit mention of it, as for instance the Heidelberg Catechism: "Why must he be a true and righteous man?"[42] This question, which will concern us in the treatment of the work of Jesus Christ, is not the fruit of speculation or the product of an attempt to indicate on rationalistic grounds the manner in which God *had to* accomplish redemption, but rather an *a posteriori* analysis of the unities of God's work as known to us by revelation. These unities, as the first Lord's Day of the Catechism confesses, come to a focus in the comforting work of Jesus Christ. In this Lord's Day already, we understand something of the fact that, in the course of redemption, nothing happens by chance or accident but all by divine wisdom. From the witness of Scripture it is plain that the church may never submit to a monophysite view of Christ, however much it be emphasized that salvation is exclusively of God. For in any number of passages, Scripture speaks of Jesus Christ as truly God and truly man. He is one of us, like us in all things, our brother, sharing *our* flesh and *our* blood. He did not come as a heavenly ambassador to frighten us with his surpassing divine power or, in spectral form, to bring us a message from heavenly realms. No, he entered into the reality of our world and life, having assumed the form of a servant. Repeatedly our attention is called to this fact, not in order that "man" be somehow honored for redemption, but in order that we should honor the *way* in which God redeemed the world. Hence Paul speaks in terms of a parallel between Adam and Christ. For, as through one man sin entered into the world, so the grace of God consists in the grace of the one man, Jesus Christ (Rom. 5:12, 15). Again we confront the mystery of the incarnate Logos; the seeming logic of monophysitism and of all forms of Docetism does violence to Scripture. Our conclusions, built up independently, cannot help us to understand the way of salvation. Only reflection on the thoughts of God as laid down in Holy

42. Question and answer 16.

Scripture preserves us from confusion. The issue is not a sort of speculation on the "being" of Jesus Christ as Mediator: "For there is one God, one mediator also between God and men, himself man, Christ Jesus, who gave himself a ransom for all" (I Tim. 2:5, 6). The divine act of redemption is here placed in immediate and undetachable relationship to the *man* Jesus Christ. The human does not compete with the divine; God's way is revealed in wisdom and mercy. Bouma points out that Paul does not say here that Christ is also God, "although Paul presupposes the truth of his Deity and its acknowledgement in the same epistle."[43] On the basis of the whole of God's truth he can speak in this fashion stressing now this, now that element, in order to picture the fullness of the riches of Christ. In Scripture the one element does not compete with the other, since the presupposition is the revelation of Christ as truly God and truly man. Therefore the humanity of Christ can sometimes be pointed out with unusual earnestness. Thus the epistle to the Hebrews pictures him as the merciful high priest, tempted in all things; and his equality with us is oriented precisely to the propitiation for the sins of the people (Hebr. 2:17). His humanity can hardly be expressed more strongly than it is in the declaration: "For which cause he is not ashamed to call them brethren" (v. 11), as God is not ashamed to be called their God (Hebr. 11:16). People entered upon a dark and dangerous path when they thought that, in view of Christ's deity, his humanity could be neglected as something secondary in his person and work. The result is estrangement from the witness of Holy Scripture which places the possibility of communion squarely in the humanity of Jesus Christ, and squarely in our flesh in which, upon assuming it, he has brought about redemption, so that he might be the first-born among many brethren (Rom. 8:29).

Indeed, Christ is also the first-born of all creation, in whom all things are created and consist. It is plain from what Scrip-

---

43. C. Bouma, *Commentaar*, page 112.

ture says (Col. 1:15-18) that these words do not mean that Christ himself belonged to creation,[44] but when he is also called the first-born among many brethren, then the reference is to his communion with his brethren. In this communion he precedes them as their leader and preserves them in his redemptive fellowship. In view of the clarity of Scripture it is plain that the battle of the church for the confession of the true humanity of Christ has not been meaningless. The importance of this confession has seldom been more sharply perceived than when the Belgic Confession, in harmony with the ancient church, confessed that our salvation depends upon the true humanity of Christ.[45] It cannot be a question to one who yields to the testimony of Scripture that we are here entering through that door of the confession of the church through which we gain full view of the riches of salvation and reconciliation in him, in whom the fulness of the Godhead dwells bodily.[46]

*   *   *

Baillie begins his book on Christology with a chapter on "the end of Docetism" and rejoices over the fact that prac-

---

44. Cf. Athanasius on this text as one of the texts to which the Arians loved to appeal, in his *Redevoeringen tegen de Arianen*, edited by C. J. de Vogel, 1949, pages 188 and 219.

45. Article 19 of the Belgic Confession.

46. Very recently the phrase "one of us" has been interpreted in a peculiar manner by Karl Barth in his attempt to base anthropology on Christology. On his view, we can arrive at a knowledge of man only on the basis of a previous knowledge of Jesus Christ and his reconciliation. Christ's participation in our human nature, in Barth, occurs in reverse order, namely as our participation in him (*Kirchliche Dogmatik*, III, 2, page 69; cf., page 169). Scripture points in a different direction as regards the relationship between our humanity and that of Christ: "Since then the children are sharers in flesh and blood, he (namely Christ) also himself in like manner partook of the same" (Hebr. 2:14), while a bit later there is added that it "behooved him in all things to be made like unto his brethren" (Hebr. 2:17). The core of Barth's anthropology, which has many implications, lies in the reversal of the thought of Hebr. 2:14. See on this my article (*Christologie en Anthropologie*) in the memorial volume dedicated to Prof. Dr. J. Waterink.

tically all schools of theology today acknowledge fully the humanity of Christ and increasingly realize its significance. He believes that "all serious theological thought has finished with the docetist, Eutychean, monophysite errors, which explain away the humanity of our Lord and thus the reality of the incarnation. No more Docetism! Eutyches, we may say, is dead and he is not likely to be as fortunate in finding an apostle to revive him!"[47] One can with reason ask the question whether in fact all danger of Docetism has been fully apprehended. But it cannot indeed be denied that present-day theology placed strong emphasis on the human nature of Christ. I am not at all referring to the discovery of "the historical Jesus," however; the bare acknowledgement of the historical existence of Jesus of Nazareth does not mean endorsement of the confession of the church regarding Christ's true humanity. But in theological reflection today one can note an unusual sensitivity in resisting the dangers of Docetism.

There is nowadays a strong tendency to draw Christ deeply into the flesh, to use Kohlbrugge's expression, and not to view him as a messenger from a far country whose manners are foreign to us. In such a situation there is always a danger, of course, that people completely humanize Christ and fail to do justice to his true deity. Thus might occur, not a resurrection of Eutyches, but a renewal of Adoptionism. In addition there arises the danger that, as we shall see more explicitly in the next chapter, people will so interpret Christ's humanity and *kenosis* that his sinlessness, or positively, his holiness must be neglected.

Still every attempt to point out the danger of Docetism must be gratefully welcomed. For this Docetism, as history has clearly shown, is a matter of life or death for the church. Every doctrine teaching a "divine" Christ who has nothing to do with the genuinely human is a threat to the faith of the church. It will be to the advantage of the church, therefore, to

---

47. Baillie, *God was in Christ*.

regard with interest those tendencies in our day which seek to
do justice to Christ's human nature. But only when this confession is inseparably united with that of his true deity will it
be a true blessing to the church.[48]

*   *   *

In the emphatic declarations with which people nowadays
speak of the humanity of Christ we repeatedly encounter a
phrase in which the confession of Christ's human nature is, as
it were, summarized. It is Pilate's utterance embedded in the
history of Christ's public condemnation: Behold, the man!
(John 19:5). This is all the more striking to us because the
name of Pilate occurs also in the creed of the church; the
church apparently saw more in his actions than the caprice of
a Roman governor. Some people regard the reference to Pilate
merely as an indication of the true historicity of Christ's appearance and suffering. The interpretation of the Catechism,
however, relates the condemnation of Christ by Pilate to the
authority with which God had clothed Pilate. Thus the church
confessed that, in the condemnation by Pilate, Christ was
struck by the divine verdict and thus he freed us from the
severe judgment of God.[49]

------

48. In general one can say that the anti-Docetism of present-day theology
tries to inter-mesh itself especially with the ideas of Calvin about Christ's
condescension, not in majesty, but in the humility of the flesh (see his
commentary on I Tim. 2:5). Lord's Day 6, Question 16, of the Heidelberg Catechism, has a different slant on the matter. The true humanity of
Christ is here related to the justice of God and regarded as necessary because "the same human nature which has sinned should make satisfaction
for sin." Many a theologian is inclined to accept the views of Calvin
(from majesty into humility; Christ our brother) but not that of the
Catechism which relates the "necessity" of the Incarnation to Christ's
expiatory work. See, for this antithesis, G. Aulen, *De Christelijke ver-
zoeningsgedachte en Het Chr. Godsbeeld*, 1929. There can, however, be no
contradiction between Calvin and the Catechism on this score. On the
"necessity" of the Incarnation, see Calvin's *Institutes* II, XII, 1 *and* 3!
Here both thoughts are posited in complete harmony.

49. *Heidelberg Catechism*, Question 38; cf. Calvin, *Inst.* II, XVI, 5.

In this connection it is important to note what Pilate says before the Jerusalem crowd: Behold, the man! Must we, in view of Pilate's position, regard also this utterance as a very special characterization which gives the statement extraordinary revelational significance, and put it on a level with Caiaphas' declaration that it was good that one should die for the people lest all the people should perish? Is it possible that Pilate, like Caiaphas, did not speak *of himself?*

In our day there are several who are strongly inclined to answer this question in the affirmative. In order to find a sound Scriptural answer to this question, one must first of all take account of Scriptural limits and be careful in drawing inferences from certain facets of the gospel story. In the case of Caiaphas, Scripture itself refers to the connection with his high-priesthood. If one should demand such a divine illumination for Pilate's utterance and regard it as *a priori* necessary, the issue would be swiftly settled, since Scripture does not so interpret Pilate's statement. But the explanation of Pilate's condemnation of Christ in terms of his authority already points up the necessity of our asking whether Pilate's statement, though it is not expressly indicated, contains any special meaning, which could be seen as parallel with the superscription above the cross: Jesus of Nazareth, the King of the Jews (John 19:19).

H. Vogel has pointed out the "ecce homo" with emphasis. The phrase "Behold, the man!" was not uttered, as he avers, by a private individual, "but by one authorized thereto, as a finger-pointer to an innocent man."[50] Hence he wishes to interpret these words as the Catechism interprets the condemnation, namely, in terms of the power and authority of Pilate which Christ himself recognized when he said: "Thou wouldest have no power against me, except it were given thee from above" (John 19:11). It is not enough to ask what Pilate meant, says Vogel, but we must note the specific relationship exist-

---

50. H. Vogel, *Christologie*, I, 1949, page 248 ff.

ing between Pilate and Jesus. Rather than be blinded by the psychology of Pilate, we should be wide open to the situation described in the text, a situation which is full of mystery of the Incarnate Word. Vogel refuses to let his fancy run about the meaning of Pilate's words but tries to get further by way of the context, even if concealed from Pilate. The point of the "Ecce Homo," if we truly read the Scriptures, is not a figure on the gallery of men, nor is it the pity or eventual sympathy of Pilate which is implicit in these words or an overtone in them, nor a sad "Behold, a man," but a pregnant "Hinweis" : Behold, *the* man! From this premise Vogel then reasons to the *"Ecce homo of the prophetic testimonies."* The phrase becomes a reference to the Abased one, who had neither form nor glory, in whose substitution lies our redemption. Only faith can see this and hear "'the mystery of the Ecce." It is not a human but a divine pointer to "the mystery of his real humanity."

Van Niftrik too sees more in Pilate's exclamation than an expression of human feeling and sympathy. He also draws a parallel between Pilate and Caiaphas who prophesied of Jesus' death. In Pilate he observes the break-through of a higher order of revelation than can ever be observed in the psychology of a man.[51] In spite of himself and without knowing it, Pilate prophesied when he said to the people: Behold, the man. Van Niftrik regards this interpretation, not as a discovery of human imagination, but as the plain intent of the gospel.

Hence both Vogel and Van Niftrik intend to indicate the design of the Gospel. When we ask however where in the context this design is made plain, the harvest is pretty meager. The views we encounter in this interpretation of the "Ecce homo" are rather dogmatic than exegetical. They broach matters in themselves important and stress the true humanity of Christ. But they do not provide an answer to the question

---

51. G. C. Van Niftrik, *Zie, de Mens! Beschrijving en verklaring van de anthropologie van Karl Barth*, 1951, page 7.

whether, in this passage, Pilate really turns "prophet," as Caiaphas once in spite of himself became a "prophet" of Christ's substitutionary suffering.

But these views are not limited to dogmatic literature. Exegetes too have always been strongly attracted to Pilate's utterance. On the one hand they see in it an attempt, in the difficult situation in which Pilate had come, to arouse the sympathy of the crowd, but on the other hand they regard it as coming from a higher Source. In Grosheide, for instance, we find a consideration of Pilate's motives but also the suggestion of prophecy: "It is as if Pilate is prophesying here, just as Balaam and Caiaphas have prophesied of Jesus. Jesus is the Son of man — man par excellence. And now he confronts the Jews, just as sinful man confronts God. He stands there in the place of his own."[52] Bouma not only stresses the background of Pilate's motives but puts Pilate's declaration in a more general context. "Behold, the man — the history of the world in two words. They picture the sinner, jeered at by devils in this text in order to mock the Creator. But now that Jesus stands there in the place of his own everything changes. Along with Balaam and Caiaphas, Pilate takes his place in the gallery of unbelieving prophets of the Christ."[53] Smelik too wants to get beyond the psychology of Pilate. Having taken the element of pity into account, he then posits the view: "Behold, the man, the Adam, the new man, the new image-bearer of God! His appearance is the new standard and embodies the new commandment."[54]

In order to come to a decision on the *Ecce homo,* we must first of all make a few distinctions. We would first point out that in the Gospel we often perceive how the order of God is established in a truly majestic manner: in the suffering of

52. F. W. Grosheide, *Commentaar op Joh.* II, page 479.
53. C. Bouma, *Het Evangelie naar Johannes* (Korte Verklaring) II, page 169.
54. E. Smelik, *De weg van het Woord. Het Evangelie naar Johannes,* 1948, page 261.

Christ also, and that directly through human actions and words. A clear example is the speech of Caiaphas. His words in themselves and on his part are perfectly transparent as a manifestation of vehement opposition to Jesus; and still God's overruling power reveals itself too in every last literal word of his "prophecy." The same cross-purposes we find in Pilate's condemnation of Christ, who recognizes Pilate's authority over him. Directly through the injustice of Pilate's verdict, God accomplishes the justice of *his* verdict. In the superscription on the cross we find the same convergence of human motives and divine intent, however, divergent these may be. Grosheide takes these converging cross-purposes into account when he says that this superscription is an insult to Jesus and detracts from his kingship. But he adds: "On the other hand, the superscription contains truth. Jesus is the true king of the Jews, Pilate's intention to the contrary notwithstanding." Schilder also asserts that the sarcasm of Pilate against the Jews helped him conceive this succinct designation.[55] But there is more in this cross-identification. The power of Christ's exaltation asserts itself from the side of God in this deep humiliation of Christ. In the ecumenical language of the superscription is a sermon of great power. "And above the writing of Pilate stands the written epigram of God. God's voice spoke in, through, and above the voice of Pilate . . . What you, Pilate, have written, you have not written: God wrote and writes always, He alone.[56]

Schilder, as the others, had his eyes wide open for the divine *style* of the passion of Jesus Christ; in it God alone is Ruler, and he takes up the actions and words of men, however intended, into *his* Counsel for Christ. Thus he demonstrates his sovereign power also in making men involuntary witnesses of the truth about Jesus Christ.

---

55. K. Schilder, *Christus in Zijn lijden,* 1930, III, page 173.
56. *Ibid.,* page 179.

With the exception of Caiaphas, Scripture does not point out these relationships in so many words. It tells us only what people say and do. It tells of the attestation of the innocence of Jesus Christ in the very hour of his final condemnation. But in the example of Caiaphas, Scripture does teach us to note carefully the connections between human thought and action and divine thought and action. To observe these connections is a far cry from speculative imagining. Only, one must be conscious of the limits to one's conclusions. When the Heidelberg Catechism points out a connection between Pilate's condemnation of Jesus and our acquittal, and hence regards Pilate's verdict as the divine verdict upon our guilt-laden Savior, it draws this conclusion directly from the Scriptural context.

But the question still remains whether we can and may regard Pilate's *Ecce homo* as the speech of God. In the first place, one must acknowledge the difference between Pilate's act of condemnation and the words which he uses, in his impasse, to arouse the sympathy of the Jews. The words *as such* were not spoken by Pilate in his capacity as judge; one cannot draw any conclusions from them on the ground that Pilate spoke as one who had been given authority of God. Such conclusions would not be warranted in view of the context, especially in view of Pilate's hesitations. The pronouncement is not *official*. One can say only that the church classified this statement with the words which the enemies of Christ spoke when they witnessed to his innocence. In the *Ecce homo*, the gospel breaks through human motives and machinations. *Ecce homo* is a message far surpassing Pilate's intent. It is an expression the church can use in a sense entirely different from that in which Pilate spoke of Christ. On his way to the cross — so the church viewed the *Ecce homo* — Christ was truly man and as man he was jeered at and committed to the cross.

This *Ecce homo* is identical with *Man of Sorrows*. He lived the genuinely human life as, in him, it lies under the curse of

God. In his disgraced humanity we see what it means to be man and how, in the midst of disgrace, God reconciles and redeems this humanity.

Indeed, this *Ecce homo,* in the language of the church, is inseparable from the confession of Christ's true deity. In the unity of the two lies the secret of the church's joyful praises. The Son of God, Light of Light, is also the man with the crown of thorns, one of us, laden with the guilt of his people. This way of redemption is incomprehensible. At this point the confession of Christ's true humanity touches upon the fulfillment of his task. The motives of Pilate in uttering his *Ecce homo* and in composing the superscription above the cross cannot prevent the disclosure of the great secret that this man belongs to the whole world, to all tongues and languages, and to all cultures. Here is the transmission of the message of salvation for the world. Here appears the *man* Jesus Christ, who is Lord — and every idea that salvation can come from man is eliminated. The church's defense of Christ's true humanity is not a round-about way of deriving salvation from human effort. The preaching of Christ's humanity is surely something other than camouflaged humanism. When Christ is referred to as "the man," we see humanity stand behind this disgrace; everyone hid his face from him. All Pilate could do at the last moment was to try to arouse sympathy. Only in the light of faith it is possible to see in *this* Christ the real man with his crown of thorns, and thus our brother who "counted not the being on an equality with God a thing to be grasped," but who assumed the form of a servant and was made in the likeness of man. In this world of our humanity Pilate's meager statement is the last thing human beings had to say about the great controversy between God and human guilt.

Nowhere else is humanism condemned as strongly as in the crucifixion of Jesus Christ, precisely in the *man* Jesus Christ.

And nowhere else is he so close to us, not in a common humanity, but in its reconciliation to God.

*   *   *

Again we are angered at every form of Docetism which alienates us from him who is truly the Mediator between God and men. This Docetism preaches a "divine" salvation but it is and remains alien to us. The message is not that of the Scriptures. In its victory over Docetism the church did not utter a cry for salvation by "a man," a passionate cry for self-liberation, but its victory was the victory of the Scriptures. Thus the church preserved its treasure. We may say: God himself preserved it for us as a necessary and abiding reference to the text: "And the Word became flesh, and dwelt among us."

The Sinlessness of Christ

CHAPTER X

The Sinlessness of Christ

N ow that we have discussed the true humanity of Christ
we arrive naturally at another problem — a problem
often posed in connection with the human nature of Christ —
namely, that of his sinlessness. From the truly human in
Christ people repeatedly inferred that he necessarily shared in
the sinful structure which is the lot of all that is human in this
world. Does not the sinfulness of every human life lie in the
mere fact of its existence; and is it correct to elevate Christ
above the "structure" of the human and thus, practically,
above the "struggle" of man? And if one should eventually be
prepared to accept that Christ did not in fact sin, should he
not be content with this factual sinlessness without proceeding
to the position that Christ, in virtue of his union with the
Logos, *could* not sin? Especially against this last thesis there
arose continual opposition, since people regarded this "inability
to sin" a threat to Christ's reality and to the value of his struggle. One can understand that these questions arose especially
in connection with the struggle of Christ's entire life — in suffering and death and particularly in his temptation. Could
this temptation still be viewed as real if it were regarded in
terms of the *a priori* proposition that Christ cannot sin?

The importance of these questions is plain. In the objections
just mentioned people stress that the sinlessness of Christ,
though a fact, is a fact to be empirically ascertained in view
of the course of his life and of his holding his own in the face
of temptation. Preceding his victory over temptation there
must necessarily be a cross-roads: two possibilities, of which

the one is the way of obedience, the other the way of disobedience.

In connection with the confession of Jesus Christ this is an extremely important problem which deserves separate attention. In the consideration of these questions it is good to proceed from the plain witness of Holy Scripture to the sinlessness, or to put it positively, to the *holiness* of Jesus Christ. The witnesses are so numerous and unanimous that a serious conflict over this holiness can hardly arise.[1]

This holiness is presupposed in many passages and occupies a dominating place in the Scriptural witness to Christ. Repeatedly one encounters emphatic and explicit references to it. Paul, for instance, speaks of the Christ "who knew no sin" (II Cor. 5:21), while Peter says that he "did no sin, neither was guile found in his mouth (I Peter 2:22). Christ's relation to sin is unique and can be summarized in the words of John: "And ye know that he was manifested to take away sins; and in him is no sin" (I John 3:5). Christ died as "the righteous for the unrighteous" (I Peter 3:18). He is the high priest, holy, guileless, undefiled, separated from sinners, and made higher than the heavens (Hebr. 7:26), the righteous one, whom men have killed (James 5:6).

This witness of the apostolic kerygma is harmonious and repeatedly becomes doxological in tone. It is intimately related to the witness of the gospels which declare that Christ is the Holy One of God (cf., Acts 3:14; 4:27, 30). In the announcement of the birth of Christ to Mary he is called "the holy thing which is begotten" (Luke 1:35) and Peter confesses: "We have believed and know that thou art the Holy One of God" (John 6:69).

The power of Christ's holiness also elicits from the unclean spirits the acknowledgement: "I know thee who thou art, the Holy One of God" (Luke 4:34). From all directions people

1. Bartmann points out that ancient heretics, however divergent they were in Christology, did not attack the sinlessness of Christ.

witness to him whom the Father sanctified (John 10:36) and who, in all his thought and action, in all his being, is absolutely above the unrighteousness of sin. Spotless was his submission to the scepter of divine law. Striking also is the witness of those who surround him on his way to Golgotha. Many of them attest his innocence: Pilate finds no crime in him, Judas says he has betrayed innocent blood, the centurion speaks of him as a righteous man.

We are profoundly impressed, too, when we note the public action of Christ and his holy self-consciousness which filled him throughout the entire course of his life. This fact probably appears most sharply in the question Christ once asked his opponents: "Which of you convicteth me of sin?" (John 8:46).

He was of course accused of breaking the first and fourth commandment but there was never any evidence that held water. The accusation of Sabbath-violation was based on an incorrect, legalistic interpretation of the law of Moses and in reply to this accusation Christ, who is lord of the Sabbath, pointed out the deep meaning of the divine law of the Sabbath. And the charge of blasphemy was based on a complete denial of the mystery of his person. For this reason Christ could ask, with so much emphasis, for proof. He was conscious of having fulfilled the commandment of the Father. He knew he had not broken it. This comes to striking expression in Jesus' conversation with the Jews who accused him of violating the Sabbath. Christ says in reply: "If a man receiveth circumcision of the sabbath, that the law of Moses may not be broken, are ye wroth with me, because I made a man every whit whole on the sabbath? Judge not according to appearance, but judge righteous judgment" (John 7:23, 24). Such a *righteous* judgment can only recognize the holiness of Christ: as he himself indicated the direction of his total life by saying: "My *meat* is to do the will of him that sent me, and to accomplish his work" (John 4:34). His deeds are not incidental, discrete actions but form together one act, one deed: The Father's work, to which he is called and to which he knows he is called. He glorified the Father on earth (John 17:4), manifested his name (John 17:6), and watched over those the Father had given him (John 17:12). In prayer, thanksgiving, and sacrifice he performed the will of the Father and he "loved his own that were in the world unto the end" (John 13:1).

From various directions, however, arguments have been adduced to demonstrate that the New Testament also points in another direction which indicates that the sinlessness of Christ is enveloped in a peculiar set of problems. Three of these arguments we wish to treat with some explicitness. The arguments are derived from the story of the rich young ruler, the baptism of Christ, and the Christology of the epistle to the Hebrews.

In the story of the rich young ruler the point at issue is the answer which Christ gives to the young man's question: "Good Teacher, what shall I do to inherit eternal life?" This answer runs: "Why callest thou me good? none is good, save one, even God" (Luke 18:19; Mark 10:18). From this pronouncement people have inferred that Christ himself did not proceed from his absolute sinlessness or holiness but rather places himself in the rank of sinful human beings. Does not Christ refer to the One who alone is good, namely, God in heaven? Moreover, people refer to the parallel text where we read: "Why askest thou me concerning that which is good? One there is who is good" (Matt. 19:17). They assert that Matthew, in order to eliminate the offensive implication that Jesus could sin, corrected the text of Mark. According to Windisch the idea of the sinlessness of Jesus originated in theological considerations. "An explicit attestation to his sense of sinlessness" we do not find until we encounter them, as the fruit of the Logos-theology, in the pronouncements of the Johannine Christ. "Thus the gospels show that the conception of the sinlessness of Jesus arose perhaps already under the immediate impression of certain features of the personality of the historical Jesus, but it received its permanent dogmatic formulation under the influence of views which arose elsewhere, earlier, and independently of the historical appearance of Christ, and that this conception, in its turn, influenced the evangelical tradition, if only in isolated passages."[2]

It is plain, however, that the inference drawn from Jesus' question ("Why callest thou me good") is quite unjustified. It may be true that Matthew, to avoid misunderstanding, has quoted Jesus' words in a somewhat different form, but from the words as such one cannot conclude that Jesus here denied his absolute holiness. What he says here is perfectly intelligible from the historical context. Implicit in the attitude of the rich young man there is plainly a superficial view of the good. He believes he has fully accomplished the law while he nonetheless cannot meet the demand which Christ makes upon him. In this light we must see the words of address: Good Teacher. And in this light also the words of Christ are intelligible: Why callest thou me good? Whoever would deduce from this answer a denial by Christ of his sinlessness must, in the first place, isolate it from the context and, second, from all those pronouncements of Christ in which he shows himself fully conscious that he is doing the will of the Father. In his answer the Savior points out to him the absoluteness of the truly good and immediately places his life under the searchlight of the absolute. It need not surprise us that this utterance of Christ goes counter to the confession of his sinlessness.

The alteration of the text in Matthew may indeed be intended to cut off a misunderstanding; but the idea still is to reject a *genuine* misunderstanding. For what Christ says does not call his own sinlessness in question but is rather a searching criticism of the superficial morality of the rich young ruler. Grund-

---

2. H. Windisch, *Der Hebr. brief, page* 40.

mann correctly says: "The question of the sinlessness of Jesus is not the point of the discussion."[3]

In the second place we must treat the baptism of Jesus. This event also has been repeatedly related to the problem of the sinlessness of Christ. The point here is that the New Testament clearly points out the character of the baptism of John. We read, namely, that John appeared in the wilderness and preached "the baptism of repentance unto remission of sins" (Mark 1:4). In *this* context we read that John baptized also Jesus. The emphasis is even laid on that which Jesus underwent *in common* with other people: ". . . it came to pass, when all the people were baptized, that, Jesus also having been baptized . . ." (Luke 3:21-22). Thus the problem could emerge as to how Jesus Christ could ever have anything to do with this baptism of repentance unto remission of sins. The problem was all the more acute because also John the Baptist felt confronted by the question whether he had the authority to administer this baptism to Jesus of Nazareth. We even read of an explicit refusal: he tried to hinder Jesus (Matt. 3:14). According to John, the request of Christ implied a reversal of the right order: "I have need to be baptized of thee, and comest thou to me?" Is not this question of John fully comprehensible, and does not the light which the rest of the New Testament sheds on baptism confirm the acuteness of the problem whether this baptism of Christ does not place him in the ranks of sinners called to be baptized and, hence, to repent? To put it differently, is not baptism founded in the redemptive work of Christ and is it not, for this reason, the exclusive possibility of those who are blessed by this work of Christ in the redemption of all their sins?

Of great significance for all the questions which emerge here is the answer Christ gave to John. For he not only reasserts his request for baptism by John but adds that this is a matter of fulfilling righteousness: "Suffer it now: for thus it

becometh us to fulfil all righteousness" (Matt. 3:15). Before
this answer John capitulates and baptizes Jesus.

Noteworthy in these things is that Christ was obedient to
the divine law *in precisely this manner*: ". . . *thus* it behooves
us . . ." To this law Christ was already subject in his circumcision and in his presentation in the temple[4] and in nothing
was he distinguished from the other children of his people. He
was "born of a woman, born under the law" (Gal. 4:4).

The important question is, however, whether the baptism of
Jesus — like the presentation in the temple, which was directly
related to Israel's deliverance out of the house of bondage —
signifies that the relationship of Jesus Christ to sin was identical with that of all Israel. If one should deduce such an
identity from the fact that people came to this baptism confessing their sins, he has decided the issue without taking into
account the unique relationship of Christ to sin. This relationship was not one of personal sinfulness but one involved in his
humiliation, in his being under the law. It must be evident
that Christ's wish to be baptized is not a concession to a
general tradition or rule to which he wishes to submit but is
grounded on a strong foundation.[5] Christ submits to an ordi-
nance of God and is in this respect no exception. He belongs
to this people and has come to do the will of the father. Hence
he wishes to receive baptism, too, and this does not mean that
he himself has succumbed to the power of sin and therefore
needs the baptism of repentance unto the forgiveness of sins.
But he is bound to this people and thus bound he will bear its
guilt. "He overrules the objection of the Baptist."[6] But this
will to be baptized, far from being a purely formal submission
to a rule valid for a given community, has a deep meaning
because at this baptism Christ publicly appears as "the Lamb
of God who taketh away the sins of the world." There is

4. Compare J. Kapteyn, *De Losser gelost*. In: *Hoogfeest naar de
Schriften*, pages 117 ff. and C. Veenhof, *De besnijdenis, Ibid.*, pages 151 ff.
5. Compare Zahn, *Des Evangelium des Matthäus*, 1910, page 144.
6. *Ibid.*, page 144.

profound harmony between the work of reconciliation and Christ's being baptized. It is the fulfilment of righteousness consonant with Christ's coming to fulfill the law in his messianic work and capacities. At bottom, Christ's baptism must be regarded as a phase in his humiliation, just like circumcision or his presentation in the temple. In many a discussion of his baptism the element of humiliation is overlooked. Goguel, for instance, says that the baptism of Jesus did not suit Matthew's taste at all because it placed Jesus in a position of subordination to John. For this reason Matthew placed a protest in the mouth of John against the baptism of Jesus.[7] This construction is thoroughly arbitrary since Matthew records also Christ's reply to John's refusal. People have pointed out that "the fathers" already did everything in their power to give an interpretation of this baptism which "accords with the Christology of the Church."[8] But the gospel, with the quotation from Christ about his fulfilling all righteousness, points into the right direction. And we must say that all sorts of objections against the historicity of the baptism issue from a lack of insight into the unique significance of the person and work of Christ.[9]

* * *

In the third place we must still speak about the sinlessness of Christ in connection with his purely human development. Scripture refers with emphasis to the development of Christ, and in this connection it is natural to ask whether the fact of development in general does not imply *ethical* development, and whether *such* development accords with the Church's teaching on the sinlessness of Christ. The question is all the more pertinent because Scripture mentions not only the

7. Maurice Goguel, *Au seuil de l'Evangile. Jean Baptiste,* 1928, page 147.
8. *Ibid.,* page 139.
9. Compare with what Goguel says about objections of certain theologians against the historicity of Jesus' baptism: "The baptism of John was a baptism of repentance while tradition presents Jesus as having been without sin," Goguel, *Ibid.,* page 141.

development from childhood to maturity but also a concomitant struggle. We are referring particularly to the much-discussed passage recorded in Hebrews: "Who in the days of his flesh, having offered up prayers and supplications with strong crying and tears unto him that was able to save him from death, and having been heard for his godly fear, though he was a Son, *yet learned obedience by the things which he suffered*" (5:7,8). Especially these last words attracted attention and people asked themselves whether this development did not imply a stage in which Christ was *not yet* obedient. The question was all the more acute because Hebrews 5 emphatically mentions the *Son*. In the treatment of his high priesthood we read of his suffering and death, by which he became the author of eternal salvation to all that obey him. What, in this connection, is the significance of the fact that though he was a Son, he nevertheless *learned* obedience by his sufferings? Does this presuppose a stage antedating Christ's obedience, a stage in which one could not speak of an absolute obedience? Windisch expressed the opinion that the Christ pictured here differs from the Johannine Christ who indeed repeatedly commended his obedience to his divine father but conceives it as something perfectly natural and self-evident, something he did not first have to learn with great effort.[10] In Hebrews 5:7 and Phil. 2, the situation is somewhat different. Here we already detect a trace of later problems; in the words "though he was a Son" the doctrine of the two natures lurks in the background. Even if one does not accept a contrast between the various descriptions of Christ in Scripture, he still confronts the difficulty of how to understand Christ's learning obedience. In any case, in the word "though" we are concerned with the mystery of the Son of God in the flesh. Though he was the Son, nonetheless he had to bear the full brunt of suffering.

The author fully acknowledges that Jesus is genuinely human. It is not in conflict with his Sonship but mysteriously

---

10. H. Windisch, *Hebr. brief*, 1931, page 44.

one with it. Why did he, who was the Son, have to learn obedience and how could he? Grosheide speaks of a riddle: "That he, who was the Son and whose equality with God had been asserted in the beginning of the letter, still had to learn obedience is something we cannot understand.[11] This does not mean, however, says Grosheide, that this text cannot be exegeted. There is development, he says, not in the sense of ethical improvement but in the sense of a growing capacity for the fulfillment of his office.[12] Christ saw his work ever more clearly before him, and proceeded to do it. This must be seen in the light of the opinion that Hebr. 5 is related to the suffering of Christ in Gethsemane.[13] *There* occurred the struggle of Christ, when he prayed: If it be possible let this cup pass from me. Nowhere more clearly than here do we sense the reality of Christ's suffering. The gospel mentions the angel who came to strengthen him, and Christ's agonies in the garden. In this connection the epistle to the Hebrews speaks of *learning obedience.* It is plain that to the author the transition is not one from rebellion to obedience but rather one of maturing in the task imposed on him. In Hebrews 4:15 we already learned of the tempted Christ who became like us in all points, yet without sin. According to the author of the epistle to the Hebrews also, the life of Christ can be characterized with the words: "Lo, I am come (In the roll of the book it is written of me) to do thy will, O God" (Hebr. 10: 7, 9). This he says —in fulfillment of Psalm 40—at his coming into the world (Hebr. 10:5). This life is completely devoted to the Father and full of his good pleasure. It is surely not an instance of contrast to the Johannine picture of Christ. In Hebrews, too, the course of his life is seen under the aspect of absolute obe-

---

11. F. W. Grosheide, *Commentaar,* page 152.

12. "The greater the demand upon him, the more he could give," Grosheide, *Ibid.,* page 152.

13. See Grosheide and compare Van Oyen, *Christus de Hogepriester,* page 90.

dience. But this obedience is not a *static* quality. It is rather a dynamic *reality* in the daily life of the Son of Man who was led from one situation to the other and was called in each new phase of the judgment of God to practical, existential obedience. This progression we note most clearly in his struggle in Gethsemane. In the record of this passionate struggle we read first of his fear and his agony, his repeated prayers, and his plea for the removal of the cup, but then—after a prayerful struggle—of his splendid willingness to drink the cup.

Through prayer and fear, profound anxiety and tears, the reality of suffering takes place. That the issue is not a transition from disobedience to obedience appears also from what we read in the sequel, since his prayer is heard "for his godly fear" and thus he learned obedience from the things he suffered. "His prayer is now heard, not indeed by the removal of the cup, but by the fact that the Father convinces him of the necessity of this cup and takes from him the terror of it, because to do the will of the Father was after all the greatest bliss of Jesus."[14]

In his response to suffering and in the reality of obedience Christ was truly man. In his struggle to do the will of God his obedience was not a placid and abstract something that lay hidden on the bottom of his soul but consisted, rather, in being driven onto the way of judgment as the bearer of a guilt that was foreign to him. Before his final sufferings he already spoke of having accomplished his work (John 17:4), certainly, but Christ still had to learn obedience in the reality of the *passio magna*. The necessity of the learning process was implied in his true humanity.[15] In making this remark we do not at all pretend to be able to solve the mystery of the person of Christ. Like Grosheide, we sense the impossibility of penetrating this secret, and satisfy ourselves in the end with the striking words of Scripture: *Though he was the son.* But we are confronted

14. Van Oyen, *Ibid.*, page 91; Bavinck, *Geref. Dogma.*, III, page 300.
15. K. Schilder, *Heid. Catech.*, II, page 176.

in this mystery by the reality of the suffering of Christ and by his genuinely human way through suffering to glory. And if anywhere, then in this passage, the escape into some form of Docetism is blocked.[16] No speculation on the basis of the deity of Christ may be permitted to confuse us. Only the scriptures should guide our thinking and lead us in the acknowledgement of Christ as the Son of God and truly man.

*　*　*

Hence the objections adduced against the confession of Christ's sinlessness cannot diminish by one whit the clear testimony of Scripture concerning him who knew no sin and committed none.

Not a shadow falls over his life—at least no shadow issuing from his own sins and weaknesses. The Bible does not picture for us an ideal man who reached one of the top rungs on the ladder of human development and was thus appointed as a brilliant example to us; instead it witnesses to the Son, the course of whose entire life was absolutely oriented to the will of the Father and therefore, even in the most painful moments of his life, spread the radiance of absolute personal holiness. At no point in Scripture does the guilt of the world as borne by Christ cast a shadow upon his personal devotion to the Father. Precisely his guilt-bearing elevates his holiness above every doubt. The mystery of the Son of man is precisely that his guilt-bearing and spotless holiness can go together.

The mystery of reconciliation and substitution is indicated most incisively by Paul when he says that Christ was made "to be sin" on our behalf (II Cor. 5:21). Anyone wishing to distill from this text an argument against the confession of the sinlessness of Christ forgets what Paul expressly says in this context: "Him *who knew no sin* he made to be sin on our be-

---

16. K. Schilder, *Ibid.*, II, page 581: "Christ himself, though not inconstant in the sense of less faithful, was nonetheless as bearer of natural, creaturely, human life, subject to the natural law of undulation, capable of "learning," susceptible of accretion in his temporal human existence. In his fidelity he was constant, but not impassive; he was not a petrifaction."

half." This can be understood only in view of God's reconciling work in Christ. Inseparably united we find them here: Christ's holiness and his being made "sin" on our behalf. The church will have to defend its confession of Christ's sinlessness against every attack. One may say of the Son what John says of God: He is light, and in him is no darkness at all (I John 1:5). Christ himself spoke of this when he called himself the light of the world. About this light the shadows fall, the shadows of death, even the death of the cross. This relationship between light and darkness is not paradoxical; it is the opposition of sin which created the reality and possibility of this contrast in his life.

* * *

The witness of Scripture to the holiness of Christ is so plain and incontrovertible that people were often obliged simply to acknowledge it. But it did not make them reverence and accept the confession of the Christian church. For they acknowledged only an empirical holiness essentially no different from that of others who, by self-cultivation, had attained this high level. Now we must ask: is it sufficient merely to acknowledge this factual holiness of Christ? People have frequently refused to go beyond this recognition.

They refused to proceed to the proposition that sin was an impossibility to Christ: the reason was that this thesis, if true, would make his life-struggle a pretty bloodless sort of thing. The background of this argument is plainly the Temptation in the Wilderness. On this occcasion, they grant, Christ triumphed over temptation, but the fact of the temptation presupposed the confrontation with two genuine alternatives; and they add that the temptation would cease to be meaningful if one should drop the reality of this crossroads and argue on the assumption that Christ could not sin in any case.

We must start by acknowledging that Scripture emphatically speaks of the reality of the temptation. It was not just an accidental occurrence in which all initiative came from the evil one. According to the Gospel it was the Spirit of God who drove Jesus into the wilderness to be tempted of the devil. The event is all the more loaded for the fact, recorded by Luke, that Christ was full of the Holy Spirit. Other indications of the intensity of the struggle are the length of Christ's stay in the desert, the varied attempts of the devil, and the angels who come and minister to him. All this is a warning to us not to underestimate the depth of Christ's probation. The Scriptural data are very sober. We learn that Christ was tempted of the Evil one and triumphed by the force of the thrice-repeated "It is written." But it is plain from Scripture that the temptation does not end here. When Satan had completed his attack and decided to leave Christ alone, "he departed from him," says Luke, "for a season" (Luke 4:13). Later Christ says that the "prince of this world" is on his way; but he adds, "and he hath nothing in me" (John 14:30). We may not limit the temptation to that which took place in the wilderness. At the Last Supper Christ says to his disciples: "But ye are they that have continued with me in my temptations" (Luke 22:28). Particularly the last few weeks of Christ's sojourn on earth were full of temptation. The words of Peter, for instance, were a decided medium of satanic temptation: "Be it far from thee, Lord: this shall never be unto thee" (Matt. 16:22). In these words Christ himself recognized the satanic import—the avoidance of the via dolorosa—since the voice of Peter and the voice of the evil one were hardly distinguishable. "Get thee behind me, Satan: thou art a stumbling-block unto me: for thou mindest not the things of God, but the things of men" (Matt. 16:23). By way of Peter's mediation, Satan here casts a scandalon, a stumbling-block, on the road of Christ's suffering. Christ emerges victor, to be sure, and Satan fails to get a foothold in his soul, a point of support on which to build further with a real chance of success, but the reality of the temptation, precisely because Christ must choose *for* intense suffering and *against* an "attractive" alternative, remains undeniable.

In view of the seriousness and reality of the temptation the question arose whether all this does not presuppose a genuine cross-roads. Because the Scripture speaks with so much emphasis of that temptation it seemed self-evident that Christ had stood at the intersection of two roads; hence people thought they could say of Christ that he was *able not to sin* but certainly not that he was *not able to sin.*

Arguments were derived mainly from the epistle to the Hebrews. There we note that Christ was tempted in all points "like as we are" (4:15); and also the circumstance that this high priest can sympathize with our weaknesses because he has been tempted in all points. Hence he is not far from us when *we* are tempted. One could, in the light of this text, speak of a sacred recollection in him who knew the power of temptation by experience. Must we not conclude then that Christ's sanctity cannot consist in an *a priori* incapacity for sin but must rather be an act in which Christ, under pressure, *demonstrates* himself to be the Holy One?

Windisch was a strong opponent of the theory that Christ could not sin. With reference to the cited passage in Hebrews, he says: "If Jesus can now sympathize with our weaknesses, since once as man he was exposed to the entire scope and all the species of temptations to which we are liable, then according to Hebrews he possessed the *posse peccare;* that is, the capacity to yield to the charms of the Tempter, and it is necessary to state explicitly that he remained sinless."[17] Hence, according to Windisch, the sinlessness of Christ is not an *a priori datum* of his existence but an empirical fact to be viewed against the background of the ability to sin. "The sinlessness which the author ascribes to Jesus was, therefore, not the simple consequence of his divine nature, but the result of conscious decision and strenuous conflict." To Windisch the ability to sin follows unconditionally from Christ's being in all things "like unto us."

---

17. Windisch, *Ibid.,* page 39.

It is natural that for him the exegetical crux lies at this point. For, comes the query, how can this capacity for sin be harmonized with his divine origin? In his opinion, the author of the epistle to the Hebrews did not succeed in offering a view concerning the Incarnate Son of God "which will seem tenable to modern logic and psychology with their demands of inner unity."

One cannot in any case escape the thesis, says Windisch, that the fact of temptation implies the ability to sin. From his reasoning it is plain that he is engaging in this study in an abstract manner and does not fully take into account the mystery of Christ. From the fact of temptation he infers a capacity for sin as if the matter concerned an abstract truth applicable to all men. He fails to see the fact that the author of the epistle to the Hebrews is concerned with the mystery of Christ and hence abstains from speculation.

In Windisch the *posse peccare* is a deduction from the reality of temptation, a deduction he regards as necessary lest the temptation lose its force and meaning. If the temptation is to be meaningful it must take place at a crossroads, the decision must still have to be made, and as yet no one knows how it will turn out.

Again and again people found themselves cornered by the dilemma either fully to accept a capacity for sin in Christ or to exclude from his life every element of conflict and temptation. Schleiermacher who proceeds from Christ's "essential sinlessness and his utter perfection,"[18] infers from it that the development of Christ must be regarded as completely free of conflict. "For it is not possible that, wherever an inner conflict has once taken place, all traces of it would be quite gone."[19] In this manner one cannot avoid a collision with Scripture which emphatically mentions the struggle of Christ. From the preceeding it is evident that people regard the sinlessnesss of

18. Schleiermacher, *Der Chr. Glaube,* paragraph 98.
19. *Ibid.,* 93, 4.

Christ, and the reality of the temptation as mutually exclusive. They proceed on the assumption that what applies to us applies to Christ; that if there be a close connection for us between our capacity for sin and our struggles, then there must be such a connection for Christ. In our hearts there is always a point of contact for temptation. And as the resultant of temptation and our sinfulness arises evil. On this basis one can hardly take account of that which is unique in Christ. In him we witness the temptation of the Sinless One. When someone places a stumbling-block on his path to crowd him away from his cross, he enters into a very real conflict, as it comes to expression for instance in Gethsemane. We notice nothing here of a human soul which, to the surprise of all, retains its impassiveness and continues its way without conflict. For this reason few followed Schleiermacher and many were impressed by the conclusion of Windisch (who argued from the reality of temptation to the ability to sin). On the basis of the intensity of the temptation people whittled away at the absoluteness of Christ's sinlessness. Of this we have clear indications in Althaus. While he does acknowledge that Christ is the Sinless One, he does have a peculiar view of the relation between the sinlessness of Christ and his temptation: "Out of the human nature of Christ, too, out of the nature which he has in common with us, there arises the pull to self-dominion over against God and self-seeking over against the will of God. Whoever regards this already as sin cannot, indeed, hold to the sinlessness of Jesus.[20] Christ distinguishes himself from us in the crisis of sin by fleeing for refuge to the Father. "By the inner movement which would lead him from the Father he allows himself, conscious as he is of his own impotence, to be driven rather to God." Indeed, "Jesus so strongly feels the inclination to decide against God that he knows he can fall, but in this state he *prays*: that is, in all seriousness, the temptedness of sinlessness." On this view one may speak, it seems to

20. Althaus, *Die Chr. Wahrheit,* II, page 249.

me, of the triumph of prayer over temptation but hardly of sinlessness. Every act of obedience here becomes an act of conquest of self and of the rebellion rising up in the self. In order to maintain the reality of temptation people talk in the categories of psychology and then, as a matter of course, enter upon the area of the sin of desire and of rebellion. On these presuppositions one must arrive at conclusions which are flagrantly in conflict with the testimony of Scripture. The Bible certainly speaks, not of a final victory over sinful, rebellious desire, but of a holiness which pervades his entire existence, inside and outside.

* * *

According to the Gospel, this holiness is not at all in conflict with the emotions of Christ, with his struggle, with his horror of death, and with his desire for the glory which he had with the Father before the world was. But in all this there was no conflict between his profound readiness to set foot upon the road of suffering and the will of the Father. All Scripture tells us about the struggles of Christ and the reality of temptation in his suffering is related to the fact that he, precisely as the Sinless One, must bear a guilt not his. Thus, as the Sinless One, he associates himself with the sins of his people, the sins of the world.

This relationship is most clearly expressed in the struggle of Christ in Gethsemane, because there he asks that the cup may pass from him. Superficially considered, there seems to be a conflict here between the will of Jesus and the will of God, since Christ distinguishes the two wills when he says: " . . . nevertheless not my will, but thine, be done" (Luke 22:42).

But the striking thing is that at the moment in which Christ distinguishes the two he subjects his will to the will of the Father in an act of supreme obedience. To be sure, in the garden Christ gains the victory in the struggle of prayer; but this victory differs from that conceived by Althaus, who posits a victory over inner *rebellion* in Christ's prayerful struggle. However, the victory Christ wins is something different and unique.

This uniqueness is evident in the progression of the conflict. First Christ asks: " . . . if it be possible, let this cup pass away from me: nevertheless, not as I will, but as thou wilt" (Matt. 26:39). When a moment later he prays again his formulation has changed: "My father, if this cannot pass away, except I drink it, thy will be done" (Matt. 26:42). Schilder has correctly pointed out that in the first prayer the main petition is that the cup may pass away, while in the second the main petition is: Thy will be done.[21]

In the progression of the prayers we witness the progression of Christ on the road of suffering.

This progress can be interpreted, though not exhaustively, only because Christ vicariously bore the punishment of sin as the Sinless One. Thus his struggle was unique; and the accompanying tensions are meaningful only in terms of his sinlessness. "Christ's task was different from that of anyone else in the world. His task is to undergo what sin merited in the way of *punishment*."[22] For this reason we cannot psychologically comprehend the struggle of Christ, and here lies the error, too, of those who construed a tension between sinlessness and temptation. Only in terms of the reconciliation and vicarious suffering of Christ can we get some inkling of what took place in Gethsemane. On this view one can understand the absence of all impassiveness—the presence of grief and fears as they show up in the repetition of Christ's prayers. The cup is like no other cup; and the Father himself reaches it to him who is the Sinless One. But in the fearful battle involved in it for him, a battle in which even the last remaining evidences of human fellowship disappear from his life, the surrender of his fears to the will of the Father is the way to the end. Rising from the conflict Christ is completely ready for the final phase of his journey to the cross. The hour is at hand (Matt. 26:45).

21. K. Schilder, *Christus in zijn lijden* I, second edition, 1949, page 444.
22. Van Oyen, *Ibid.*

* * *

Now we are somewhat in a position to treat the problem whether Christ could or could not sin. Immediately we confront the criticism which has recently been made of a line of thought which has played a role as well in Reformed as in Roman Catholic theology: the approach to the sinlessness of Christ by way of the personal union. On the ground of the reality of the union of the two natures and the genuine deity of Christ people reasoned to his sinlessness.

We shall offer a few examples. In Roman Catholic theology we clearly observe the reasoning which argues from the deity to the sinlessness of Christ. On the ground of the hypostatic union of the two natures a capacity for sin in Christ is excluded. Philip says, for example, "The personal union with the Logos is as it were a substantial sanctification in the sense of perfect dedication to God."[23] By way of the "sinlessness" of God we thus arrive at the sinlessness of Christ. Bartmann is very lucid on this point: "Christ would have been able to sin only by a completely free opposition of his will to the divine. But that was not possible since the managing possessor of the human will was the Logos; hence God would have had to apostatize from himself—which is an absurdity."[24] This, according to Bartmann, is the decisive ground. Against the theologians who accept the possibility of sin as a necessary corollary of the humanity of Christ, Bartmann observes that he cannot see where they get the courage to subordinate the theological to the anthropological difficulty. Schmaus' reasoning is in a similar vein: "The inner incapacity for sin results from the fact that the "I" of the human nature is the Logos."[25] According to Schmaus, Christ does have a free human will but the "I," active through it, is God. It is not a human but a divine self who is responsible for the deeds performed through the human will. Pohle regards the problem of Christ's sinlessness in re-

---

23. Winkler Prins' Encyclopedia VI, page 57.
24. *Lehrbuch der Dogmatik* I, page 360.
25. Schmaus, *Kathol. Dogm.*, II pages 655.

lation to his freedom of choice as one of the most acute in theology. If Christ were not free his death on the cross would have no merit but "if he were free, then he could rebel."[26] In Reformed theology Kuyper and Bavinck may be taken as representative. Kuyper says that owing to the human nature of Christ there was in him the possibility of sin (as it existed in Adam before the Fall). "But since Jesus did not assume a human person, a 'homo,' but human nature, and since there was in him no human ego (to realize this 'possibilitas') but, on the contrary, the human nature remained eternally united to the second person of the Trinity, therefore the control of this divine person makes it absolutely impossible for the 'possibilitas' to become reality."[27] Bavinck, too, speaks of a "necessary" sinlessness in distinction from an "empirical" sinlessness.[28] "He is the Son of God, the Logos, who was in the beginning with God and who was himself God; he is one with the Father and always accomplishes his will and work. To one who confesses this of the Christ the possibility of sinning and falling is an atrocious idea." And he adds: "For then God himself must have been able to sin—which it is blasphemy to think; or the union of the divine and human nature is regarded as severable and practically denied."

Particularly H. Vogel was a strong opponent of this line of reasoning. He declares that in confessing the sinlessness of Christ the issue is not a physical or metaphysical quality of Christ; says he, "at this point may lie the Achilles' heel of the orthodox conceptions of this mystery."[29] In the sinlessness of Christ we are concerned with the person of Jesus Christ and not with the sinlessness of God. Thus alone one can plumb the depths of this confession. His sinlessness is that he accomplishes the will of the Father and takes up his cross, not regarding the

---

26. Pohle, *Dogmatik* II, page 120.
27. Kuyper, *Loci* III, Cap., III, par. 6, page 11; compare his *Werk van den Heiligen Geest*, 1927, page 138.
28. Bavinck, *Geref. Dogm.* III, page 299.
29. H. Vogel, *Christologie*, I, pages 391 and 396.

shame. "He could not sin, as truly as he is, and remains, who
he is: Christ for us." From this point of view he criticizes
the orthodox insight which he obviously regards as a logicistic inference from the deity of Christ. We must be cautious
here in order to remain fair. For the issue in the orthodox
view is not a logical inference from the "metaphysics" of
Christ. This impression may sometimes be created when people
speak as do the Roman Catholic theologians who treat of the
sole responsibility of the divine subject or ego; but one must
not forget the possibility that this line of thought, in which the
sinlessness of Christ is seen in intimate association with the
Incarnation, concerns not *merely* the *abstract* sinlessness of
"the divine nature" of Christ but his person. That is the background of Bavinck's remark about the "atrocious idea." When
he says this his mind's eye sees the image of the son of God who
became flesh. Behind the ostensibly theoretical conclusion lies
the confession that Christ is the Holy One and that in him we
confront the activity of God. The criticism of Vogel is therefore unfair; it is a denial of the profound religious motif in
these views. The error which is easily made in confessing
Christ's sinlessness is not the reference to the union of the two
natures but rather the transference of the sinlessness of Christ
into a sphere of theoretical matter-of-factness and matter-of-
courseness which eliminates the tensions of the temptation and
in which people are content to say that God is far from godlessness and that the Almighty abhors injustice. By way of
this *a priori* it is no great trick to eliminate all tensions and
conflict from the life of the man Jesus Christ, but it is not
necessary thus to expose the confession of Christ's holiness to
confusion; and orthodox theology is certainly innocent of pet-
rifying theories in this respect. Reformed theology at least has
put full emphasis on the true humanity of Christ and his fearful conflict. In Roman Catholic reasoning at this point, more
than in the Reformed and Lutheran arguments, one can easily

see how the genuinely human development and conflict of Christ's life more than once caused trouble in theology.

In the course of Vogel's argument there is nonetheless an element which must not be neglected and which can warn us against arid theorizing on the subject of Christ's sinlessness. For in Holy Scripture the holiness of Christ and his resistance to temptation are environed by a special revelational context. Indeed, the point of Christ's life is the mystery "that he cannot sin." And one must hold, with the church, that those are wrong who are content to say that Christ was able not to sin. But one must be on his guard against an abstract mode of reasoning about the confession of Christ's sinlessness and against playing down the reality of the temptation. One who is preserved from abstractions here, will more and more appreciate the riches of the fact that Christ could not sin. This "inability" is not a metaphysical quality to be recognized as self-evident but something closely related to the situation of the Incarnate Word. The issue is not the general confession of the sinlessness of God, but rather that of the Incarnate Son. In his case there is not, as with us, a cross-roads, a junction, without further qualifications. The moment the Scripture introduces the temptation in the wilderness it mentions Christ's being filled with the Holy Spirit. In his life there is a mysterious incapacity for sin stemming from his love and mercy. Scripture refers to the sinlessness of Christ as his permanent *deed*. This deed can never be separated from his work as Mediator. The purpose of the temptation in the wilderness is not that Christ should commit some *ethical* aberration but that he should be dissuaded from entering upon the road of suffering. "All three temptations are clearly related to Jesus' Messianic task and form a contrast to it."[30] This was the one great temptation in the life and death of Christ: that he should depart from this Messianic pattern of life.[31] In this light one must

---

30. Giuseppi Riccioti, *Leven van Christus*, 1959, page 303.
31. Compare K. Schilder, *Christus verzocht om den tempel*. In: *Om Woord en Kerk*, I 1948, particularly page 117.

understand Christ's sinlessness: he could not elude this course
of suffering: he *could* not sin. He could not elude his suffering because he did not want to elude it. One must see this "inability" in line with the mockery of the spectators on Golgotha:
"He haved others; himself he cannot save" (Matt. 27:42). The
inability to sin is that of his person, of his full and inviolable
willingness to do the will of the Father. It is the inability to
desist from his love, which he brings to its final, it con-
summating realization. When we speak of the sinlessness of
Christ we are most easily inclined to think of his fulfilling the
law of God but in Scripture it is related to his work as Mediator; and therefore the temptation as we can readily see, is
not general but one involving *glory*.[32] Hence one can never see
the inability to sin in its true light unless one thinks of this
attitude and this act. And this is not a new argument, one
which comes in addition to the one derived from the personal
union, but it is the same ground, which orthodoxy at bottom
intended: it is the person Jesus Christ who came to do his work
and who personally overcomes temptation in an act of not being
able to sin. The temptation was that he should avoid the way
of suffering. ". . . What shall I say? Father, save me from
this hour?[33] But for this cause came I unto this hour" (John
12:27). What shall I say? This utterance, born of deep emo-
tion, indicates — not hesitation, for a moment earlier he announced his death in lucid reference to the dying grain of
wheat — his struggle and readiness to go to the extreme limit
of his humiliation. Therefore we can never say that the reality
of the temptation is nullified by his Messianic ability to sin.
The Scripture discloses nothing of the dilemma between the
sinlessness and the freedom of Christ — the difficult problem
broached by Pohle. For in Jesus Christ we see that his free
will manifests itself precisely in His sinlessness. Of any concept of sovereign freedom there is no mention. His freedom

---

32. Compare Bavinck, *Geref. Dogm.*, III, 300.
33. See footnote in the American Revised Version.

is to do the will of the Father and not to stand neutrally at the cross-roads of two diverging possibilities. Christ's sinlessness does not nullify the temptation but rather demonstrates its superiority in the teeth of temptation.

In faith one might speak here of the "necessity" of his victory. By "necessity" we mean only that which God has disclosed to us about him and his work: we mean the redemptive intent of the personal union in Christ. The "inference" of the sinlessness of Christ from the personal union is not the Achilles' heel of orthodox theology but, when not understood abstractly, a direct datum of the revelation concerning Christ.

In the hypostatic union the chief point is not a theoretical interest in the union of a sinless divine nature with a human nature but the *act* of him who assumed the form of a servant and who did not cling to his prerogatives as God's Equal but humbled himself to die the death of a criminal. Christ himself mentioned this "necessity" when he said: *Behooved* it not the Christ to suffer these things, and to enter thus into his glory? (Luke 24:26). *Thus* to enter into his glory was his task and not by way of the avoidance of suffering. Here is the radiance of Christ's sinlessness, of his absolute holiness, which is one with his mercy and compassion. *He* could not fall, not from a lack of freedom, but precisely because of his freedom *before God*, the freedom consisting in obedience, which could therefore bring liberation and salvation to man. ". . . Jesus knowing that his hour was come that he should depart out of this world unto the Father, having loved his own that were in the world, he loved them unto the end" (John 13:1). In the way of this love he "cannot" save himself but only others. And here he fulfilled all righteousness as it also behooved him. In this he cannot deny himself: therefore "as a lamb that is led to the slaughter, and as a sheep that before its shearers is dumb, so he opened not his mouth" (Isaiah 53:7):

And so the confession of Christ's sinlessness belongs to the confession of the church: both his not-having-sinned in fact and his not-being-able-to-sin. In this not-being-able the church confesses the mystery of Christ: it confesses *this* personal union, and this "motive" of the Incarnation of the Word.[34] This confession refers us to the unshakable foundation that was laid in *this* love and in *this* obedience which culminated in the death of the cross. Christ rose superior to all temptation in the highest freedom through fear and sorrow. This is the comfort of the church and its witness in the world. *This* gospel may be preached to all nations.

* * *

There is, in this connection, one text still left for our consideration. If the sinlessness of Christ is really connected with his readiness to drink the cup of suffering down to the last bitter dregs, we think involuntarily of an utterance of Christ, which, though spoken on the way to the cross, seems to indicate another possibility. We are referring to what Christ said to Peter at the time of the arrest. In this phase of the suffering Peter reached for the sword. With it he wishes to clear a path which would take suffering out of Christ's way. It is the same Peter who, as the instrument of the evil one, had said earlier: "This shall never be unto thee!" This Peter reaches for his sword. But then the Saviour commanded him to place the sword back in the sheath. Until now we have seen the line of Christ's obedience run steadily on, straight through the considerations of men and the temptation of Satan. But Christ added: "Or thinkest thou that I cannot beseech my Father, and he shall even now send me more than twelve legions of angels?" (Matt. 26:53).

Does he not now speak of another "possibility"—one which does not involve suffering? Is Christ really confronted by a

---

34. We are alluding here to the question whether the Incarnation of the Word would have taken place also if there had been no fall. In the treatment of the work of Christ this question will be dealt with more fully. At this point we shall merely assert that this idea is a speculative emasculation of the biblical message. The confession of Christ's sinlessness would be speculatively detached from his work as Mediator. See Calvin's *Institutes* II, 12, 4.

cross-roads, by two possibilities, even in connection with the will and help of his Father? The entire context makes clear, however, that Christ does not here refer to such an intersection, that he is not weighing other possibilities. Having gone through the struggle of Gethsemane, he now encounters the feeble effort of Peter to deflect him from the path of suffering. In response to his attempt at intervention Christ speaks to Peter, who has his hand on his sword, about the power of God who rules all things and before whom Peter's help seems ridiculous. There is here no repetition of the agonizing struggle of Gethsemane: witness what Christ says next: "How then should the Scriptures be fulfilled, that thus it *must* be?" (Matt. 26:54). The picture of Isaiah 53 here rises before the eyes of the Man of Sorrows; and he knows the Scriptures must be fulfilled and thus the will of God for his life. And in that hour he still administered the Counsel of God to the multitudes: "But all this is come to pass, that the *scriptures* of the prophets might be fulfilled" (Matt. 24:55, 56). Amidst the crisis of swords and staves he remained true and, though abandoned by all his disciples, went his way *alone*.

*   *   *

The confessions of the churches have spoken clearly of the holiness of Christ. "Without sin" is a phrase we hear at many an ancient council. In 431 the Council of Ephesus, for instance, repudiated the idea that Christ should have sacrificed himself, not just for us, but also for himself: he who knew no sin has no need of a sacrifice.[35] The Council of Chalcedon in 451 repeats the words of Scripture that Christ became like us in all things sin excepted.[36] And in later periods the confession proved to exert a strong and lasting influence on the thinking of the church about the Lord Jesus Christ. The Council of Florence confessed that no one can be freed from the domination of the devil by any means other than the merit of Jesus

---

35. Cf., Denzinger, *Enchiridion Symbolorum,* 122.
36. *Ibid.,* 148.

Christ our Lord whose conception, birth, and death were without sin.[37]

In all sorts of variations this confession occurs in the Protestant creeds also. In the Heidelberg Catechism, when it discusses the two natures of Christ, we read that Christ had to be a *righteous* man; here the holiness of Christ is plainly implied. In Lord's Day 14 the holiness of Christ is explicitly mentioned when Christ is referred to as the true seed of David, like unto His brethren in all things, sin excepted. This confession is, of course, part and parcel of the redemption of God which comes to us in Jesus Christ. For he—we read—is the Mediator who "with his innocence and perfect holiness covers, in the sight of God, my sin wherein I was conceived and brought forth." The same expression "sin excepted" occurs in Article 18 of the Belgic Confession and again in Article 26 with reference to the intercession of Christ. It is clear that passages from Scripture occupy a large place in the confessions. There is in them little dogmatic deduction but instead a single-pitched, and still doxological, repetition of many undeniably lucid passages from Scripture. And so we can understand why the confessions, like the Gospel itself, regard the holiness of Christ as intimately connected with the expiation of our sins.

Both as regards formulation and the appeal to Scripture on this point there is great unanimity in the creeds of the churches. This is true of Reformed, Lutheran, Roman Catholic, and Anglican confessions. The direction of the thinking of the churches was clearly determined by the lucidness of Scripture which pictures Christ as the Holy One although men hid their face from him. From the agreement of the confessional formulation we may not infer, of course, that the agreement of the churches is complete. It always depends on whether the confession touching the phrase "though without sin" is seen and articulated in a truly Scriptural light. For one can accept the phrase "without sin" and still speak of Christ in the flesh

---

37. *Ibid.,* 711; cf., 710 and 224.

and of his conquest of rebellion in such a way as to do violence to it. And one can virtually equate the holiness of Christ with the holiness of other men, so that it becomes clear that he does not mean to say that which the Bible, in its numerous testimonies, reports. When we remember that in the Roman Catholic church and its theology the immaculate conception of Mary, elevated to the status of dogma in 1854, takes its place next to the sinlessness of Christ, we understand that the words "without sin" cannot function properly in the confession of the church, unless the entire witness of Scripture be brought to bear on it. Only then the holiness of Christ will truly belong to the doxological repertoire of the church. It is not a revelation of an ethical ideal and cannot sufficiently be described in the words "dedication" and "consecration." It is the mystery of him who was made to be sin. In this context only, one can truly confess him as the Holy One. Outside this context one may momentarily be impressed with the spotlessness of his earthly life but one will fail to hear the gospel in it.

When Jesus Christ encounters a man with an unclean spirit in the synagogue at Capernaum, this spirit cries out: "What have we to do with thee, Jesus thou Nazarene? Art thou come to destroy us? I know thee who thou art, the Holy One of God" (Mark 1:24). This acknowledgement of the Holy One of God, whose superior power is feared by the demons has nothing to do with the *confession* of Christ's holiness. Only he can truly confess that holiness who understands that Christ was made to be sin and thus conquered all temptation and obediently fulfilled the will of the Father when he, for the joy that was set before him endured the cross and despised the shame. (Hebr. 12:2).

The Unity of the Person

CHAPTER XI

The Unity of the Person

HAVING discussed the divine and the human nature of Christ, we would now proceed to a consideration of the problem of the relationship between the two natures in the unity of the person. By thus speaking of "discussion" and "proceeding to a consideration" we may seem to leave the impression that we are now concerned with an abstract problem of human thought. In reality, however, we are concerned only to reflect on what the Scriptures reveal to us regarding the person of Jesus Christ. This reflection issues naturally from our taking account of the ancient confession of the church: truly God and truly man. In what sense did the church mean to speak of these things in its confession? It was conscious of the fact that in this confession it was broaching an incomprehensible mystery, the great mystery of which Paul spoke. But this mystery was nevertheless not something which eluded all formulation. It concerned the living person of Jesus Christ who was the content of this confesssion of the church. Hence, in the face of heresy, the church again and again took account of its confession touching Christ without intending to abandon the mystery of the person. At the Council of Chalcedon the church confessed that the union of the two natures of Christ was without division, separation, mixture, or change, declaring at the same time that in this union the two natures retained their properties. Quite naturally all sorts of questions arose as a result since, certainly, the doctrine of the two natures did not imply the existence of two persons, two independent subjects, but was concerned with the *one* life of

271

Jesus Christ. To this fact the church gave expression when it spoke of the two natures in the unity of the person. In close connection with the preceeding there arose, in the period of the Reformation, a controversy over the *nature* of this union. It was the conflict between the Lutherans and the Reformed: a conflict concerning the so-called *communicatio idiomatum*. In this discussion the participants concentrated their attention particularly upon the Lutheran confession of the omnipresence of the human nature of Christ, a thesis which played a dominant role especially in Luther's doctrine of the Lord's Supper. It is not our intention extensively to treat all aspects of this conflict but the point at issue is nonetheless important enough to merit our full attention, since the Reformed view of the communication of properties, through this conflict also, comes clearly into view.

We shall leave to one side the much-discussed question whether Luther formed his doctrine of ubiquity in the interest of his views on the Lord's Supper or whether it assumed an independent place in his theology. For whatever one may think of the historical development of his doctrine, there can be no difference of opinion about the fact that Luther adhered to the doctrine of ubiquity. And it is plain too that the problem has ramifications beyond this ubiquity. Basically we are concerned with the character of the union of the two natures in the unity of the person of Christ; and in connection with it, the significance of the union for the properties of the divine and the human natures.

In describing this controversy between Lutheran and Reformed theology, one must be very cautious. It is incorrect, in any case, to say that the doctrine of the *communicatio idiomatum* as such is already monophysite, hence involves a mixture of properties. Lutherans, as will appear, have polemicized with emphasis against monophysitism. One can understand why people believed they detected in Lutheranism a monophysite tendency, but it will certainly be necessary, especially with regard to the Lutheran Formula of Concord, to read carefully and to distinguish sharply.

We can assume in this connection that it is incorrect so to contrast the Lutheran and the Reformed confessions that the one is made to teach a *communicatio idiomatum* while the other is not. This would be as wrong as it is to say that the Lutherans did, and the Reformed did not, teach the real presence of Christ at the Lord's Supper. Bavinck correctly says that between Lutheran and Reformed men an important difference arose about the effects of the union.[1] He presents a reproduction of the Lutheran conception by saying "that the properties of both natures were communicated, not only to the one person, but those of the divine nature were communicated also to the human." Thus the human nature was elevated to a position of divine omnipotence and omnipresence. By the communication of divine properties to the human nature, Bavinck feels, the communication of gifts to the human nature has ceased to be significant. "Lutheran theology still mentions 'gifts,' but it is embarrassed in finding a place for them and lacks room even for the anointing of Christ with the Holy Spirit." Moreover, by this communication of the properties of the divine nature to the human in Lutheran theology, a Docetic element creeps into Christology: "The purely human development of Christ does not come into its own."[2] In Reformed theology, on the other hand, the union of the divine and the human natures was grasped more correctly, says Bavinck; particularly in the doctrine of the communication of gifts, a "beautiful doctrine," he discovers this superior insight, since by it the genuinely human nature of Christ is kept inviolate. Reformed theology principially overcame the Lutheran doctrine of the

1. Bavinck, *Geref. Dogm.*, III, page 293...
2. *Ibid.*, III, page 294.

"mingling" of the two natures.[3] Reformed theology did aus-
terely maintain the unity of the person but in this unity it insisted, for the human nature, on the rule that the finite cannot
contain the infinite (*finitum non capax infiniti*). At the same
time, says Bavinck, Reformed theology circumvented Nestorianism by asserting that the union of the two natures was
embedded in the unity of the person.

The most important question to be considered here is whether the Lutheran doctrine of the communication of properties
may in fact be called a doctrine of "mixture." There is every
reason to consider this question seriously because the Lutheran
Formula of Concord expressly concerned itself with it. The
question could not but arise since both the Lutherans and the
Reformed wished to adhere to the Chalcedonian doctrine of
the union "without mixture and without change." The Formula of Concord points out that the ancient orthodox doctors of
the church, both before and after Chalcedon, more than once
used the word "mixture"—be it with discrimination and good
sense—in reference to the hypostatic union and the communication of properties.[4]

According to Luther also, the two natures come together
and are mingled in one person. Still one may not infer from
the acceptance of the term "mixtio" that we are here confronting pure monophysitism (the one theanthropic nature). For
even though the term be kept, the important thing is: what is
meant by it? Certainly not a "confusio" of natures, that is
"a mingling (*Vermischung*) or equalization (*Vergleichung*)
of the (two) natures as when honey and water is made into
mead, which is a mixed beverage and no longer either water
or honey, since the relationship between the divine and the human nature in the person of Christ is quite different." And so
there is obvious reference to Chalcedon: the distinction between
the two natures is mentioned as well as the fact that in the per-

3. *Ibid.*, III, page 237.
4. J. F. Müller, *Die symb. Bücher der ev. luth. Kirche*, 1928, page 678.

son of Christ the natures are neither separated nor mixed.[5] On the contrary, each remains in all eternity in its own nature and substance. Thus, in the combination of these two aspects— mixture but no confusion—we confront the central problem of Lutheran Christology. Is this an inner contradiction or a meaningful synthesis? And does Lutheranism really main- tain Chalcedon?

*　*　*

In order rightly to answer this question we must first of all notice that in the Formula of Concord we repeatedly witness that motif which Bavinck refers to as specifically Reformed: that the communication of properties means, not a fusion of them, but a communication of them to the one person of the Son. There lies the point of contact between Lutheran and Re- formed theology. By way of the personal union Luther still comes to speak of a mixture, that is, in the person of the Son. A simple mingling of the natures as in the theanthropic nature of monophysitism is regarded as contraband; hence the doc- trine of Eutyches is rejected as heresy. But Luther's symbol at the same time rejects a simple duality in the person; the na- tures are not related as "two boards glued together" without intercommunication. Hence also the Nestorian heresy is re- jected, because in it the two natures are separated and two Christs are construed. The Lutheran doctrine, therefore, as also the Reformed, *intends* to reject the Nestorian as well as the Eutychian heresy. And *still* (here lurks the real problem), on the basis of this rejection, and in view of the personal union, the symbol teaches that the properties of the divine nature are communicated to the human nature. The symbol itself posits the problem "whether, because of the personal union, the divine and the human nature have genuine intercommunication, and

---

5. "nunquam vel separantur vel confunduntur, vel altera in alteram mutatur," Müller, *Ibid*, page 675.

hence also whether the properties of the two have genuine intercommunication."[6]

Thus the problem stands squarely before us. The point of departure is the confession of Chalcedon, at least by intention; while the problems cluster around the nature of the communication of the properties within the unity of the person. It is emphatically said that the one nature does not change into the other. Each nature retains its properties and the properties of the one can never become the properties of the other. The properties or attributes of the divine nature are said to be: almighty, eternal, infinite, omnipresent, omniscient, and these can never become the attributes of the human nature. The "properties" of the human nature are: being a physical creature, flesh and blood, finite; suffering, death, movement from one place to another, hunger, thirst, experiencing cold and heat; and these can never become properties of the divine nature. At this point one would think, and not without reason, that the Lutheran and Reformed view of the union of the two natures, having the same Chalcedonian starting-point, point in precisely the same direction. But now enters in the specific and peculiarly Lutheran idea from which the Reformed confession has dissociated itself.

In what does this peculiarly Lutheran point of view consist —the point of view which ignited such a spirited controversy in the sixteenth century?

To some extent we detect it when we listen to the pointed polemic against Zwingli's view of the union of the two natures. The Formula of Concord specifically combats the Zwinglian idea of "alloeosis." By this term is expressed the idea that, though one can say *with words* that the entire person has performed something, he still means that only one of the two natures has in reality performed it; one may say, for instance, that the person of Christ has suffered for us but still mean that the human nature by itself suffered for us.[7] Against this

6. *Ibid.*, page 544.

Zwinglian doctrine numerous quotations from Luther's works
are adduced; as for instance the well-known passage: "Beware,
beware, I say, of the *alloeosis;* it is a mask of the devil, for in
the end it produces such a Christ as I should not care to follow as Christian." Once the "alloeosis" is taught, one must inevitably teach also the doctrine of the two persons in Christ.
The work of Christ, and hence also the person, is split up. "If
it should no longer be said: God died for us, but, instead, only
a man, then we are lost." Of the divine nature by itself this
cannot be said and is impossible, but now that God and man
have been united in the one person of Christ, it is possible (to
say it), so that of the suffering of Christ it can truly and correctly be said: "God died" and one can speak of "the suffering
of God, the blood of God, and the death of God."[8] "Now that
God and man are united in one person, it is correct to speak of
the death of God when that man dies who, with God, formed
one thing or one Person." According to the Lutherans one may
not conceive of the expressions "God suffered" and "God died"
as a "verbal predication;" that is, as merely in words and not
in deed.   In view of this, one can understand the reference
in the Formula of Concord to James 1:17, where we read that
in God there can be no variation. The divine nature in Christ
is not changed by the incarnation but one must maintain the
unity of the Person, and one must dare to speak of it as realistically as possible, lest one endanger the mystery of the true
union.   Now it was the intent also of Reformed theology to
maintain the unity of the person and Reformed theology can
certainly not be identified, on this point, with that of Zwingli.
But a difference nevertheless arose between Lutheran and Reformed theology, because in the Lutheran conception, despite
its rejection of a monophysite mixture, certain deductions were
made from the union of the two natures for the human nature

---

7. *Ibid.,* page 682.
8. *Ibid.,* page 683: "vere et recte de ipsius passione dici possit: Deus
mortuus est, Dei passio, Dei sanguis, Dei mors."

in Christ. The opinion of those who oppose the idea that the human nature in union with the divine should have something more than its natural and essential properties is called a false opinion with reference to what seem to be the obvious implications of the Word of God. For Scripture teaches that the human nature in Christ, having laid aside the form of a servant and being glorified at the right hand of God, received, in addition to its natural properties, also "special, exalted, supernatural, unsearchable, inexpressible, heavenly prerogatives and eminence in majesty, glory, power, and dominion over all that can be named."[9] In Christ we are not merely concerned with created gifts of finite qualities occurring also in the saints. Indeed not: so great is the glory in which the human nature in the union is permitted to share, that is, at the glorification, that one should not try to decide "of what the human nature in Christ, without damage to itself, could or should be capable."

The Scriptures ascribe majesty to the human nature; the glory of the regeneration of things, executing judgment, having all power in heaven and on earth. The communication of properties takes place, not merely in a manner of speaking, but in reality. This does not imply confusion, for the power which according to John 5 and 6 belongs to the flesh of Christ, is not identical with that of his divine nature. The properties of the human nature are not laid aside or changed into those of the divine nature. But the human nature does receive majesty, because the fullness of the Godhead dwells in Christ bodily. Majesty, power, and glory radiate through the human nature as fire in a red-hot piece of iron, or the soul in a body. During the period of humiliation this majesty was hidden and kept in the background but after the servant-form has been laid aside the majesty of Christ becomes fully manifest. Hence there is in Christ a divine omnipotence belonging to the divine nature alone but "it . . . proves itself fully, though voluntarily, in, with, and through the assumed and now exalted human nature in

9. *Ibid.,* page 685.

Christ."[10] The fire which glows in the iron is a property of
the fire, but because the fire is united with the iron, the iron
has the power "to glow and to burn without a change in the
essence or natural properties of either fire or iron."

Through the union the human nature does not indeed receive
the divine omnipotence, for this it cannot receive, but it does
receive all power and knowledge. Hence there follows a polemic with the Agnoetes who teach "that the Son does know
everything but his assumed human nature is ignorant of many
things." Everything must be viewed in the light of the personal
union and then one can say that Christ is among us with more
than just his Godhead. In virtue of the union he received the
majesty and power "to be present also according to and with
the human nature he assumed"—present with his entire person, both in the divine and the human nature.

To summarize: we can say that the Formula of Concord
condemns:

(a) The "confusio" of the two natures.
(b) The idea that the human nature should be omnipresent
     in the same way as the divine nature, that is, as an
     infinite being.
(c) The idea that the human nature could be like the divine
     in essence and substance.
(d) The idea that Christ with his divine omnipotence,
     should not be able to be physically present wherever
     he pleases.
(e) The idea that Christ should have suffered for us only
     in his human nature.

The Lutheran church and Lutheran theology are obviously
concerned to teach that, after the union, the two natures can no
longer be thought of as existing apart from each other but both
are to be conceived as at every moment wholly together without
giving rise to a mixture.[11]

10. *Ibid.*, page 689.
11. Schmidt, *Die Dogmatik der Luther Kirche,* page 213, 222. Compare
H. Grass, *Die Abendmahlslehre bei Luther und Calvin,* 1940, page 61 ff.

There is real and irrefragable fellowship between the natures in the one person. With an appeal to Col. 2:9 it is emphatically asserted that the divine nature penetrates into the human. What is said of the one nature can also be said of the other and not merely in a manner of speaking. Every attribute concerns the entire person, so that one can say without scruples that God died and that the man Jesus is almighty.

The intention of all this is to stress the unity of the person and not to let it fall into two halves. *Mixtio,* but no *confusio!* The human nature retains its essential properties. To avoid possible misconceptions Lutheran doctrine even means to point out from which nature the attributes added to the Person are derived. This is the noteworthy element in the Lutheran doctrine, as appears plainly in the Formula of Concord where we read that "the same thing is not simultaneously an attribute of both natures but is separately explained according to the nature from which each is ascribed to the person."[12]

Then comes the reference to I Peter 3 and 4 where we read that Christ died in the flesh and suffered for us in the flesh. Again we note a point of contact between the Lutheran and Reformed Christology. In both we note a strong emphasis— over against Nestorianism—on the unity of the person. But Lutherans again and again saw in the "Calviniani" those who failed to do justice to the indissoluble unity of the two natures. But this criticism is hardly justified by the facts. For the decisive element in Reformed theology is precisely that it meant, against all Nestorianizing tendencies, to proceed from the union of the two natures in the one person of Christ as the one subject of all the works of the Mediator. They never meant to treat the works of Christ as the actions of the abstract human nature of Christ. There is every reason to assume that Luther, in his resistance to the spiritualistic tendencies of Zwingli, drew Calvin too much into Zwingli's Nestorianizing atmosphere. To Luther *this* Christology and the doctrine of

---

12. Müller, *Ibid.,* page 682.

the Lord's Supper were inseparably linked together. He believed that Calvin also paid tribute to spiritualism and that, in fact, he repudiated the "real presence."

But in reply one may say precisely that Calvin remained loyal to Chalcedon and that in this line he was able to overcome spiritualism in the doctrine of the Lord's Supper.

The heart of the matter, which casts its light both upon Christology and the Lord's Supper, is pointed out in Dankbaar: "Calvin found the way of escape from subjectivism and spiritualism without lapsing into an unspiritual depersonalization of the sacrament and without doing violence to the 'finitum non capax infiniti.' And Luther did not understand this or perhaps he understood it when it was too late."[13]

It is perfectly true that Calvin (in harmony with Chalcedon) laid strong emphasis on the distinction of the two natures in the person of Christ.[14] The whole question is whether Calvin, in stressing the distinction, lost sight of the unity The answer to this question determines the controversy between the Lutherans and the Reformed. Clearly and elaborately Calvin discussed these questions in his *Institutes*. It turns out that he never concerns himself with the two natures by themselves but always with the Person in which Christ reveals himself as both God and man.[15] Christ as God and man is our Lord and the true Son of God. Calvin polemicizes against Nestorius who, rather than distinguish the two natures, tore them apart. The Scriptures, according to Calvin, cry out against the theory of Nestorius "where the appellation of 'the Son of God' is given to him who was born of the virgin." Still one must not imagine a mixture of natures in the unity of the person.[16] In adoring the one Christ Calvin is always concerned about unity and distinction. As we have seen, this is also a dominant motif in Lutheran Christology, Where then lies the

---

13. Dankbaar, *De sacramentsleer van Calvin,* page 162.
14. Emmen, *De Christologie van Calvijn,* page 40.
15. *Institutes* II, 14, 4.
16. *Ibid.,* II, 4, 7.

difference? Calvin also recognizes a communication of properties. In it, he says, lies the key to an understanding of Christ's redemptive work. Here the communion of the natures appears. "Let this maxim, then, serve us as a key to the true sense, that those things which relate to the office of the Mediator, are not spoken simply of his Divine or of his human nature."[17] Hence Calvin wants no division between the two natures, but he does stress, more strongly than the Lutherans, that there can be no confusion. In Christ there is only one acting subject, but in it lies the distinction between properties—the mystery confessed at Chalcedon.

In this connection the adage "finitum non capax infiniti" frequently turns up in the discussions. It was generally regarded as a specific motto of Calvin. One can demonstrate, however, that it does not occur in Calvin himself. Calvin had no need of reflection about the finite and the infinite, in order, from this point of view, to elucidate the union of the two natures in Christ. But he did stand on guard against any crossings of creaturely boundary-lines—also in Christ. His concern was not a philosophical, cosmological theory into which he tried to fit his Christology; but from the gospel he learned that the riches of Christ consisted in the fact that he redeemed us as one of us. For this reason he stood on guard, also in Christology, against anything that threatened to erase the true humanity of Christ—even the humanity which Christ had after his glorification.

The Son of God assumed human nature in an act of love and reconciliation, and this human nature is in all things truly like us. And it remains like us in the union, so that Calvin will not allow it the ascription of omnipresence. The hesitation, which we note in the Formula of Concord in this connection, is cleared up in Calvin. He cannot admit that the human nature of Christ should have communicated divine properties which

17. *Ibid.*, II, 14, 3.

are not, as in the divine nature, real divine properties. Refusal to admit this is not the fruit of rationalistic criticism but the recognition of mystery. Calvin is pronouncedly anti-Docetic and does not wish the human nature, in its union with the Son of God, to be driven beyond its creaturely limits.

In this connection Calvin was repeatedly accused of Nestorianism. Bauke and Korff and many others have so accused him. It is interesting to see how the issue of Nestorianism again and again turns up. Korff's objection is particularly that Calvin repeatedly tries to illumine the Gospels in terms of Christological dogma. In this manner that which is one in the person of Christ is separated: the Nestorianizing element in Calvin. These questions arose earlier too. Voetius points out that the Reformed tried to parry the accusation of a Nestorian division addressed to them by the Lutherans.[18]

The Lutherans saw in the Christology of Calvinism an undeniable dualism. The dualism would be that the divine and the human nature in Christ function independently. The same charge of Nestorianism has returned in the twentieth century—also among those who by no means meant to accept the Lutheran view. Bauke says, for instance, that Calvin retains the "finitum non capax infiniti" and the "extra-calvinisticum" and from this appears the "Nestorianizing of Reformed theology."[19] As long as one confesses the "extra-calvinisticum" and hence refuses to allow the Logos to be enclosed within the finite human nature, then one must according to Bauke, remain caught in a dualism. Korff in particular revived this criticism of Calvin. He does admit that Calvin stresses the unity of the person and that the two natures do not coexist as separate entities. But he cannot see how Calvin can be cleared of the Lutheran charge of Nestorianism.[20] The manner in which Calvin operates with the doctrine of the two natures shows a ten-

---

18. Voetius, *Disput. Sel.*, Edition of Kuyper, 1887, page 231.
19. Bauke, *R. G. G.*, see under Christology.
20. Korff, *Chrikstologie*, I, page 262.

dency in the direction of Nestorius. Chalcedon, with the phrases "without division" and "without separation," does not quite come into its own in Calvin.

This charge against Calvin has practically been disqualified by Bavinck already[21] and later also by Emmen.[22] Dominice is mild in his verdict but he nevertheless sees in Calvin two parallel lines; he wonders whether to speak of the deity of Christ as resting during the storm at sea is not "purely Nestorian" and whether Calvin did not split the unity of the two natures into "two mutually incompatible entities, each having a significance of its own."[23]

He is strongly of the opinion that Calvinism will always run the danger of Nestorianism while Lutheranism runs the danger of monophysitism. Still Dominice acknowledges that Calvin did not arrive at two Christs since in him we note a movement from God to man and from man to God, "so that in the end it is still one person with whom we have to do, Jesus Christ, Immanuel."

This last paragraph indeed offers a correct reproduction of Calvin's thought. For, while Calvin does repeatedly distinguish between the two natures in Christ, he does not speculatively draw out the logic of it, but is concerned rather to give expression to the testimony of Scripture. Hence he refers to the statement of Christ "Before Abraham was born, I am" and ventures to comment that this statement was very inapplicable to his humanity because Christ clearly distinguishes here the day of his manifestation from his eternal essence. On the other hand it is also plain, says Calvin, that Christ's increase in stature and wisdom, his not knowing the day of the Lord, his not doing his own will, and his being handled and seen, belong to his humanity. Still Calvin speaks of a communication of properties by which "those things which were per-

---

21. Bavinck, *Ibid.*, III, page 238.
22. Emmen, *Ibid.*, page 40.
23. M. Dominice, *Die Christusverkündigung bei Calvin.* In: *Jesus Chrustus im Zeugnis der H. S. und der Kirche*, 1936, page 243.

formed in his human nature are improperly, yet not without reason, transferred to the Divinity."[24]

This communication is apparently very important to Calvin because he declares that Nestorius was justly condemned in the council of Ephesus, [25] and he speaks of the "impiety of Nestorius."[26] Some have tried to catch Calvin in a net woven of certain expressions of his without taking account of the fact that our human formulations relate to mystery and may not be regarded as rationally transparent description. We notice the same thing in the criticism made at times on Lord's Day 18 of the Catechism where we read: "with respect to His human nature, He is no more on earth; but with respect to His Godhead, majesty, grace, and Spirit, He is at no time absent from us." Here too the charge of Nestorianism has been preferred. But there is not a trace here of a separation of the two natures, because the idea is merely to give expression to the words of Scripture which tell us that Christ, though ascended and hence absent from us, will be, by his own statement, with us "unto the end of the world." To this fact Lord's Day 18 tries to give expression. As in Calvin, so here, the subject is the "ineffable mystery"[27] that the Son of God assumed the human nature; and all our speech which bears on it participates in mystery. Thus Calvin distinguished, and it is extraordinarily helpful to see that no one, attempting to speak in conformity with Scripture, escapes it. We observe it with the Lutherans, who, at decisive points, speak of the unity of the person, but relate particular deeds of Christ especially to *one* of the two natures—as appears clearly in the Formula of Concord. Koopmans said once[28] that one may not say: "This he did according to his Deity and that according to his humanity." Korff, in crit-

---

24. *Institutes*, II, 14, 2.
25. *Ibid.*, II, 14, 4.
26. *Ibid.*, IV, 9, 13.
27 See Calvin's Commentary on John 1:14: "ineffabile arcanum, quod Dei filius humanam naturam induerit."
28. J. Koopmans, *De Nederlandse Geloofsbelijdenis*, page 129.

icizing Calvin, quotes Koopmans on this point. But it is striking that Koopmons, having prefaced the statement by saying we may not separate the humanity from the Deity, follows it up by saying: "In the gospel there certainly are signs pointing both to the Deity and to the humanity." This fact Calvin was concerned to point out, without thereby eliminating the unity of the person. And, anyway, Koopmans speaks in a vein similar to that of Calvin when he discusses the suffering of Christ. "In Christ's suffering as man also, the Deity is the subject taking this work upon him. It is his divine task which he fulfills as man." Calvin is of the same opinion and certainly does not intend to let the human nature function independently. He merely wants to do justice to the unity and to the distinction without doing violence to the ineffable mystery.[29]

*　*　*

A serious warning not to accuse Calvinism too swiftly of Nestorianism is implicit in the fact that the same accusation was levelled at Chalcedon itself. This charge is intimately related to the influence exerted on Chalcedon by Leo the Great. In 449 he wrote a letter, now famous, to Flavian on the doctrine of the two natures. Of Leo too it has been said, in view of the way in which he distinguished the two natures, that he leaned in the direction of Nestorianism. Harnack believes that Leo had no interest in the unity of the person. In reality Leo was sharply opposed to Eutychianism; this is not hard to understand because at that time his doctrine was the center of discussion and Nestorius had been condemned already in 431. A strong emphasis on the distinction of the two natures may of course, when this polemic with monophysitism is regarded by itself, create the impression of sympathy with Nestorius. But it is legitimate to ask the question whether one is then himself doing justice to Chalcedon. These questions perpetually play a role in the history of dogma. And Chalcedon, we notice, is repeatedly subject to criticism. According to Dorner,

29. See Calvin's Commentary on Acts 20:28.

monophysitism is to some extent justified in the light of Chalcedon. It was not till Lutheran Christology arose that the debt of Chalcedon was somewhat cancelled. Adoptionism became a warning by all means not to allow the unity of the person to be obscured. It is plain that at Chalcedon, in the eyes of some, the distinction of the two natures came to expression rather than the unity. But then they do not do justice to the fact that Chalcedon expressed itself with equal force on the "without division or separation" as on the "without mixture or change."

If one then continues fully to agree with Chalcedon he will almost naturally get into difficulty with his criticism of Reformed Christology. Korff is a good example. For he also rejects the Lutheran Christology and regards it as a danger-signal to anyone wishing to advance beyond Chalcedon. Hence he appreciates the protest of the Reformed and asserts that Calvin has here said everything that needs to be said.[30] Luther, in his doctrine of ubiquity, did violence to Chalcedon's "without mixture and without change," while German idealism made its deductions from the phrase "finitum capax infiniti." In view of this cutting criticism it is hard to understand on what grounds Korff accuses Calvin of Nestorianism; he knows that Calvin is concerned only about the distinction between the two natures—witness the examples Korff extracts from Calvin's writings. The issue is: where are the boundary-lines within which the mystery of the person of Christ may be honored. Calvin is never interested in the divine nature or the human nature as abstract entities, as Luther, for instance, insisted on the presence of the *flesh* of Christ at the Communion table to exert its life-giving power: but Calvin concerned himself with the *one* Person of the Son, who operates and is present in all his works as Mediator.

* * *

Repeatedly we have alluded to the well-known phrase: finitum non capax infiniti. It has become a custom to regard it as

30. Korff, *Ibid.*, I, page 228.

a specifically Reformed adage[31] and in the Lutheran opposition
to Reformed Christology it still plays a fairly important role.
This appears especially in the attempt of Werner Elert to show
that this slogan about the finite and the infinite practically occurs already in Nestorian theology.

The basic concept embodied in this motto, Elert says, occurs already in Antiochian theology; Theodore of Mopsuestia,
for example describes the relationship between God and man
in Christ with the concepts "finite" and "infinite." And it was
Nestorius, in his opinion, who made this motto the starting-
point of his Christology. In the motto is contained a "weltanschaulich" *a priori* intended, according to Elert, to make Christology more transparent; and this argument of Nestorius resembles, as two peas in a pod, the polemic of Reformed theology against the Lutherans in the sixteenth century. "And
wherever it turns up in theology, it is an infallible sign that,
Christologically speaking, one is on the way to or from Nestorius." The relation between God and man is conceived by it
in quantitative categories. By way of this criticism Elert makes
room for Lutheran Christology. In all this it remains a riddle
why Reformed theology dissociated itself with so much emphasis *from Nestorius*. This view of the kinship between Reformed criticism of Lutheran theology and Nestorianism is especially unacceptable because the point of Reformed Christology was by no means to establish a "weltanschaulich *a
priori*" but merely to stress the reality of the human nature of
Christ. The polemic against Lutheran theology did not imply
a restoration in honor of Nestorius, but was a continuation of
the polemic against monophysitism and an insistence on the
fences erected against Docetism. One may believe that the
motto "finitum non capax infiniti" creates the impression that
it represents a rational, philosophical approach to Christology
and observe that in the Incarnation we are confronted, not

31. W. Elert, *Ueber die Herkunft des Satzes Finitum infiniti non capax*,
in Zeitschr. für syst. theol., 1939, page 500.

with an unqualified "infinitum" associating itself with some "finitum," but the divine act of the Incarnation of the Word. And in view of these considerations, one can be grateful that Calvin did not construe his Christology on the basis of this motto. But it is utterly incorrect to imagine that everyone incidentally employing this motto is guilty of a philosophical schematization of Christology. For Reformed theology, even when in its polemics it employed the concepts "finite" and "infinite," was at bottom interested in nothing other than what Chalcedon had long ago confessed. It must be pointed out with emphasis that Lutheran theology also, when it spoke of the communion between the two natures, asserted more than once that the issue was a communication of divine properties to the human nature *insofar this nature was susceptible* of it. This is essentially the same problem which Reformed theology confronted when, in its opposition to the excessive formulations of Lutheran theology, it meant to observe the limits of human nature. Therefore, as we witness the polemics, contemporary or past, of Lutheran theologians against Reformed Christology, we cannot escape a renewed confrontation with the question whether Chalcedon is indeed the expression of the faith of the church.   *   *   *

Before closing the chapter we wish to call attention to a point which gains special importance in the controversies touching the unity of the person. We mean the adoration and worship of Christ.

In Reformed theology the question was discussed whether this worship might be accorded Christ *as Mediator.* Here too the controversy with the Lutherans played an important role. Of Lutheran theology it was said that there could be no problem at this point because the communication of divine properties to the human nature belonged to the essential elements of this Christology. Reformed theologians, however, concerned themselves explicitly with this problem because they wished in no respect to mix the two natures. Thus for them the problem arose, not from a secret sympathy for Nestorius, but from their attachment to Chalcedon. It was said, for instance, that worship of the human nature was possible only if one should teach, with the "Ubiquists," that the divine properties are given to the human nature. And in this connection it was emphatically asserted that only God could be worshipped.[32] Scholten who regarded Reformed theology as being in too close proximity with Nestorius, once posited the thesis that in Reformed liturgy the church abstains from prayer to Jesus, the exalted Mediator.[33] But that is something which was never, in this form, an issue in these churches. The issue was not whether one might worship Christ but what is the *ground* of this worship. Indeed, Reformed theologians meant to guard against deifying the human nature of Christ in any form; and Bavinck, for this reason, says that the ground for this worship could not be derived from that which was creaturely in Christ.[34] Not that they preferred, instead, the worship of the "divine nature" but rather approached the problem in terms of the irrefragable unity of the person. The worship of the church is addressed to the *one* person, Jesus Christ. Hence all Nestorianism was rejected as well as all deification of the human nature: In our *faith* we address ourselves to him who is our Mediator in the unity of the person and to whom Thomas, freed now from his doubts, cries out in adoration: My Lord and my God.[35]

Another question remaining on the agenda of this chapter is that which may be summarized in the word "theotokos," the name given to Mary: Mother of God. As is well-known, this word, among others, ignited the Nestorian conflict, since

---

32. See the pronouncement of the fifth ecumenical council. Denzinger, *Enchiridion Symbolorum*, 221. In it an anathema was pronounced upon anyone who taught that Christ must be worshipped separately in two natures.
33. Scholten, *Leer der Herv. Kerk.*
34. Bavinck, *Ibid.*, III, page 304.
35. Cf. Kuyper, *Locus* de Christo, Cap. II, page 39 ff. Bavinck, *Ibid.*, III, page 301.

Nestorius expressed his preference for the name "Christo-tokos." Against him the council of Ephesus in 431 emphat-ically insisted on "theotokos," while Chalcedon (451) and Constantinople (553) followed its example.

It is of some importance to compare the use of this word in the ancient church with the later appraisal of it in Protes-tantism. According to Roman Catholic theologians, the in-frequent use which Protestants make of the term, and, indeed, their aversion to it, prove that Protestantism has distanced it-self from the ancient church. One can compare the aversion of many to this term with what Bruce says of Nestorius: "Nestorius was jealous of the heathenish tendency of the name, mother of God."[36] Hence the Roman Catholic charge is to be taken seriously. It seems to me that the altered appraisal of the designation "Mother of God" is to be seen against the backdrop of the development of Mariology in the Roman Catholic Church in which this term (as also that of *aeiparthenos*) was given such a pronounced character. We do not mean that Rome consciously proceeded to a deification of Mary[37] but that Mary has been assigned a place in the doctrinal system and practice of the Roman Catholic church which tended increas-ingly to erase the limits of creaturehood. Especially in re-sponse to this Mariological development, which culminated for the time being in 1854 (immaculate conception) and 1950 (the assumption into heaven), Protestant resistance to this designation "Mother of God" arose and developed.

But this does not at all mean that Protestantism would not be responsible for that which the council of Ephesus protected and maintained in 431 against Nestorius. Reformed churches have never felt the need to repudiate the decision of this coun-cil for the simple reason that they agree with the rejection of Nestorius' views. His difficulties with "theotokos" and his preference for "Christotokos" arose from his inclination to

---

36. Bruce, *The Humiliation of Christ*, page 49.
37. See my *Conflict met Rome*, Ch. VI.

separate the two natures in Christ and to speak of the human nature by itself—the nature of which Mary would be the mother. The church rejected this dualism and used the word "theotokos" to mean that Mary was the mother of him *who was the eternal Son of God* and that the Son did not assume a human being but the human nature. Another question is whether the term "Mother of God" is the most acceptable term for the expression of this truth. There is room for a difference of opinion on this point and some may judge that in a given historical situation the term may create misunderstanding.[38] This was the case when in later periods Mary's halo grew and became brighter, and the term "Mother of God" became an integral part of Mariological adoration. It is our conviction that in one's use of terms also one is responsible for the life of the whole church and that one does not do anyone any good by using this term (however well intended by the councils in their polemic with Nestorianism) apart from its subsequent development; it is no longer obvious that the term implies a rejection of a dualism in Christology. We know that attempts have been made to break the aversion to "theotokos" and to settle the issue for good[39] but, since the term may create the impression of elevating Mary and does not add anything to the confession of the church of all ages, it is subject to serious objections. But with indignation we reject the notion that Protestantism is secretly dissociating itself from the confession of the church, which always repudiated, against Nestorianism and Adoptionism, the idea that he who was conceived of the Holy Spirit and born of the virgin Mary, should not be the eternal Word, and Light of Light.

---

38. By this standard one might judge the formulation of the problem by Hans Asmussen: If Mary is not the mother of God, then the church of all ages has erred, or we who refuse to so designate Mary, have separated ourselves from the universal Christian Church," H. Asmussen, *Maria, die Mutter Gottes,* 1951.

39. See G. C. van Niftrik, *Kleine Dobmatiek,* page 108.

When Bavinck begins his treatment of the communion of the two natures in Christ, he refers to a familiar distinction which used to play a role in theology: communion in properties, in actions, and in gifts.[40]   One might call in question whether this distinction does justice to the revelation concerning the communion of the natures.   In the communion of properties and of actions we are in fact confronting the same reality.   The properties of the one person Jesus Christ become manifest precisely in his actions, so that we can condense both distinctions in the statement that there is a communion of properties in the reality of the life of Christ.   We may never isolate a given deed or property of Christ from his divine or from his human nature.   At stake here is the unity of the person.

One cannot say that Christ performs certain deeds in such a way that his human nature is the subject of these deeds while he performs other deeds in such a way that the divine nature is the subject.   It was sometimes described in this manner, lest one should have to say that *God* suffered on the cross.   But one may not say in any case, at least if one maintains the unity of the person, that the human nature of Jesus Christ suffered in the abstract, for the simple reason that this human nature has never existed in abstraction from the divine.   One must admit, indeed, that the church rightly stood on guard against any form of theopaschitism but the point is that we must strive rightly to understand the unity of the person.   We must be concerned to maintain that all the deeds of Christ were performed by his *one* person and that in the suffering of Christ the human nature was indissolubly united with the divine.   This communion of natures therefore comes to expression in a communion of actions.   This communion of actions is not something additional to the communion of natures, but part of it: this communion, far from being static, is a permanently dynamic reality in the life and works of Christ.   The Reformed

---

40. *Geref. Dogmatiek,* III, page 293.

creeds already give clear expression to this fact. In the Canons of Dordt we read for instance: "The death of the Son of God is the only and most perfect sacrifice and satisfaction for sin, and is of infinite worth and value, abundantly sufficient to expiate the sins of the whole world. This death is of such infinite value and dignity because the person who submitted to it was not only really man and perfectly holy, but also the only begotten Son of God, of the same eternal and infinite essence with the Father and the Holy Spirit, which qualifications were necessary to constitute Him a Saviour for us; and, moreover, because it was attended with a sense of the wrath and curse of God due to us for sin" (II, 3, 4). This creed obviously dissociates itself completely from the notion that the death of Christ was an act of his human nature in isolation from his divine nature. The infinite value of Christ's death is here associated with the fact that he, who was true God and true man, was the single person, Jesus Christ, undergoing this death. Schilder rightly declared it to be a Reformed conviction that not a single work of the Mediator, either in the past or in the present, was performed "in" or "according to" a single "bare nature"[41] and that one virtually eliminates the Mediator if one says that he performed his mediatorial work merely according to his human nature. At this point the church need not worry lest it slide into theopaschitism and lest it associate suffering too intimately with the living God. For at stake here is the unique mystery of the one Christ in the singleness of the person. He is the subject of all his deeds. And he is the object of our praise and worship as the One who performed his work in the absolute unity of and faithfulness to his office.

* * *

A moment ago we referred, in the above-mentioned distinction, to the communication of gifts. It is somewhat sur-

41. K. Schilder, *Heid. Cat.* II, page 211 — "bloote natuur."

prising to see this third "communication" next to the others.
One may rightly wonder whether it belongs here. For in the
communion of properties and actions we confronted the miracle
of the union; but in the communication of gifts we confront the
fact that God gives things to his son, Jesus Christ, in this
union. This is the beautiful doctrine, as Bavinck says, of the
communication of gifts, a doctrine which certainly cannot be
put on a par with the communion of properties as an item in
the same series. With it Reformed theology resisted every
form of the deification of the human nature of Christ. In this
doctrine they made room for the human development of Jesus
Christ whom they saw, in the Gospel, on his way from infancy
to maturity. Scripture also speaks of the anointing of Christ
and the descent of the Holy Spirit "without measure." This
is something principially different from what the Lutherans intended with their communication of the divine properties to
the human nature. With the gifts are meant those which
equipped the man Jesus Christ for the fulfillment of his official
calling. This is not a granting of the supernatural to the human nature but the equipment, by the gifts of the Spirit, of Jesus
Christ for the completion of the work assigned to him.

The confession of the communication of gifts is a direct result
of the confession of the church in Chalcedon. Christ was genuinely man, and assumed the likeness of sinful flesh—human
nature in its weakness. We witness here that the human nature
of Jesus Christ is not consumed in the union by the divine nature but that it was really united with that divine nature for the
fulfillment of Christ's office.

*   *   *

Now, however, the question arises whether we can say no
more about the nature of this union than that it is a union
which does not suspend the several properties of the two natures. Must we be content to speak of an incomprehensible
mystery or is there perhaps an analogy somewhat illuminating
the nature of this union? As is known to the reader, people

have repeatedly tried to describe that which they confessed as mystery by means of an intracosmic analogy. Thus they did with the confession of the trinity, for instance, and so, too, with the unity of the person. It is especially the analogy of the relationship between soul and body which we encounter in this area. And it is important to consider this analogy with care. Obviously it is not an analogy derived from Scripture for the Bible nowhere compares the relationship between the two natures of Christ with that existing between soul and body in man. But this fact did not deter people, even in early times, from using the analogy. This can be explained to a certain extent from the idea, then current, that the relation between soul and body also involved *mystery*. The purpose of this analogy, with these people, often was not to make the unity of the person conceivable and transparent, but rather to make plain that as the one relationship is incomprehensible, so is the other.

The Athanasian symbol already contains the analogy.[42] In its section on Christology we read: Jesus Christ is . . . "one altogether, not by confusion of substance, but by unity of person. For as the reasonable soul and flesh is one man, so God and man is one Christ." On account of the brevity of this statement it is impossible completely to fathom the intent of the author but we do realize that the symbol intends to stress the unity of the person and to illustrate it by means of the soul-body analogy in man. The question is, however, whether the intention of the author was merely to refer to a *tertium comparationis*— the unity of that which can be called a duality in another connection—or whether he intended really to help us understand the nature of this union.

One repeatedly gets the impression that the soul-body analogy is but incidentally used to stress the true unity of the

---

42. Cf. J. Stiglmayr, *Der im sog. Athanasium verwendete Vergleich von Leib und Seele mit der Einheit der zwei Naturen in Christus,* Zeitschr. für Kath. theol., 1925, page 628-632. He himself writes: "We know this comparison may not be pressed."

person without a concomitant concern with the anthropological problem of the actual relationship between body and soul. The analogy therefore repeatedly returns in the same loose connection. It occurs, for instance, in Luther when he wants to point out the intimate connection between the two natures; he then elaborates by saying that the soul exists throughout the body, so that by striking at the smallest member of the body we strike at the soul. The intention of Luther is, obviously, to illustrate the personal union; and he adds the comment that the relationship between the divine nature and the human is still more intimate than that between soul and body.[43] From the soul-body analogy Luther even made deductions with which to elucidate his doctrine of ubiquity: the human soul manifests itself throughout the body. Here we observe something of the danger of this analogy. This is not to say, however, that the analogy occurs only in Lutheran theology. Calvin also used it to illustrate the unity of the person. He too is concerned to stress the incomprehensibility of the union. He regards man as a unity composed, nonetheless, of two substances. He uses this picture in answering the question how the two natures of the Mediator constitute one person.[44] He regards man himself as "the most opposite similitude; being evidently composed of two substances, of which, however, neither is so confounded with the other, as not to retain its distinct nature." Of the soul is predicated that which cannot be applied to the body and, conversely, what is said of the body is not applicable to the soul. Calvin even proceeds further in elaborating the analogy because he discovers in it something corresponding to the communication of properties in Christ: "Lastly, the properties of the soul are transferred to the body, and the properties of the body to the soul; yet he that is composed of these two parts is no more than one man. Such forms of expression signify that there is in man one person composed of two distinct parts; and

---

43. Cf. W. Köhler, *Dogmengeschichte,* II, 1951, page 216.
44. *Institutes,* II, 14, 1.

that there are two different natures united in him to constitute that one person. The Scriptures speak in a similar manner respecting Christ."[45]

Calvin, it is plain, does not intend, by means of this analogy, to add something new to the teaching of the Scripture. He has only been struck by the peculiar relationship of the two substances and the one human being. And it deserves note that Calvin, before pointing out the analogy, says: "If anything among men can be found to resemble so great a mystery, man himself appears to furnish the most apposite similitude." The words "if anything" seem to mean that Calvin himself felt that by means of the analogy he failed to say anything essential of the unity of the person in Christ.

Certain it is that in Reformed theology this analogy has no dogmatic significance, any more than in the Athanasian symbol.[46] That would be the case only if concealed in this analogy there was a certain anthropological theory, intended to illuminate the personal union. But this is not true of Calvin. He does not mean to offer an ecclesiastical anthropology but speaks in non-scientific terms about soul and body which together form a unity. This diversity and unity constitute the occasion for him to point out, be it with some hesitation, the unity and the diversity of the two natures in the one person of Jesus Christ. But it is plain that we are not given a genuine analogy which could help us form some satisfactory conclusion about the nature of the union. For in man unity and diversity are components of creaturely coherences, while in the unity of the person of Christ we are confronted by the absolutely unique

---

45. *Ibid.*, II, 14, 1. See also Augustine, *Enchiridion* 36, (Sizoo-Berkouwer, *Augustinus over het Credo,* page 86) ; and Vincentius of Lerinum, *Commonitorium,* 14.

46. A. Kuyper, *Loci* III, Cap. III, par. 7, page 27. "Hence the hypostatic union may not be confused with the union of the Trinity or with the union between Creator and creature or . . . (then follows a series of 'unions,' Tr.). It is *sui generis,* entirely univocal."

Incarnation of the *Word*. For this reason one can correctly assert that the unity of the person of Christ, in virtue of its unique character, does not have a single intracosmic analogy. There are no analogies to the Incarnation of the Word which can make it at all comprehensible. In the absolute sense of the word it is the mystery of God. Not a mystery in the sense that the unity of a human soul and body is a mystery—merely some thing incomprehensible to us—but the "mysterion" of God revealed in the flesh.

In the past the church defended this mystery against all sorts of heresy. It defended its confession against all who detracted either from the divine or the human nature of Christ, against the heresy of the separation and the mixture of the two natures, and against all later attempts to get beyond the doctrine of the two natures. The church was not concerned to canonize the terms which it employed to designate the mystery of the Incarnation of the Word. It was conscious that the conflict was not one of terms, as if they contained the ultimate in wisdom, but one involving the reality of Jesus Christ. But opposition to the terms of the church—as, for instance, to the expression "two natures"—repeatedly proved to be opposition to the *content* of the church's confession that Jesus Christ was truly God and truly man. For this reason the church will have to watch closely the opposition to the terminology it employs.

When Bavinck considers the doctrine of the church and reviews various conceptions of it, he finally says: "For the time being theology can do no better, if it would be truly Scriptual and Christian theology, than to maintain the doctrine of the two natures."[47] The phrase "for the time being" is not meant to relativize the confession of Christ's true deity and humanity, but rather to give account of the human factor in formulation. He then posits the confession of the two natures

---

47. Bavinck, *Geref. Dogma.*, III, page 288.

squarely in the midst of modern thought: "Theology may well
be deeply conscious of the imperfection, certainly also in the
doctrine of Christ, attending its language. But all other attempts, made thus far, to formulate the Christological dogma
and to impress it on our consciousness, fail to do justice to the
riches of Scripture and to the honor of Christ. And theology
must guard itself against this first of all."

All this applies, with special force, to the confession of the
unity of the person. It is not an additional point of faith besides that of the Incarnation but an expression of it. Two
natures in the unity of the person: All objections levelled
against this formulation deny, again and again, that all depends
on how the words of the church are understood in the light
of Scripture. Throughout the history of the church there is
perceptible a sort of nostalgia for a mental picture of the unity
of the divine and the human nature. When this was not forth-
coming, people frequently escaped into a contemplation, from
a distance, of the *mysterium tremendum* and the *mysterium
fascinosum* in which the true humanity threatened to be
eclipsed. But in the light of Scripture we may say that when
the church speaks of the unity of the person, it goes directly
back to the message of Holy Scripture itself. No, we are not
called upon to try to picture the unity of "the divine" and "the
human," but Scripture does come to us with a picture of the
one Christ. At no point in Scripture does his true humanity
threaten or eliminate the true deity. The tensions in his sacred
life are not the tensions of an abstract connection between the
divine and the human, but rather those of his humiliation in the
unity of the person. It was the intent of the church to say only
this and it was aware, that its words, often spoken antithetically
in the heat of conflict, could never replace the preaching of the
entire fullness of the Scriptures. It is the *Scriptures* which still
witness of him—more richly and profoundly than the language
of the church ever could. To open the eyes of man to this fact

was the intent of the confessions, which meant, not to impoverish the treasure of the church, but against all obscuration of the image of Christ to maintain an open perspective toward the Word of God which speaks of him who, as the living Lord, stands in the midst of our lives with his cheering words "Be of good courage: I have overcome the world."

The Impersonal Human Nature

CHAPTER XII

The Impersonal Human Nature

IN THE last few decades the problems involved in the idea
of the impersonal human nature of Christ have, rather
strikingly, been a focal point of interest. People have often
spoken of the impersonal nature of Christ as if it were positive
evidence of sterile theologizing, by which an attempt was
launched to make transparent, to the reasoning intellect, the
incomprehensible union of the two natures. Recently, fresh
attention has been solicited for this idea, while at the same time
fresh attacks on it were not wanting. Several theologians of
our day have expressed their views on it; hence we are all the
more interested to know whether it constitutes an important
theological problem or a sterile *theologoumenon*. Sharply opposed to the idea of the impersonal human nature are Korff
and Althaus, while its emphatic defenders have been Barth,
Miskotte, Gilg, and Relton. Hence there is every reason to ask
whether in the confession of the "vere deus, vere homo," and
in our theological reflection on it, we are confronted by the
doctrine of "anhypostasy."

Critics have judged that the doctrine fails to do justice to the
reality and completeness of the human nature of Christ; the
doctrine would, by its stress on the superiority of the divine
Logos, cause the shrinkage of the real humanity of Christ. In
order to feel the force of the criticism somewhat, we may start
with the strong verdict of Korff who combines his criticism
with the expressed conviction that Christological reflection
should call a halt at Chalcedon. It is impermissible, according
to Korff, to start making inferences from Chalcedon.[1] One of

---

1. Korff, *Christologie* I, page 194 ff.

the false conclusions thus drawn is, to his mind, the doctrine of
"anhypostasy." The idea that the human nature of Christ
should be "impersonal" is in immediate conflict, says Korff,
with the picture of the gospels. "The Jesus confronting us in
the gospels does not at all impress us as having only a human
nature which finds its personality in the divine logos."[2] On
the contrary, the gospels show us a "genuinely human consciousness." The human nature is not just an impersonal organ
of the Logos; we rather encounter "a struggling, praying, believing, human being."

This attitude of Jesus would be an impossibility "if the human ego, with its self-determination, should be lacking." The
doctrine of "anhypostasy" is an attempt to explain the "how"
of the Incarnation. It is an attempt to make plain how the two
natures can together form one person. The reasoning was:
there are two natures and but one person; hence the two natures cannot both be personal in character. But this imper-
sonality cannot apply to the divine nature, for it is in command.
Ergo: it is the human nature which lacks personality. This
conclusion is "completely logical," to be sure, and seems inescapable. But Korff refuses to draw any conclusions at this
point, "be they logical or illogical." For we have here a "sur-
plus" of consistency. And the results of such conclusions always become immediately visible: "it is plain that by the inferences made here, something has been detracted from the integrity of the human nature—an act which cannot be squared
with Chalcedon." For it is a fact that by the decision of a council (Korff is referring to the council of 553) something has
been denied the human nature, of which everyone would other-
wise have thought that it belonged to it. Thus arises a mixture
of things similar to that of monophysitism. For thus the human nature lacks its own *hypostasis,* its own personality, but
finds it in the divine nature. Korff further elucidates his point

2. Korff, *Ibid.,* page 198.

of view by rejecting the arguments of Barth for the doctrine; he asserts that the emphasis Barth puts on the doctrine is part and parcel of his inclination to underestimate the significance of the humanity in Christ. All attempts to make this doctrine acceptable cannot annul the fact that in this doctrine the human nature of Christ is "beheaded," that is, robbed of something essential: the person. In summarizing Korff's position, we can say that he wants to maintain the integrity of the human nature and that in the doctrine of "anhypostasy" he discovers a certain form of Docetism which is radically in conflict with the picture of Christ as given in the Gospels.

Althaus is also a strong opponent of this doctrine. He thinks too, that it constitutes a violation to the genuine humanity of Jesus and thus to the genuineness of the Incarnation.[3] The doctrine is untenable. "One cannot separate the nature from the person. Human personality is an essential constituent of human nature. Hence 'anhypostasy' abolishes the true humanity of Jesus, his believing and praying human ego, the truth of his being tempted—the Logos cannot be tempted." People arrived at the idea because they could not bear the tension—the full paradox—of the "true God and true man" and wished, in a theory of the God-man, to *conceive* the deity and humanity of Christ *together* in one person. This may be consistently in line with an objective theory, but it is not the way of faith.

*   *   *

For the time being the above criticism will be sufficient to cast in sharp relief the core of the discussion and to bring out the importance of the problem. At stake, in the criticism, is the truly human nature of Christ. The important question which must be answered is whether this doctrine, if not by intention, then by consequence, detracts from the human nature. The peculiar thing is that some adherents of the doctrine also insist, with great emphasis, on the integrity of human nature of

---

3. Althaus, *Die Christliche Wahrheit,* II, page 225.

Christ. Hence it is important that we now devote our attention to the arguments of those who believe they should defend this doctrine. First of all we wish to call attention to the view of Karl Barth who presented it already in 1927. He regarded it especially as an expression of the fact that God, as acting Person, is the subject of the Incarnation.[4] The subjectivity of God is in supreme control also in the Incarnation. "His humanity is but a predicate of his deity." The reality of the humanity of Christ stands or falls with the action of God. "That is the well-founded meaning of the doctrine—defended unanimously by ancient theology, by Catholics, Lutherans, and Calvinists—of the 'Anhypostasy' and 'Enhypostasy' of the human nature of Christ."[5]

With *"anhypostasy"* is meant that the human nature of Christ cannot exist for a moment outside the Logos, while *"enhypostasy"* indicates that the reality of the human nature is concretely that of the acting Lord. That recent theology should reject this doctrine with such strong aversion proves its deep lack of realism. For this doctrine is uncannily true to life: it puts the whole problem of Christ, without ambiguity, "in the decisiveness of the divine act and of human faith." He refers in later years,[6] to the decision of 553 when, in his opinion, the doctrine was elevated to the status of dogma with this intention: "to resist the concept of a dual existence of Christ, namely, as Logos and as human being—a concept which must necessarily go back either to Docetism or to Ebionitism." Barth defends "anhypostasy" against what he considers the primitive argument: that it detracts from the human nature, hence the charge of Docetism. This argument is based on a misunderstanding of the Latin word *impersonalitas.* "What the human nature of Christ lacks according to the old doctrine is not that, however, which we call personality," for

---

4. Barth, *Prolegomena*, 1927, page 262.
5. *Ibid.*, page 264.
6. Barth, *Kirchliche Dogmatik*, I, 2, pages 178 ff.

that was called individuality and that was not denied the human nature of Christ. But *personalitas* was regarded as being "that which we call 'existence'."[7] Hence the import of the doctrine of "anhypostasy" was "that the flesh of Christ by itself has no existence (Dasein)"; expressed positively: "The flesh of Christ has its existence through the Word and in the Word which is God himself in his quality of Revealer and Reconciler." Hence "anhypostasy" refers to the reality of a divine act of sovereignty in distinction from all other events. "He *exists* as such, however, only in virtue of the divine Word." The man Jesus Christ as such has no separate mode of existence, no life or being which one could consider, or which could have significance, by and for itself; the man Jesus Christ has his existence immediately and exclusively in the existence of the eternal Son of God.[8] By means of the "anhypostasy" Barth wants to resist the danger of Ebionitism which proceeds from the personality, the apotheosis, of a man who so impressed people that they cried out: "He is God"[9]— a theory which corresponds to Adoptionism.

Hence, according to Barth, the point at issue is not at all a form of Docetism. Nothing is detracted from the completeness and integrity of the human nature of Christ but there *is* a rejection of an abstract, isolated existence of the man Jesus of Nazareth.

*   *   *

This last point of view also emerges sharply in the writing of W. J. Aalders, who speaks of the term "enhypostasy," by which theology, says he, tried to express the union of the divine and human in Christ.[10] It expresses, on his view, that the divine person is in command of the existence of the God-man. "The human person is lacking," or rather, it has its personal existence in the logos. In other words, "the human nature is

7. Barth, *Ibid.*, page 180.
8. Barth, *De Apostolische Geloofsbelijdenis*, 1935, page 83.
9. Barth, *Kirchliche Dogmatik* I, 1, 422.
10. W. J. Aalders, *De Incarnatie*, page 159.

not beheaded, but over-arched." There is nothing new in the idea; it merely says "that the humanity is not an independent person contracting a personal union with the deity. To that extent it is *anhypostatos,* without a person." The human exists in the divine logos. Leontius of Byzantium is in danger, thanks to Aristotle, of allowing the divine nature to become the form of the human nature which is matter.[11] Thus the mystery of Christ would be deprived of its splendor. But later the term "enhypostasy" meant only "the denial of a mechanical, and the affirmation of an organic relationship between the divine and the human in Christ."[12] The humanity is taken up into the personal existence of the Son of God. Aalders mentions as the adherents of the doctrine thus understood: Damascene, Thomas, Calvin, Zanchius, Bavinck, and Barth.[13] None of these would detract from the humanity, but to them it would be, without residue, the *organ* of him who took it into his service. The humanity, so far from being truncated, is elevated and glorified by its union with the deity in the person of the Son of God.

For the purpose of illustration we would still refer to Bavinck's point of view. He says that the union of the two natures cannot be thought to be other "than the union of the person of the Son with an impersonal human nature."[14] For if the human nature in Christ had a personal existence of its own, then Christ would be merely a man living in close communion with God. By an impersonal human nature Bavinck does not mean "human nature in its generality"—a Platonic idea. Indeed not: the human nature in Christ was certainly individual, as was evident in certain qualities; but he was not an individual among other individuals, for the human nature in him had no personal subsistence next to that of the Logos. From the beginning the Holy Spirit so equipped it for its union with the Logos

---

11. See H. M. Relton, *A Study in Christology,* 1929, pages 69 ff.
12. Aalders, *Ibid..* page 161.
13. *Ibid.,* page 357.
14. Bavinck, *Ibid.,* III, page 290.

and its Mediatorial task that it could represent in that Logos the whole human race and be the Mediator of God for all men, for all generations, and social levels, and ages, and centuries, and places. Bavinck's meaning is plain. The idea is not to detract even a particle from the genuine humanity of Christ but the point is simply "that the human nature formed in and out of Mary did *not for a moment exist by and for itself*" but from the earliest moment of conception was united with, and taken up into, the person of the Son."[15] Hence Bavinck resists the idea that this the human nature would be made incomplete. The human nature, though without any deficiency, is thus subordinate to the Logos.

* * *

After this survey of views pro and con it is plain that the heart of the matter consists in the problem of the genuineness of the human nature in Christ. One can condense it into the question whether the term "anhypostasy" does, or does not, lead into monophysitism. In answering the question one must make the proper distinctions. One can ask first of all what Leonitus of Byzantium thought of this problem; and then, what the church confessed and theology averred regarding "anhypostasy." In this connection it will be hard to deny that the danger of monophysitism persistently threatens. Still in one's evaluation of theology one must guard against making snap judgments. For it appears again and again that the church was keenly vigilant against the great danger of Docetism. It condemned not only Apollinaris and Eutyches but, in 680, also monotheletism. It is very remarkable that Korff rejects both the "anhypostasy" *and* the decision of the church against monotheletism. He regards "anhypostasy" as a violation of the human nature, whereas the church in 680 set its jaws against precisely such a violation in the form of monotheletism. Hence the necessity of asking what is meant by "anhypostasy" remains. But one will, in any case, have to take account of the

15. Bavinck, *Ibid.,* III page 291. Italics ours.

fact that the term is repeatedly used *without any intent of detracting even the smallest constituent from the human nature of Christ.*

This intent was clearly visible in the theory of Apollinaris. He manipulated his anthropological distinctions in such a way that the Logos took the place of *one* of the human constituents. But when, in Reformed theology, the term "anhypostasy" is used, the issue is not one of *truncating* the human nature but one of *uniting* it with the Logos. Hence several enthusiastic supporters of Chalcedon made use of the term. In Chalcedon they saw that the recognition of the true deity and the true humanity forced them to acknowledge that this union between God and man did not detract from the majesty of the Godhead. From this acknowledgement emerged the idea of "anhypostasy." They would speak of a union, but the union was specifically that of the Son of God, truly God, and Light of Light, *with the human nature.* The union was not one of two substances mysteriously associating themselves, but a union resulting from the assumption *by the person of the Son* of true humanity. Hence in evaluating the idea of "anhypostasy" one must always ask whether the rationale behind it is sound. For it is plain that it is no great trick for monophysitism to teach, under cover of this term, that the humanity of Christ is absorbed by the divine. But one may not, without further inquiry, judge every theology employing the term by this danger. Fairness in judgment must be the watch-word in this profoundly important question. This is evident from the difference between the terms "anhypostasy" and "enhypostasy." We repeatedly observe that the first is meant to carry the meaning of the second: to express that the human nature does not subsist by itself but has its existence only in the divine Logos. When this was meant it is plain that the intent was not to truncate the human nature but to respect the content of Chalcedon. In view of the dangers of monophysitism it can be understood that people frequently gave preference to the expression "enhypostasy," to avoid the undesirable connotation of the word "impersonal." By means of the term "enhypostasy" they intended to oppose Ebionitism, or its modern relatives, and Nestorianism; they wished to guard against making the human nature something independent and thus to preserve the mystery. We must remember, therefore, that the church must be concerned, not to sanction certain scientific terms, but to watch closely the *import* of the terms used to give expression to the mystery of the Christian faith.

* * *

Still it remains a noteworthy fact that many regard the term "anhypostasy" as implying an evaporation of the human nature of Christ. When Aalders spoke, for instance, of an "over-arching" of the human nature, Korff reacted by saying that he could not accept this, since the human nature would thus in the end become an impersonal organ in the service of the divine nature. That was it: the "mere organ" idea was a violation of the living, dynamic, full humanity of Christ. How necessary it is for those who believe they may employ the term to make it impossible that they should be accused of paving the way to a dangerous Docetism. In order to cultivate a community of faith on the foundation of Chalcedon we must be on our guard lest our use of terms block the way.

Here we run into a controversy within the Reformed churches which we cannot fairly ignore. We are referring to the discussion which arose on the impersonal nature of Christ. The immediate occasion of this discussion was the fact that Vollenhoven made a few Christological pronouncements and offered several objections to "anhypostatos" as a philosophical term. At the same time Vollenhoven wished fully to maintain the confession of the personal union. But he was attacked by Hepp who believed that the idea of the impersonal human nature of Christ constituted, not just a given theological construction, but a doctrine having confessional status. From this

summary it will be sufficiently clear that it is not superfluous
to consider this controversy more closely.

* * *

The point at which we must begin was a remark Vollenhoven made about the word "impersonal." He judged that
around the year 360 the term meant: "not having a (divine)
Person." In this connection he writes that there are also
others who say that the human nature was not im-Personal
but impersonal. He then comments: "The term, so conceived,
is monophysite and hence to be rejected."[16] Hence, by the term
"impersonal," Vollenhoven means; not having a human person.
Thus we are directly concerned with the question under discussion.

One could say that Vollenhoven's criticism has points of
agreement with that of Korff, since he, like Korff, perceives
in the term "anhypostasy" a tendency toward monophysitism
and believes the truly human nature of Christ to be imperilled
by it. This appears plainly from Vollenhoven's view of the entire Christological conflict, and in particular, from his view of
Apollinaris, who truncated the human nature of Christ by sub-
stituting the Logos for something belonging to the human nature. Vollenhoven regards this as a deadly danger.[17] The Cap-
padocians were right, to his mind, when they declared over
against Apollinaris "that if Christ was and is not a complete
human being, then his own are not completely redeemed by
his suffering either," and "with the satisfaction also the certainty of faith was undermined." In the background of Apollinaris' thinking he discovers the idea of the sovereignty of
the human *pneuma* which does not permit itself to be united
with the Logos. The formulations of Apollinaris must be understood in the light of this concept of sovereignty. Further
illumination of this fact comes with Vollenhoven's appreciative

16. D. H. Th. Vollenhoven, *Het Calvinisme en de Reformatie van de wijsbegeerte*, 1933, page 189 (Note).
17. *Ibid.*, page 133.

observation that Augustine distinguishes the Person from the person, and therefore does not have to wrestle with the problem of two "wills," "hypostases," and "egos" of equal rank. Vollenhoven speaks therefore of the "unique relationship between God and man in the Mediator." And so he also rejects Nestorius who posits only a moral union between two persons, both of them sovereign and hence capable only of a moral union. In these conceptions, to our mind, lies the background of Vollenhoven's criticism of the "anhypostatos." If "anhypostatos" means: not having a human person, then the reality of the human nature is compressed into something less than human and one runs into monophysitism. Then the mystery of a full union is violated. He believes that the word "impersonal" issues from a theory of two equally sovereign personal entities. In view of these conceptions it is plainly unfair to charge Vollenhoven with having done an injustice to the fullness of the union of the two natures in the person of the Mediator. All depends on the meaning assigned to the terms used. The problem also became significant for the church because Hepp came to the conclusion, in view of Vollenhoven's criticism, that he departed from the confession with regard to the person of the Son. Hence, at this point of our discussion, we must consider the dogma of the church. Without going into all the aspects which have historical significance, we must confront the question whether the repudiation of the impersonal human nature does not indeed conflict with the Christological dogma of the Reformed Churches. Therefore we must now proceed to weigh the arguments adduced by Hepp.

* * *

Vollenhoven, says Hepp, is in conflict with the Reformed confessions. We can limit ourselves to Article 19 of the Belgic Confession where we read: "We believe that by this conception the person of the Son is inseparably united and connected with the human nature; so that there are not two Sons of God, nor two persons, but two natures united in one single person; yet each nature retains its own distinct properties." In view of the expression "nor two persons," Hepp asks: "Can one ever interpret this in any other way than that the one person is that of the Son?"[18] Though the term "anhypostatic" does not occur here, it is still plain, in his opinion, that the circumscription given can only mean that Christ's human nature had no human person; so that Vollenhoven's opinion on this point constitutes a serious departure from the confession. This argument returns also at other places: the unipersonality of Christ is practically equated with the doctrine of "anhypostasy."

If Vollenhoven were consistent, says Hepp, he should also proceed to call the Reformed confession monophysite. And so Hepp refers to Vollenhoven's position as "semi-Nestorian." With unequivocal clarity the confession teaches the impersonal human nature, thinks Hepp, and does not regard the absence of a human person as something which renders incomplete the humanity of Christ. Vollenhoven's position breaks up the unity of the person, according to Hepp. For if he disbelieves in an impersonal human nature, then he must regard this nature as personal and posit a divine and a human ego in Christ.

But this does not complete the picture. For the important point now is what one must understand by the word "person." Hepp observes that behind Vollenhoven's criticism there lurks a wrong concept of personality—the presupposition, namely, that a human being without personality is incomplete. The discussion at this point suddenly veers strongly into a non-confessional, scientific direction. According to Hepp, the absence of personality constitutes no threat to the genuinely human, because personality does not relate to humanity as such but to the human mode of existence. In man the personal always carries onesidedness with it. For this reason also it can be understood why there was in Christ no human person. "Were there in Christ a human person, then as man he would be

---

18. V. Hepp, *De vereniging van de beide naturen van Christus*, 1937, page 32.

necessarily onesided and need a complement." But that is not
the case. On the contrary we would deprive Christ of his glory
if we were to ascribe human personality to him and burden
him with human onesidedness.

In this discussion everything depends, patently enough, on
the content of the concept of personality. The whole argument
of Hepp rests upon his idea that personality implies onesidedness. One observes the difficulty of a position which would
demand that, for an understanding of the confession of the
church, one would have to operate with a given scientific concept of personality (wetenschappelijk persoonsbegrip). Hepp
and Vollenhoven obviously have diverse concepts of personality.
If the confession were really giving expression to such a scientific concept, we should have to make a choice. But it is our
conviction that this is not at all the case. Even without such
a choice it is possible to understand the non-scientific confession
of the church.[19] The confession says with emphasis that there
are not two Sons nor two persons, and clearly rejects all Nestorianism. The Son did not unite himself with an independently existing human being but with the human nature,
and that in a most mysterious manner. Hence there can be no
two Sons or two persons. This antithesis is today what it
was the fifth century. The confession does not declare what
belongs and what does not belong to the human nature, nor
does it describe the anthropology of its compositors. But it ex-

19. When the church condemned the teaching of Apollinaris it did not, by
that token, condemn his anthropology. When he said that the Logos assumed a human soul and a human body but not a human *pneuma,* the church
condemned his teaching as a threat to the completeness and genuineness of
Christ's human nature. But this condemnation did not imply at all that the
church sanctioned a trichotomous anthropology. The confession of the
church as regards the human nature of Christ — the *vere homo* — does not
rise and fall with the anthropologies of the day. One could take as a parallel the words of Paul in I Thess. 5:23: "And the God of peace himself
sanctify you wholly; and may your spirit and soul and body be preserved
entire . . ." Here Paul merely wishes to stress the *totality* of man without
implying a trichotomy. Compare the command of Christ to love God with
all one's heart, soul, mind, and strength (Matt. 22:37; Mark 12:30).

presses the confession of the entire church; and the church must continue its confessional conflict with anyone who separates the two natures or does violence to the mystery of his Person.

There is nothing in Article 19 of the Belgic Confession which indicates that the personal always implies onesidedness. For this we may be grateful, since now the confession is preserved from becoming a shuttle-cock in an anthropological debate. The Person of the Son is mentioned indeed as the One, who assumed the human nature from the flesh and blood of the virgin Mary. It is not a union, managed from without, of two substances but an act proceeding from the divine initiative of the Logos. He takes the human nature up into himself. Hence one may not infer from the formulation of Article 19 that the impersonal human nature of Christ is a doctrine of the church, but one may infer that the Logos did not unite himself with an independent human being. The difference is plain. In the first instance one is bound to indicate the concept of personality from which one proceeds in his thinking. Hepp is perfectly consistent when he promises to publish an account of his conception of personality later on. His criticism of anyone who objects to the term "impersonal" is part and parcel of this conception. In the second instance no scientific concept of personality is presupposed but there is an insistence on the mystery of the union of the two natures against all who regard the human nature as self-subsisting. The mystery resides in the fact that Christ, though he was not the *adopted* man Jesus of Nazareth, could still be a true and complete human being in the hypostatic union.

Vollenhoven is not concerned, as he writes with emphasis, to stress the personal in the human nature of Christ. But he does reject the dilemma: personal—impersonal.[20] His repudiation of the impersonal human nature does not issue from a desire to give independent significance to the human nature;

---

20. Vollenhoven, *Anhypostatos*, Philosophia Reformata, 1940, page 75.

and against Nestorians and Adoptionists he prefers the charge that they regard the human nature of the Mediator as a person even though it never existed independently.   This Vollenhoven regards as a plain and serious error, and he declares that he has always sincerely confessed the unity of the person.

*   *   *

In this connection it is important to note that Vollenhoven, with his views on the Person and the person, is perfectly well satisfied with the term "enhypostasy." He asserts that "anhypostasy" and "enhypostasy" may not be regarded as identical. "Enhypostasy" need not, on his view, be monophysite while in the term "anhypostasy" he always senses an element of "truncation." One will have to grant, however, that in Reformed and Lutheran theology the terms have been used repeatedly without any sharp distinction. In the word "anhypostatos" was then expressed that the human nature did not exist independently, while the word "enhypostasy" expressed that the human nature existed in the Logos.   And from the use of the term "anhypostatic," as current in these circles, one may certainly not infer monophysitism. All depends on the content of the term, specifically of the prefix "an."

On the other hand we can understand that from a historical point of view Vollenhoven senses a danger in the term "anhypostatic." How easily the term can serve as a cover for doing less than justice to the human nature! But the terms as such are not necessarily dangerous. Therefore one cannot regard a difference in the use of them as a confessional difference.[21] As long as it is plain why the church opposed the reduction of the human nature to something independent, people will be able to endorse the words of Article 19 "not two Sons of God, nor two

---

21. A. G. Honig, *Handboek van de Geref. Dogmatiek,* page 461: Honig believes that, though the term "impersonal human nature" is not *per se* objectionable, it is worth asking whether by avoiding it one does not prevent misunderstanding.   Article 19 of the Belgic Confession is perfectly lucid without it, page 402.

persons." When Polman discusses the Christology of Calvin and De Brés, both of whom acknowledge the mystery of the union, he adds in comment: "It has always struck me in their writings that they do not, or that they very seldom (and then only in discussion), speak of the impersonal human nature of Christ. Their thinking was too much Scripture-governed for them to get around to the term."[22] Their use of the term precisely in discussion is understandable in view of their polemics against an independently conceived human nature. "Impersonal" can then be used indeed without the connotation that some essential constituent of humanity is lacking in Christ. The obviousness with which the Belgic Confession speaks, according to Hepp, is a fact: but it is an obviousness, not of endorsing some scientific anthropology, but of rejecting every form of Adoptionism and Nestorianism.

* * *

Did the church in some way or other give the term "anhypostatos" confessional status? Everyone will agree that the creeds of the Netherlands do not have it. Hepp acknowledges too that though, in his opinion, the matter itself is clearly taught in the Belgic Confession, the term is not in it.[23] But the question remains whether an earlier council did not sanction the term. Candidates, eligible for consideration, are the Council of Constantinople convened in 553 and that of Frankfort convened in 794. No elaborate research is needed, however, to see that they did not use the term either. W. J. Aalders, the only man who appears to doubt whether or not this is true with respect to 794, obviously treats of the matter itself and not of the term. But it is very informative to see that in this conflict the church is concerned to reject the Adoptionism current in Spain during the eighth century. Against those who taught a human nature with an independent existence the church posited the inseparable union of the two natures in one

22. A. D. R. Polman, *Geloofsbelijdenis,* II, pages 308.
23. Hepp, *Ibid.,* page 32.

person. The same antithesis appears in the pronouncement of
785 which says of the errors of the Adoptionists that no one
but Nestorius dared voice such blasphemy—that of the *adopted*
son of God.[24] In this area one never encounters the problem
of a scientific anthropology but one does meet the resistance of
the church to an independently conceived human nature of
Christ.

* * *

The conflict over the impersonal human nature can be placed
in still bolder relief by reference to the polemic conducted by
Kuyper in a chapter bearing the expressive title: "No Assumption of a Human Person.[25] Kuyper regards it a question of the
greatest moment whether or not Jesus Christ assumed a human
person. In this chapter he opposes those who, with Fichte, dote
on the idea of personality—an idea which the Scriptures do not
mention. This concept became more and more important to
theology when the humanity of Christ began increasingly to
occupy the foreground. Then Kuyper polemicizes against those
who speak by preference of the humanization of God and mean
that the essence of God becomes manifest in a human being.
He also opposes those who put the human personality of Jesus, through which God manifests himself, at the center of their
theology. But thus, says Kuyper, we lose our Mediator. In
the place of these theories Kuyper places the personal union of
the divine and the human nature. That is the meaning of this
thesis that Christ did not assume a human person. His polemics was directed against the modern form of the heresy
which conceives the union in Christ as an act of revelation in
the independent person of Jesus Christ.[26]

* * *

It should be sufficiently plain now that it is of surpassing
significance *how* the assumption of the human nature is spoken

---

24. Denzinger, *Ibid.*, page 299.
25. "Geen menselijke persoon aangenomen," in *Vleeschwording des
Woords*, Ch. VIII.
26. See also his *E Voto*, I, pages 323 and 370 ff.

of. The danger of Adoptionism is a constant one to the church. Repeatedly it was confronted by the question as to how to escape Adoptionism without becoming monophysite. The problems under discussion emerge clearly into view when we consider the Spanish Adoptionism already mentioned. The key-word employed to give clarity to Christology, was the word "adoptio." Felix of Urgel, for instance, taught that the human being adopted by the Son of God must be sharply distinguished from Christ who, as God's own Son without adoption, was the second person of the Trinity. The man Jesus was predestined to be united with the Son of God. This Adoptionism was condemned by the Western Church in 792 (Regensburg), in 794 (Frankfort), and in 799 (Aken), because the church regarded this as a doctrine of two persons and spoke explicitly of the Nestorian impiety by which Christ was divided into two persons: God's own Son and the adopted son.[27] Seeberg calls this condemnation of Adoptionism fatal for the development of Christological dogma. His judgment is that the church, in this conflict, was guilty of a one-sided fixation of the confession of the deity and excluded further reflection on the humanity of Christ. Harnack virtually comes to the same conclusion. In his opinion, Elipandus was a faithful adherent of the Augustinian-Chalcedonian Christology, and every Westerner still spoke of the *assumptio hominis* and certainly not just of the *assumptio humanae naturae*. To Harnack, as well as to Seeberg, it is a question why the church repudiated Adoptionism. It would have been intelligible, were the Greek conception predominant, since it so stressed the participation of the human nature in the Logos and its glory that barely any duality was left.[28] Here Greek mysticism, with its complete and inseparable fusion of the divine and human, is in charge. But in the West? Harnack believes that in the West also the mystical view of unity increasingly gained ground and

27. Seeberg, *Dogmengeschichte*, III, page 57.
28. Harnack, *Dogmengeschichte*, III, 257.

that the rejection of Adoptionism in Spain is to be understood in view of this mysticism. But there, in his opinion, lies the tragedy of this development. Elipandus and Felix still wanted to stress the complete humanity in Christ. The result of the condemnation of their doctrine was that the Western-Augustinian Christology with its last, but significant, remnant of a historical view of Christ was sidetracked. Not that Harnack himself accepted this Christology. On the contrary: its defeat in Spain was its own fault since it still operated with the Divine Logos as existing behind the adopted man Jesus. But at least there was in it some reminiscence of the vital human picture of Jesus of Nazareth. The rejection of Adoptionism completely mutilated this picture. Though Elipandus warned passionately against the violation of the real humanity of Christ, hence, against the danger of Docetism, the church—in the clutch of mysticism—refused to listen and in an unhappy hour abandoned the valuable elements of the Augustinian tradition. And so they teach that the divine Logos "assumed the impersonal human nature and amalgamated it in the full unity of his being." And Alcuin [29] makes just as clean a sweep of the data of the gospels as the monophysite and crypto-monophysite Greeks. To the Western theologians Christ was no longer in any respect a human person, since the humanity had been deified in the mystery of the Incarnation.

In all of his criticism Harnack's strong aversion to Chalcedon comes to expression. He believes Adoptionism to be continuous with Chalcedon and thinks he can maintain this view by generalizing the concept "adoptio." He is undoubtedly right when he says that the term "adoptio" already occurred in the Christology of Augustine. But he must himself agree that this term did not occur too frequently in the older literature. But Harnack's construction, generated by his aversion to the church's Christology, makes him ignore this fact; and he takes

29. Court theologian of Charlemagne, and opponent of the Adoptionist Christology.

it ill of Alcuin that he regards the term "adoptio" as a novelty. In his opinion, it is essentially Augustinian and correct. He fails to see that in the use of that word there may be a radical difference—as, for instance, between Augustine and a pure-bred Nestorian. Harnack has to agree, too, that Felix went further in this respect than Augustine. Felix was not content to speak of adoption and to unite this idea with the personal unity, but "he sharply divorced the two natures and tried at the same time to picture clearly how the adoption was accomplished." Thus, on the basis of adoption, he arrived at the concept of a man united with the deity and asserted that Christ had two fathers: a natural father, David, and an adoptive father, God, and that one could therefore speak of a double birth. Harnack acknowledges it all but he still maintains that the West abandoned both Augustine and Chalcedon (!) for the sake of a mystical concept of the Divine mystery. From the preceding it is plain that Harnack seriously fails to do justice to the true motives of the Christological struggle. The church rejected Adoptionism, not because this heresy championed the reality of the human nature of Christ, but because it violated the mystery of the unity of the person in Christ by positing a duality of persons.

*   *   *

In the controversy over Adoptionism lies the most obvious suggestion, expressed historically, for the solution of the conflict concerning the impersonal human nature. If Harnack be right, the church, both in the Middle Ages and in the period of the Reformation, lapsed into a monophysite Docetism. But if one is not prejudiced against Chalcedon, one may see also another possibility. That was the position of the church when it opposed Adoptionism, not from monophysite motives, but from respect for the Incarnate Word. Adoptionism stressed the person of Jesus; and monophysitism sought the mystery of the unity in the one theanthropic nature in which it adored the "mystery."

Against both heresies the church was on its guard. Since that time the danger of either heresy is still real. In the history of dogma one can see warnings in either direction. From dualistic motives one can employ the concept of adoption with the intent to save the humanity in Christ and, despite this good intention, still get lost in a consistent Adoptionism. One can *also* employ the concept of the impersonal human nature because one regards the humanity of Christ more or less submerged in the divine nature. Chalcedon avoids both errors. For this reason the issue in the struggle for a sound Christology can never be settled by the term "impersonal nature." There is too much difference in its use and interpretation, and if the issue were to be settled here, the church would be called upon to determine its position in the fixation of a concept of personality. We must learn to see that the terms, by which the church in its laborious struggle expressed its position, are historically and often antithetically conditioned. The term "impersonal nature" repeatedly carried with it the threat of a genuine Docetism. But it has also on several occasions been employed to mean "in-personal," that is, to maintain that the natures retained their distinct properties (Chalcedon).

The idea was not to add a new element to Chalcedon, but to express that in the union of the two natures the Son of God actively assumed the human nature. There was not a monophysite or Docetic element in this train of thought. But for this reason the church had no need at all of the dogmatic or confessional fixation of the terms "enhypostatic" or "anhypostatic." The ways in which one can withdraw his consent from the "vere Deus, vere homo" are too dangerous and too subtle for the church to comfort itself with the scientific fixation of a given term. The church *had* already confessed that the divine nature retained its properties in the union. Christ was truly

God when he united himself with the human nature—this the church confessed.

This union is incomparable with anything else because it was the Son of God who assumed the human nature. The incarnation is an act of the Logos and apart from this act the human nature cannot for a moment exist or even be conceived. Hence the rejection of Adoptionism; hence the rejection of Docetism. It has been a blessing for the church, as we remarked earlier, that it did not, in view of the importance of the divine nature, depreciate the human. But it was also a blessing that it did not regard the Incarnation as an irrational, paradoxical mystery, a contradictory association of two substances, but rather as an act of the Son of God. And when in the Reformation period the problem of the union of the two natures was again a live issue, now in response to the Lutheran Christology, the Reformed churches, and Reformed theology, again took seriously—not some irrational superiority of the divine but—the truth of Christ's deity according to the Scriptures; and it is a dark page in the history of dogma that this defense came to be known by the horrible name "extra-Calvinisticum." In reality the issue is that of the truth which is preached in the church of Christ, and not one belonging merely to the field of theology. It is the proclamation of the "truly God and truly man"; and the church did not attempt to make this mystery transparent but rather preached in the Scriptural contexts of reconciliation. Only by faith can the unity of the Christ, as the Scriptures present it to us, be understood. And this understanding is not a comprehension of the great mystery, but rather a life of communion with him who, though he was the Son, yet became one of us. And one can reverence the mystery only by faith in him, whom to know is eternal life.

Christ Incognito?

CHAPTER XIII

Christ Incognito?

UNTIL now we have been concerned with various aspects of the confession of the church as touching Jesus Christ. This confession can be summarized in the words "vere Deus, vere homo." Again and again we encountered that which Calvin designates as the "ineffable mystery" of the act of God in the Incarnation of the Word. Always the church was conscious that it could not comprehend the Incarnation and was constantly on the alert against various attempts to make transparent to the rational intellect the union of the two natures in Christ. In the history of dogma one may observe plainly that wherever such attempts are made there is involved a detraction either from the duality of the two natures or from the unity of the person. But this does not mean that the mere assertion of the mysteriousness of the Incarnation will exorcise all dangers. It does seem plain from that assertion that the mystery is not exhaustively penetrable to the rational mind, but it is also possible, by means of an appeal to mystery, to derogate from the confession of the church; this confession is then charged, in view of its positive pronouncements, with the attempt to give a rational explanation to the mystery. Hence the mere acknowledgment of mystery is no sufficient guarantee. By means of it one can oppose rationalism but also detract from the revelation of God. The word "mystery" sometimes becomes a very vague indication of the suprarational or irrational and no attempt is made to do justice to the revelation concerning Jesus Christ. By this we do not mean that every use of the word "mystery" is illegitimate unless it refers directly to the fact of the Incarnation or the cross. In Scripture itself, the word "mystery" is employed in various ways. Most frequently it occurs with immediate reference to Christ whom Paul calls the mystery of God (Col. 2:2). Paul also preaches to the church the mystery of the crucified Christ, the word of the Cross (I Cor. 2:1,7; Col. 1:27), and speaks of the mystery of God revealed in the flesh (I Tim. 3:6). But the word mystery also occurs in a more general sense. Bornkamm is right when he says: "The concept 'mysterion' does not in all places of the New Testament derive its content from the revelation of Christ."[1] The word varies in its specific meaning within the context of the Gospel, but is also used with reference to the Anti-Christ: the lawless one is already operative in the mystery of lawlessness (II Thess. 2:7) which, in its full scope and true nature, is still to be revealed; and in Revelation we read that the woman sitting on the scarlet-colored beast has the name "Mystery" written on her forehead (Rev. 17:5). Hence also in the kingdom of the Anti-Christ there is a "mystery"—a peculiar and dangerous mode of working against which the church must be warned with eschatological seriousness.[2]

With this antithetic exception, the word "mystery" in the New Testament relates to the mystery of Christ, to the acts of God in Christ; and there is a danger that when the general concept of mystery—as something exceeding our powers of understanding—is applied to the redemption of God, the central facts of revelation are obscured. In popular usage, one must admit, the word has this formal and general significance. It is used in varied contexts to indicate the incomprehensible aspects of a given matter. Then the intent is not to state concretely what the content of the "mysterion" is, nor that it is the

---

1. In Kittel, *Wörterbuch*, IV, page 829.
2. Compare the *mystery* (II Thess. 2:7) with the *revelation* (apokalupsis) of the lawless one (II Thess. 2:8).

mystery of *God,* but merely to give a formal qualification of the irrational. Hence arose the danger of approaching the dogma of the church with some such formal concept of mystery. If only people had limited themselves to the way in which Scripture speaks about the mystery of Christ in a relation of antithesis to the mystery of the works of the Anti-Christ, then this danger could have been resisted. But they began to apply this word, in a vague, undefined sense, to salvation, and so it became possible for Heering, by means of the formal concept, to oppose the church's confession of the Incarnation—a supposed attempt to transcend the mystery. We then arrive at what Bornkamm has said: "In the church of a later day a dogma was sometimes plainly called 'mysterion' because it was not accessible to the intellect, even to that of believers, and would be profaned by discussion or heretical opposition." And he adds: "The dubious result which could flow from this conception of dogma evinces itself in the fact that the mystery was now separated from the kerygma with which Paul had decidedly classified." Thus the mystery of salvation could become a phenomenon on a level with intriguing mystery-religions. In the Eastern church especially we see the danger written large when in the consequences of monophysitism it becomes evident that the mystery is experienced as something irrational.

Hence the big question in any discussion of mystery is: what is understood by it and is it possible by a reference to it to offer resistance to the reduction of faith and dogma to something irrational.[3] In this reduction there is an appearance of Christian humility, but at bottom it is an emptying of the confession of the church. Without denying anyone the right to use the word "mystery" with reference to the incomprehensibilities of life, one will have to ask whether, in using the word with reference to the Christian faith, one does not stand in continual need of checking it with the New Testament which asks of us

3. As an example we refer to Rudolf Otto, *Das Heilige,* and *Reich Gottes und Menschensohn,* page 205.

that, in confessing mystery, we stand truly on the one foundation: the word of the cross, the mystery of God, Jesus Christ. This does not mean that the element of incomprehensibility does not play a role in the biblical message. Scripture warns repeatedly against the overestimation of the human mind which tries to penetrate rationally into the work of God. The Old and New Testament erect a high wall against anyone who tries intellectually to overmaster God and warn that "there is no searching of his understanding" (Isaiah 40:28). Paul cries out in amazement at the ways of God: "how unsearchable are his judgments, and his ways past tracing out." (Rom. 11:33).

But one may never approach or qualify the redemption of God in terms of the general concept of incomprehensibility. The incomprehensibility of God's work is not on a level with the puzzles in which human life abounds. It is the incomprehensibility of the work of God, which was disclosed to us in his Word. Hence we may never, by means of a vague appeal to mystery, oppose the man who believes on Scriptural grounds in the plain, though incomprehensible, reality of the mystery of God.[4]

* * *

All this is of great significance for the confession of Jesus Christ. And therefore we wish to devote special attention to a problem which has recently come to repeated expression and which has a direct bearing on this mystery. In our day we recurrently encounter the attempt to approach the union of the two natures in terms of mystery. The subject of special consideration is, then, the relationship between the two natures in connection with the revelational significance of Jesus Christ. The aim is not to make this relationship transparent but rather

4. See also Calvin on "human curiosity which no barriers can restrain from wandering into forbidden labyrinths," on the one hand (*Institutes* III, XXI, 1); and, on the other, on the excessive moderation which would "teach men to avoid all questions concerning it." "To observe, therefore, the legitimate boundary on this side also, we must recur to the word of the Lord, which affords a certain rule for the understanding" (*Ibid.*, III, XXI, 3: chapter on Predestination).

to point out the incomprehensibility of the revelation of God in the hiddenness of the *flesh*. Hence we wish to treat the idea of the *Christological incognito*.

*   *   *

In the treatment of the confession of Jesus Christ we cannot, obviously, avoid this question. All that we have discussed till now converges, as it were, on the questions still to be considered in connection with the revelation touching Jesus Christ. One can provisionally describe the idea under discussion by saying that the humanity of Christ does not as such *reveal*, but rather *conceals*, God. It is again a question of the union of the two natures but now particularly under the aspect of its revelational significance. In order to get some notion of the import of this idea we shall consider the views of Emil Brunner who has elaborated it. His basic thesis is that the Incarnation of Christ is directly antipodal to all pagan religion and mythology because in paganism the idea is always the "immediate knowability of God."[5] The transcendent deity suddenly appears to men in a marvellous theophany and is, by this act, directly knowable. The God of the biblical revelation is quite different and approaches us in quite another mode. His revelation is always concealment also. The point is not to provide a divine oracle but "the condescension of God, the theme of the whole Bible," which implies a complete entering into of human, earthly reality. The great mystery is the Word become flesh; and in the flesh is manifest the absolute humility, for it is most distant from the divine glory. Paul, says Brunner, even reached for a still stronger word: in the likeness of sinful flesh. "The concealment of the divine in the non-divine—in that which was not only dissimilar but also antithetic to him—cannot be expressed more strongly." In this revelation of Christ we confront the complete concealment of his glory and "absolute unknowability." God reveals himself in Jesus

---

5. E. Brunner, *Der Mittler*, 1927, page 294.

Christ but he does it in the total hiddenness of the flesh. Hence the immediate vision of him is excluded, and only by faith can one overcome the offense and learn to understand the revelation in the concealment. Brunner appeals with emphasis to Kierkegaard who spoke in this connection of "the most profound Incognito or the most impenetrable unknowability."[6] Revelation does not suspend the concealment, but comes to us in the form of mystery. Thus it places man before the decision between acceptance or offense. God never reveals himself directly, but always indirectly: that is in a human being. The main revelational category of Christ's entire life is that of the incognito: revelation in absolute concealment.

In this connection Brunner refers to the picture of Christ given in the gospel of John.[7] This picture is by no means one which can be observed by the senses. Were this the case, it would be an example par excellence of a direct revelation, of a direct knowability which would suspend the incognito. This would imply a mingling of the divine and the human in Christ. The bridge which theology crossed in this direction is the "fatal doctrine of the communication of properties." The glory of the Son of God would then glitter without concealment before the eyes of all. Brunner is grateful to historical criticism

---

6. *Ibid.*, page 296; Brunner's dependence on Kierkegaard appears not only from his references to Kierkegaard but also from the writings of the latter himself. See Kierkegaard, *Einübung in das Christentum* (Gesamm. Werke, second printing, vol. 9; Gottsched und Schrempf) in which the incognito-idea plays a dominant role. In this work we encounter all the concepts which play a role in dialectic theology and which Brunner has taken over: the possibility of offense in connection with this revelation (65); the paradox (20); the servant-form and revelation (18); contemporaneity (83); incognito (115 and passim); direct communication (115) and its impossibility (117); see, for this last idea, Brunner's quotation from Kierkegaard: "If there is to be direct communication — really direct — then one must, if possible, drop the incognito," Brunner, *Ibid.*, page 117. See *Einübung*, page 123: "The possibility of offense consists in the refusal to grant a direct communication" and "direct communication is paganism," page 127. The incognito-idea, according to Kierkegaard, was one of his most important. Compare W. Ruttenbeck, S. Kierkegaard, *Der Chr. Denker und sein Werk*, 1929, page 197. About the offense, see Kierkegaard, *Die Krankheit zum Tode.*
7. *Ibid.*, page 306.

for having broken through the crust of theology and having opened our eyes to the true humanity of Christ in the flesh. Thus the idea of the incognito could assume its prominence and, against this background, the decision of faith could come into its own. Here, too, lies the ground for Brunner's strong aversion to the doctrine of the virgin birth; for by this doctrine the deity of Christ is explicated and made metaphysically evident. The Incarnation of Christ, in theology, is made into a miracle which radically eliminates the incognito.[8]

We confront here a certain conception of the significance of the human nature of Christ.[9] The core consists in the dialectical relationship between self-disclosure and concealment. Concealment, to Brunner's mind, is a strong motif in revelation, as appears from his comparison between Paul's phrase "in the likeness of sinful flesh" (Rom. 8:3) and the words "without sin" in the epistle to the Hebrews (4:15). And he poses a remarkable question: "Is this the same that is meant by the strong Pauline expression?"[10]   But he cautiously adds: "We cannot be exactly sure, but there is no ground for thinking that Paul wished to cross this boundary-line." One might ask what he means by this comparison between Paul and the epistle to the Hebrews, and refer to other statements in Paul which indicate plainly that we need not be in doubt about Paul on this point. But the example is very illustrative of Brunner's views. He is continually afraid that somehow or other people will detract from the hiddenness of God in the flesh of Jesus Christ and, by positing a direct encounter, a direct theophany, undermine the seriousness of the decision of faith. Revelation in concealment means to Brunner that "Christ can be mistaken for any man at all: hence one can only believe in

---

8. *Ibid.*, page 309.

9. The chapter in which Brunner develops his views on the idea of incognito is entitled: *The Significance of the Humanity.*

10. Brunner, *Dogmatik* II, page 378.

him."[11]   Therefore the believer is no less interested in Christ's true humanity than in his deity.   And his true humanity implies concealment in the flesh without direct knowability and without glory.   The church has too much neglected this truth and regarded the gospels too much as reportorial description instead of regarding them as the testimonies of what faith has discovered amidst concealment.[12]   And when this is neglected, Christ's humanity becomes a direct revelation of his deity.   The light radiates in all directions and the hidden glory seen by faith is exchanged for the real appearance of Christ which is visible to all.   But then one has lost the gospel since this is intrinsically bound up with the possibility of regarding Jesus as an ordinary human being.[13]

If the glory attested to in the kerygma had belonged visibly to the earthly life of Jesus, one could no longer maintain the true humanity in Christ.   The God-man would have been the *God*-man, recognizable as such to all and . . . the indirectness of communication would be eliminated.   The incognito would be no more.

*   *   *

Despite all the difference existing between Barth and Brunner, we nonetheless encounter in Barth the same Christological climate.   This becomes evident particularly when he treats of the instruments of revelation.   For then he speaks of the "Welthaftigkeit" of revelation, by which it is absolutely necessary that revelation take place in the hiddenness of the flesh. It is not visible to the senses but becomes manifest in folly and weakness.   It is concealment; it never takes us by surprise in a superficial, miraculous, and obvious manner but places us before an unavoidable decision.   Revelation always takes place in such a manner that without faith one can never distinguish

11. *Ibid.*, page 302.
12. Brunner, *Der Mittler*, page 306: "A false picture emerges as soon as it is read with the eyes of the secular historian and it is mistaken for a biography."
13. *Ibid.*, page 160.

it from that which is non-revelational. The nature of revelation is not such as to impress us with its striking character. On the contrary: it assumes human forms and enters into the world of the flesh. There is even a certain tension between the revealing God and the "material" in which he reveals himself. This material is not in the least suited to be instrumental to·revelation. This concept of revelation has certain consequences, not only for his views on general revelation[14] and his views on Scripture, but also for his Christology. He wants to make his deductions from the Incarnation of the Word[15] and then quotes Luther to the effect that "the deeper we can draw Christ into the flesh, the better it is."

One might get the idea that Barth wishes only to stress the fact of the Incarnation of the Word against all forms of Docetism. And, indeed, to illustrate his opinion he quotes a large number of passages from the Reformers to stress the reality of this Incarnation. Calvin also spoke emphatically about this mode of God's coming and said, for instance, that being God, Christ "might have instantaneously made a conspicuous exhibition of his glory to the world; yet . . . he receded from his right, and voluntarily debased himself, for . . . he assumed the form of a servant, and content with that humble station, suffered his Divinity to be hidden behind the veil of humanity."[16] In his infinite grace Christ associated himself with those who are contemptible and ignoble. Calvin too would reject what Barth somewhere calls "embellishment"—the movement from the assumption of flesh to the assumption of the mere humanity.

---

14. Compare my *De Algemene Openbaring*, 1951, page 246 ff.
15. K. Barth, *Kirchliche Dogmatik*, I, 2, pages 162 ff. and I, 1, 177 ff. Schilder's characterization of Barth's conception of the "Welthaftigkeit" of revelation is right: "Now Barth detaches the paradox from the relationship between the communication and the receiver in order to make it an attribute of the communication itself without also taking account of its concrete relationship to the receiver," K. Schilder, *Zur Begriffsgesch. des* "*Paradoxon*," 1933, page 338.
16. Calvin, *Institutes* II. XIII. 2: compare, in the same passage: ". . . for a time his divine glory was invisible, and nothing appeared but the human form, in a mean and abject condition . . ."

Still it would be wrong simply to identify these ideas of Calvin with those of Barth. Barth himself has asked the question whether people fully realize and accept the consequences of the Incarnation. One must be sure to take account of the fact that the human nature assumed by Christ is identical with the post-Fall nature of man. Only *so* the Incarnation has meaning, because it is only in the post-Fall situation that we confront God. Barth believes that Calvin also failed to see the implications adequately, because when he discusses the Incarnation he says that "flesh" applies not so much to the corrupt nature as to mortal man. Barth wonders why the Scriptures then speak so contemptuously of the flesh. The church meant of course to make an absolute separation between Christ and sin but it did not fully see the complete solidarity of Christ with us all in this earthly flesh.

Hence Barth, as was Brunner, is concerned with the hiddenness of revelation in the flesh. Hence we must face the decision between faith and offense with respect to an indirect revelation in a world which leaves the *impression* that it has nothing whatever to do with revelation.[17]

After this short reproduction of how Barth and Brunner conceive the incognito, one might think that he has run into a completely new complex of problems which has emerged, in particular, from the basic motifs of the dialectical views on revelation and concealment. It is true that these views, particularly under the influence of Kierkegaard, have come to the fore, but one cannot say that they have no connection with a certain tradition. Kierkegaard may have fathered the incognito idea but there is another motif in dialectical theology which goes back to Kohlbrugge and his followers. The old conflict between Kuyper and Böhl suddenly achieves new relevance to

17. In Barth's *Prolegomena*, 1927, we already run into the word incognito. Here he associates the incognito of Christ with the life of believers in this world. "Not only the Son of God proceeds incognito through the world; the same applies to that which really makes his own to be his own: their life is hid with Christ in God," page 293.

the student of present-day Christology. This conflict began when Kuyper attaacked Böhl who, in his *"Von der Inkarnation des göttlichen Wortes"* (1884), crossed the limits, according to Kuyper, which Hebrews 7:26 had posited against the development of the Son of God in guilt and sin.[18] In his opinion Böhl seriously detracted from the fact that Christ was "holy, guileless, undefiled, separated from sinners" (Hebr. 7:26). Kuyper discovered this error especially in the dogmatics of Böhl and focussed his objections accordingly. He acknowledges that Böhl is right in stressing that Christ, to be our redeemer, must assume *our* nature and not another; and plainly asserts that Böhl denies that Christ ever fell into personal sin. But he demurs when Böhl teaches that the guilt of Adam is imputed to Christ as well as to us. He quotes Böhl as saying: "In virtue of his birth Christ had just as complete a human nature as we and, as such, shared the imputation of the sin of Adam with us."[19] Against this view Kuyper ranges all the passages of Scripture which incontrovertibly teach the absolute holiness of Christ. At this point we plainly run into the problem of original guilt. Christ, says Böhl, placed himself at his conception under the imputation of Adam's guilt.[20] He poses the question: "Must the main thing be withdrawn from him at the conception—we mean: the unabbreviated human nature?" At the time of his birth Christ allowed that to come upon himself "which we all have and that by imputation, not inherently, so that something sinful adhered to him." And so Christ places himself under the judgment of God. "Can a substance purified by the Holy Spirit still be an object of God's judgment?" The Incarnation, says Böhl, is not at all surrounded by a halo. Christ was not personally guilty, to be sure, but he bears the burden of the wrath of God by imputation and the imputation

---

18. A. Kuyper, *De Vleeswording des Woords,* 1887, page VI.
19. *Ibid.,* page LV.
20. E. Böhl, *Zur Abwehr,* 1888, page 43; compare his Dogmatik, page 299 ff.

was a horrible reality. He became a curse for us and suffered terribly under this curse. Böhl obviously interprets the imputation of Adam's guilt as a transfer of guilt in a special sense. The sins of others came to lie upon him. And this must be taken with final seriousness, so that Kuyper's jeremiad is groundless.

Even though Christ was without sin, Böhl thinks it is a pity that so many Christian teachers are worried when they think of a *tempted* Savior. Against Rome, Luther was the man who saw Christ descended deeply into the flesh. Böhl regards him as "the first and, unfortunately, also the only one among the champions of the Reformation who fully accepted the mysteries of the Incarnation of the Logos." Here lies Böhl's deepest concern: the reality of the Incarnation. And then we witness in Böhl the emergence of the problem of the sinlessness of Christ in connection with the guilt laden upon him. We might have discussed this controversy between Kuyper and Kohlbrugge in the chapter on the sinlessness of Christ, but it is increasingly apparent, in our opinion, that the fundamental issue here is the hiddenness of Christ in the flesh. In his work on the Holy Spirit Kuyper broaches this defense of Böhl and points out the importance of the issue which separates them. He agrees with Böhl that with respect to Christ also, there is imputation. "Christ bore, not his own but another's guilt, and this strange guilt he could not bear unless it were imputed to him."[21] And Kuyper acknowledges too that Christ's guilt-bearing began with his Incarnation, and not later on. But Böhl asserts also that the imputation in the case of Christ takes place "as with one of us." Against this Kuyper objects that the imputation to Christ is quite different from the imputation to us. The imputation of guilt to Christ is vicarious. Böhl talks of an imputation of guilt involved in his birth in the flesh. From Böhl's reply it is clear that Kuyper's reproduction of him

---

21. A. Kuyper, *Het werk van den Heiligen Geest*, page 28.

is correct. Kuyper, says Böhl, imperils the unabbreviated human nature of Christ. This is even more plain in the following statement of Böhl: "What an impossible thing, moreover, that God the Lord should, in the case of Christ, have held back one factor in the great account: that of the imputation of Adam's guilt; and that he should have permitted the Redeemer to come into the world through a back-door." Böhl is worried that Kuyper is not doing justice to the truly human nature of Christ and solidarity with us implied in this nature. With Luther he wishes to draw Christ fully into the flesh—a flesh which bears the likeness of sin. It would be hard to assume that this passionate discussion was based on a misunderstanding. And from later developments this seems still less likely. Van Niftrik, too, regards the issue as important and stresses the fact that Christ did not come to us as an ideal man but *in the flesh*. He knows he is liable to the charge of violating the sinlessness of Christ, but he answers: "But the gospel does not say that Christ became an ideal man; rather that he became flesh and, in the Biblical idiom, this often means man as sin made him."[22] Thus, he says, Christological thought is in ferment. But one may well ask what kind of ferment this is. For an attempt is made here to point out the absolute solidarity of Christ with us. The fact that Christ did not come to be an ideal example to us is the common confession of the church. The Scripture pictures him as the Lamb of God laden with the guilt of his people. But it is not plain just what the "extra something" is which the word "flesh" provides. It is peculiar that while the authors concerned cling to the personal sinlessness of Christ they still wish to draw conclusions from "the likeness of sinful flesh," in terms of which they then charge others—Calvin, among others— with not having seen fully the reality of the Incarnation.

In the controversy between Böhl and Kuyper the central issue was the imputation of the original guilt of Adam. This

22. G. C. van Niftrik, *Protest. Christologie*. In: Winkler Prins, Volume VI, page 56.

element is no longer predominant in later discussions. The problem of original guilt has, of course, been given a new and altered position in dialectical theology. Hence in our day the neo-Kohlbruggian idea of Böhl is given the form of a dialectic between revelation and concealment, the humanity of Christ (his flesh) concealing the revelation of God. Dialectical theology, however much it has been influenced by Kohlbrugge, is certainly no rehash of his theology. That much is clear from the relationship between revelation and concealment. In Böhl this revelational point of view was still embryonic. He was concerned rather—like Kohlbrugge—about the idea of the absolute humiliation of Christ.[23] In the dialectical formulation of the problem the emphasis is much more on a special view of the *structure* of revelation. By way of the idea of participation in "sinful flesh" the argument from the assumption of the guilt of Adam has now issued into the idea of the incognito. Thus old problems come to us with new faces. The continuity in this progression is evident from the common criticism by Böhl and Barth of Calvin. Theology is presently pondering the implications of the Incarnation of the Word. Special emphasis is again laid on the fact that Christ was born in the human nature of the post-Fall situation—an idea which Reformed theology has always accepted and which Kuyper affirmed. But it seems as if a search is on for an "extra" something. This "plus-element" is currently the hiddenness of the revelation of God in the flesh. Böhl strongly stressed the lonely nights of Christ and the horror of his actually bearing the guilt of others. This idea still plays a role today. But the dominant role is that of the structure of revelation. The Incarnation of the Word and the idea of incognito are regarded as correlative. The issue here is whether the correlation is genuine; and

___

23. For Kohlbrugge, see his *Betrachting over het eerste kapittel van het Evangelium van Mattheus*, 1842.

whether the idea which Kierkegaard fathered can be justified before the tribunal of Holy Scripture.[24]

* * *

Perhaps we are not exaggerating when we say that we are now treating one of the most important questions of Christology: the significance of the humanity of Christ in the revelation of God in Jesus Christ. The core of the discussion consists in the relationship between revelation and concealment. In the dialectical view we witness again and again that God reveals himself precisely in concealment: one might say that in his revelation he conceals himself by the manner in which he reveals himself. Both in Barth and Brunner we can find striking examples of this. And the most striking element of all is the fact that this relationship between revelation and concealment is regarded as a *necessary* consequence of the biblical concept of revelation.

Not that they want to apply an extra-biblical concept of revelation to the revelation of Christ. Indeed, they assert, this conception is given in revelation. But they do posit that revelation can take place only in the absoluteness of concealment because only then is there room for the possibility of offense. This view may be conceived most sharply by reference to the recurrent idea of indirect revelation by which it is impossible, by sense-perception or the imagination, to recognize in him the unambiguous revelation of God. No, it remains possible to contradict this revelation. And now the issue is: what is the relationship between this possibility of contradiction and the nature of the revelation of God in concealment? Between the two the thesis of indirect revelation posits a necessary correlativity. It seems that we are very close to Scripture here: it likewise speaks of the impossibility

---

24. Here we can only refer to the relationship between this idea and Luther. Compare Böhl's appreciation for Luther and Barth, *Ibid.* I, 1, pages 175 ff. A study of Luther and Kierkegaard would be important. Something on this score is given by Pierre Mesnard, *Le vrai visage de Kierkegaard* (Bibliotheque des archives de Philosophie) 1948, pages 367 ff.

that the natural and unenlightened heart should recognize in
Jesus Christ the revelation of God. When Peter, amid a multiplicity of views concerning Christ, confesses that he is the
Son of the living God, then Christ immediately refers this
confession back to a revelation of God. It cannot arise out of
the human heart, nor out of human reflection or intuition, nor
from sense-perception. The true knowledge of Christ can issue
only from the illuminated heart. One can harden his heart
against the Christ and even, while one knows the Scripture,
pass him by without worship (Matt. 2:4-6).

Thus one regarded him as a prophet and another says: we
have seen strange things today (Luke 5:26); still another
says that he is mad (John 10:20) or that he is born of for-
nication.[25] His miracles, according to the interpretation of
some, are accomplished with the aid of Beelzebub, the prince
of demons (Luke 11:15). The epistles also make plain that
the knowledge of Christ is by no means a matter of course; it
is not something easily understood in terms of human life.
They rather tell us that no man can say that Jesus is Lord, but
in the Holy Spirit (I Cor. 12:3). To the natural heart the
cross is not transparent in its deepest meaning and can become an offense or foolishness to Jews or to Greeks (I Cor.
1:18, 23).

But now the decisive fact is that this response, issuing from
blindness, this being offended, is never correlative with a concealment inherent in the structure of Revelation.

In the revelation of Christ we are not concerned with a mystery conditioned by the category of "Welthaftigkeit" and the
attendant "unfit" instruments of revelation. Christ's reaction
to unbelief and opposition points in another direction. He
never construes this opposition, even theoretically, in terms of
the structure of revelation. When unbelief interprets the signs
and wonders of the Messianic kingdom as having been per-

25. Cf. John 8:41 and Grosheide, *Commentaar* I, page 45.

formed by demonic assistance, then Christ, knowing the
thoughts of the sceptics (Luke 11:17), unmasks the folly
of their interpretation. "Every kingdom divided against itself is brought to desolation; and a house divided against a
house falleth. And if Satan also is divided against himself how
shall his kingdom stand?" The Kingdom is come and Christ
cast out demons by the finger of God. Of the possibility of
a wrong and unbelieving interpretation, one can say only that
the "form" of revelation is not responsible for it, but stamps it
rather as folly and unbelief. When Brunner says that, in virtue
of the incognito, Christ can be mistaken for any other man
at all, his error is that he argues theoretically in terms of the
structure of revelation instead of thinking in terms of the con-
victing force of the revelation of God.[26] The Scriptures make
plain, moreover, that we are not confronted by a dual possibility given with the form of revelation but rather by the rejection of the content of the revelation. This rejection is continually placed in a glaring light, because the rejector is confronted by the Son of man who is surrounded by the voices of
God: the prophetic and apostolic witness. The flesh which
Christ assumed does not eclipse the radiant light of God. The
most profound reason for the offense as a reaction to the revelation of God in Christ is not the "form" of this revelation of
the power and wisdom of God but rather the resistance of the
whole man who refuses to admit the revelation of reconciliation into his life.

* * *

In I Cor. 2:8 Paul speaks of the mystery which has in it
the hidden wisdom of God "which none of the rulers of this

26. In criticizing Brunner (the "possibility" of mistaking Christ for anyone else) we do not detract from Phil. 2 where we read that Christ
assumed the form of a servant and was made "in the likeness of man." Paul
does not call in questionn the genuine humanity of Christ. Compare Greydanus, *Commentaar op Phil.*, page 194; G. J. Streeder, *De gemeente in
Jezus Christus, De brief aan de Philippenzen*, 1848. page 38; and in general:
C. Van Til, *The Intellectual Challenge of the Gospel*, 1951, pages 36 ff.

world hath known: for had they known it, they would not have crucified the Lord of glory." Here, too, the theory of incognito is missing. For in the revelation of the mystery of Christ we are not concerned with a secret doctrine kept in utter concealment but with a mystery, though hidden for many centuries, which is now revealed. The appearance of Christ may never be seen as an isolated mystery, for the man Jesus Christ appeared in the floodlights of the revelation of God. Hence the fact of the Incarnation may not give rise to a schematism characterized by the idea of an impenetrable incognito. By this formal concept of revelation one narrows the scope of revelation and runs the danger, willy-nilly, of lessening the responsibility of unbelief.

The influence of the incognito-theory can be explained only from the fact that it took up the element of the humiliation of Christ and seemed thus to be in line with the biblical revelation. But it is clear that the theory was introduced as an independent factor issuing from the structure of revelation and that the revelation of the humiliation was not the sole determinant. The revelation of Christ was reduced to logical categories, which brought Kierkegaard, for instance, to the idea of the intellectual *skandalon* of the God-man paradox in Jesus Christ. This logical treatment of the possibility of faith and offense was possible only in terms of a given conception of the structure of revelation, and could not have arisen if from the beginning the argument had been in terms of the content of revelation itself.

* * *

What does Brunner mean when, in connection with the significance of the humanity of Christ, he introduces the problem of the kerygma? Does he want to bury every element of Christ's deity under the flesh and then to explicate the Gospels in terms of the absolute hiddenness of the flesh? to eliminate the Transfiguration on the Mount as a projection which should it be taken biographically, would violate the incognito and the indirect revelation? Does he mean that one can speak of concealment only when everything in his life has its "normal" course and everyone could take him to be anyone else? Does he want to eliminate the miracles of Christ, the darkness on Golgotha, the opened graves, and the tearing of the temple-curtain? And if he wants to retain the miracles, can he consistently hold to his theory of indirect revelation?

But the Scriptures speak differently. They never formulate the problem in terms of the incognito—as does Brunner—or in terms of the "Welthaftigkeit" of revelation—as does Barth —but they picture for us the Son of man in the flesh of his humiliation standing in the flood-light of the Word which interprets him: the Word which in the mouth of John the Baptist was meant to clear away all uncertainty concerning him and to disclose him as the Lamb of God which came to bear the sins of the world. This we find also in the instruction of Jesus Christ when he reads the book of Isaiah and speaks of the "Now" of fulfillment: hence also his "Woe unto you" addressed to Pharisees who ask for signs because they do not believe his words and thus try to escape the directness of his revelation. They are the ones who try, again and again, to thrust him back into obscurity and secrecy. The New Testament will never validate the incognito-theory, for the determinative fact about incognito is absolute secrecy and concealment.

The incognito-theory is something different from the idea of the self-concealment of Christ in the progression of his Messianic action—a subject treated by Ridderbos. Indeed, this concealment is part of a holy pedagogy serviceable to the *revelation* of his Messianic mission. But the theory of incognito implies absolute and, as long as he is on earth, uninterrupted concealment. Here, in my opinion, lies the fundamental error of the incognito-theory.

When those who encounter Christ manifest unbelief, they are rebuked for this unbelief because they have not believed the Word. Outside of this Word Christ cannot be seen or known. The men of Emmaus are deeply depressed because they have not understood the cross *in the light of the Word.* They lived in the consciousness of the loneliness which was caused, to their minds, by the cloaked action of God in their lives. But Christ speaks of hearts filled with unbelief toward the Scriptures which have pre-interpreted the coming of the Christ. Hence the incognito-concept is not fruitful as an interpretative principle for the gospels. He who wishes to employ it must proceed to eliminate, with ruthless consistency, all the moments of glory (doxa) from the earthly course of Jesus' life. Such consistency has seldom been practiced though a tendency in this direction may definitely be observed. The incognito-theologians practically feel obliged to systematize the life of Christ in terms of humiliation and hence cannot approach the gospel without bias.

Brunner is the most illustrative case in point, since he regards the virgin birth in conflict with the incognito. Here system rules and assumes a critical function even toward text-critically inviolable passages. He no longer listens to the much-lauded kerygma but subjects it to norms of his own. He pictures Christ, not as he appears in the gospel, but as he *must* have been in terms of the incognito-concept; that is, "a weak man, who suffers, who experiences hunger, who trembles and is afraid."[27] But Christ's appearance in the world is not a sudden and perplexing act: there are authorities who can say who he is. Unbelief is without excuse since his advent was announced. Even after his resurrection Christ still refers to the prophetic word of the Old Testament which is now fulfilled in his progression from suffering to glory. If one wishes consistently to apply the theory of the incognito one must eliminate from the gospel many stories which speak in one way or another of the glory of God which was manifested intermittently in Jesus' earthly existence *for a special purpose;* as, for in-

---

27. Brunner, *Der Mittler*, page 309.

stance, at his baptism or his transfiguration. In terms of Brunner's conception these "glorifications" can be interpreted only as the suspension of the unlimited incognito. But thus one arrives at a subjective view of revelation. Christ can be known only by faith and by the illumination of the Spirit and not by rational obviousness: *ergo,* Christ travels incognito. So runs the argument. But thus the content of revelation is conditioned by what the unillumined heart of the natural man believes he can say about it. The theory of the kerygma will not do to explain the moments of glory in the gospel. Kittel points out that Matthew and Mark use the word "doxa" in connection with the glory of Christ's return and that Luke uses it with reference to his birth and the transfiguration. But his difference exists only as far as the word, not as far as the matter itself, is concerned. We find it also in Matthew and Mark. The story of the transfiguration occurs in all three synoptic gospels (Matt. 17; Mark 9: Luke 9). Here the incognito-theory receives a new blow. "He was transfigured before them; and his face did shine as the sun, and his garments became white as the light" (Matt. 17:2). Luke expressly adds that the disciples, when they were fully awake, saw his glory; and the revelational significance of the whole appears from the voice which comes out of the cloud saying: "This is my beloved Son, in whom I am well pleased; *hear ye him*" (Matt. 17:5) In the "metamorphosis" of which the Scriptures speak the form of the Son of man in his humiliation is bathed in glory. "In a special event the unique glory of Jesus was witnessed at the transfiguration."[28] And when Schniewind ponders the question as to what event is here confronting us and calls to mind other stories which almost make us think of the resurrection, he nevertheless concludes that we must not take this story to be a backward projection of the later glory. "Still it is wrong to regard our story as an Easter-story projected back into the

----

28. J. Schiewind, *Das Evangelium nach Markus,* 1949, page 123.

earthly life of Jesus." He rejects this idea because Elijah and
Peter do not fit this scheme. But if we may then regard the
story as a reliable witness, it is plain that one must drop the incognito-theory. For then the glory of God also radiated into
the earthly life of Jesus with the obvious intention to reveal his
significance.

Not that we wish to detract from the characterization of the
entire life of Christ as a life of humiliation. Over against the
incognito-theory one can certainly not describe his life as a
life in "doxa." Scripture is all too plain on the deep humiliation
of the Son of man and reminds us that during his earthly life
Christ *was not yet glorified* (John 7:39). This reminder re-
curs in the Gospel of John. But we do reject a schematization
of the life of Christ which, by means of an *a priori* concept of
revelation, eliminates the *doxa*-element from his life in every
respect. For these incidental moments of *doxa* do not interrupt
the humiliation. It is precisely in the story of the Transfiguration that we read of the appearance of Moses and Elijah who
come to speak with him about the "decease which he is about
to accomplish at Jerusalem" (Luke 9:31).[29] Peter may wish
to extend the moment of glory by making booths, but of him
the gospel says that he did not know what he was saying. This
glorification is there, rather, to conduct him to the full depth
of his humiliation (his decease at Jerusalem); and thus the
revelational significance of this moment of glory is apparent, as
it is in the message which Moses and Elijah bring and in the
voice demanding a hearing for Christ.

Hence it is of great importance rightly to see the relationship
between Christ's humiliation and his glory. The Scriptures
speak repeatedly of his glory. Think of the wedding at Cana
where the disciples witness the revelation of his glory in a miracle (John 2:11). And it just is not true that the revelation

---

29. Compare K. Schilder, *Christus in Zijn Lijden*, I, 1949, page 95; he
also refers to the fact that Christ *received* glory (II Peter 1:17) and that
he spoke, *not with the Father*, but with Moses and Elijah.

of Christ's *doxa* would make the reaction to it any the less decisive. For this *doxa* is not that of a miracle which takes one by surprise and whose true significance is seen by all. Indeed not; it is in the story of the miracle at Cana that we read that the disciples *believed* on him. It was not accidental that the transfiguration on the Mount was not a demonstration before the eyes of the world and that this event is still to be regarded as part of the self-concealment of the Messiah, since Jesus forbade his disciples to speak of it until after the resurrection (Matt. 17:9). But here again we are plainly warned not to lay out the life of Christ and the revelation of the Father in terms of a single arbitrary scheme. On the Mount a few individuals witness his metamorphosis but on another occasion, at which Jesus speaks of his coming death, everything is changed. After he has prayed that God might glorify his name, a voice out of heaven declares: "I have both glorified it, and will glorify it again" (John 12:28). Gone here is the intimacy of the inner circle within which the revelation can and must be kept. But here the multitude is present which, though it misinterpret the voice, nonetheless comes in contact with the message of the Father about the course of his Son's life.

It is plain, to our mind, that anyone who still values the gospels must come to the conclusion that the incognito-theory leaves no room for these aspects of revelation, because they, after all, eliminate the absolute incognito.

* * *

Recently the problem has come to the fore whether the Incarnation and the cross of Christ yield an ontological or a noetic paradox; that is, whether the offense of the cross issues from a misunderstanding on the part of the subject or whether it is inherent in the ontological paradox.[30] In this connection, especially Vogel maintained the paradoxicalness of

---

30. See in connection with Kierkegaard: J. Sperna Weyland, *Philosophy of existence and Christianity*, 1951, pages 130 ff.

the Incarnation of the Word. He is not content with a reference to a noetic paradox but speaks of "an ontic contradiction,
when God abandons himself, as one of us, to the death-curse
of sin."[31]

The paradox is that "the reality of the humanity of Jesus
Christ is the humanity—assumed and sustained by God himself
—of man who, as the one to whom the curse of inhumanity
and godlessness is due, has become unrecognizable in his humanity."[32] The words "God himself" are placed in the context
of a peculiar doctrine of satisfaction within the theory of the
incognito of Christ. It is God who abandons himself in Christ
to judgment, and thus conquers sin. We are coming close here
to the idea of theopaschitism, which the church has always rejected as a violation of the trinitarian mystery.[33] The church
was always willing to speak of God acting in Jesus Christ for
reconciliation, and it never severed the bond between the Son
and the Father, but at the same time it wished to maintain
strictly the confession of the incarnate *Word*. It knew it could
never fully express the secret of God's love and never hesitated
to use the strongest anthropomorphic expressions in pursuance
of the Scriptures; but it called a halt before it contradicted
Scripture. It always understood the phrase "God in Christ" in
a different sense from that used by Vogel and Barth.[34] Perhaps
one can say that behind the theory of the incognito of God
there is a conflict over the doctrine of satisfaction—a remarkable stage in theology. The doctrine of satisfaction used to be
attacked from all directions. Now it returns as the reverse
side of the incognito-doctrine.

---

31. H. Vogel, *Christologie* I, pages 165 and 202.
32. *Ibid.*, page 242. See E. Schlink, *Zur Christologie. Verkundigung und
Forschung*, page 93. Schlink says that Vogel was contemplating the
ontological dialectics of Chalcedon through the lenses of the existentialist
dialectics of Kierkegaard.
33. E. L. Mascall, *Existence and Analogy*, 1949, page 134.
34. Compare Y. Feenstra, *Het apostolicum in de twintigste eeuw*, 1951,
pages 193 ff.

* * *

In Reformed Christology the idea of concealment—not to be confused with the incognito-idea—also plays an important role.[35] There may be a danger that in reaction to the theory of the incognito people will object to the idea of the concealment of Christ in the flesh. But one who sees what is meant by it will understand that we now confront a quite different complex of thought. First of all we wish to point out that in Reformed theology the idea of concealment arises in connection with the humiliation of Christ. This line of thought issued from Scripture itself and not from a certain schematism. Especially with a view to the relationship between the divine and the human nature of Christ the idea of "occultatio" arose. Reformed theologians would not have adopted this idea if, like the kenosis-theologians, they had believed that the divine nature laid aside its divine properties. For then Jesus Christ would be the man who had once been God but who, by kenosis, had become fully man. If one rejects this theory, however, the question arises as to what the relationship was between the divine and the human nature in the days of Christ's humiliation. And in this connection people frequently use the concept of "occultatio." Now we must ask what the concept meant in Reformed dogmatics.

* * *

It is not true that the problems of revelation and concealment play a role only in dialectical theology. There the problem was given a particular form, but in Reformed theology[36] it was an important issue for a long time.

35. A. Kuyper, *Vleeschwording des Woords*, page 199. Compare K. Schilder, *De Vleeschwording des Woords* (In: *'t Hoogfeest naar de Schriften*, pages 20, 23). Bavinck, *Geref. Dogm.* III, page 427. See also Greydanus on Philippians 2, *Commentaar*, page 192.

36 In general one may think here of Schilder's views which can be characterized by the words: "Light amidst smoke." God appeared to Abraham "in concealment" (Gen. 15). See Schilder's *Licht in de Rook*, 1923, page 259. This book dates back to a time when dialectical theology was still in its infancy. See also the newly revised edition of 1951, pages 344 ff., as well as Schilder's *Zur Begriffgeschichte des "Paradoxon,"* page 438.

This appears repeatedly in Calvin when he speaks of the Incarnation of the Word. By means of the concept of "occultatio" he wishes to express that Christ came to us, not in the glory and majesty of the form of God, but in the form of a servant.

In his commentary on Philippians he says that Christ could not abdicate his deity at his Incarnation but for a certain period he concealed it, lest it should appear in the weakness of the flesh. He laid aside his glory in the eyes of men, "not by diminishing it but by concealment." By his signs and miracles he proved himself to be the Son of God but the "meanness" of the flesh was nonetheless as a cover to the divine majesty.

And Calvin confirms this truth when he writes that Christ, being God, "might have instantaneously made a conspicuous exhibition of his glory to the world; yet that he receded from his right, and voluntarily debased himself, for that he assumed the form of servant, and content with that humble station, suffered his Divinity to be hidden behind the veil of humanity."[37] For a certain period he did not display his divine glory but "manifested himself in the condition of an abject and despised man." In his exegesis of John 1:14 Calvin says that Christ, though he remained God, cloaked it in the humility of the flesh. This "occultatio" we discover throughout Reformed theology. The concept constitutes a human effort to indicate the mystery of the humiliation of Christ. Calvin's intent is not to posit an absolute incognito, for he also refers to the fact that the splendor of Christ's glory penetrates through the weakness and concealment of the flesh. As we have seen earlier, Calvin discusses this point in connection with the *revelation* of God in Christ, but always in order to point out the comforting character of the Incarnation. God appears in Christ, not in his majesty, but in our humanity, and is very close to us. This is the aspect under which Calvin again and again discusses the

---

37. Institutes II, XIII, 2.

concealment. It is not *a priori* necessary in terms of the structure of revelation but expresses the way of God to us in the humiliation of the Man of Sorrows. Calvin could not view this humiliation in terms of the dialectics of concealment and revelation because his assumption was that this humiliated Christ was revealed, in his concealment, by the *Word of God.* His concept of revelation in connection with Jesus Christ is different—and the difference is more than one of terminology. For when the hiddenness of the flesh is placed in an intimate relationship to the Christ-revealing Word, one also gets a different slant on the possibility of offense. For then the offense, of which Scripture speaks with so much emphasis, is not isolated from the revelation concerning Christ. The dialectical theologians relate the offense too much to the fact that Christ, as God, was also a true man. This concealment of the deity under the humanity would be the real offense to the human intellect. Were this true, the humanity of Christ would have been the real source of the offense: this mode of revelation would be offensive because this man would have been at the same time truly God. In this line Kierkegaard worked out his idea of offense: the offense at God who became man. This is said to be the Christological offense par excellence. One can, as it were, ponder this offense without taking into account the message and the work of the Incarnate Word. The incognito would be the real content of the offense. From this it appears how unsatisfying the incognito-idea in Christology is. Aside from the transcendental criticism, one can also offer immanent criticism. Indeed: the idea of offense and that of incognito are mutually exclusive. If the word incognito still has any meaning, there lies in it the idea that a person wishes to remain disguised and to pursue his way unnoticed in utter anonymity. But in Christ we do not encounter any such incognito. When he conceals himself for a time, he does it with a view to his work of self-revelation and never to be able to go by unnoticed. He is concerned that people should learn to *know* the

Incarnate Word. His birth, life, and death, are all directed to publicity. His life and work were intended for the world, and not done in a corner. The mystery of the cross is broadcast throughout the world. Hence the offense at his birth and his cross does not consist in the concealment of the deity in the humanity but rather in the divinely revealed message concerning the humiliated Son. The offense is never an attitude of resistance springing from the impossibility of conceiving the unity of God and man, but one of opposition to the message of the grace of God revealed to us in the humiliated One. In him we are confronted, not just with the knotty problem of how it is possible that this man should claim to be the Son of God, but with the decision to believe or not to believe the revealed Word of God.

For this reason the concealment of Christ's deity in his humiliation is such a decisive point in Reformed Christology. The problem of revelation is always related to the fact of humilation. The humiliation of Christ does not present man with an unsoluble mental problem but with a question touching the whole man in his relationship to this action of God in Jesus Christ. Why did Christ assume our flesh? In Calvin's catechism of 1537 we read the answer: He took our poverty upon him in order to give us his riches, and our mortality to give us his immortality; he descended, in order to elevate us into heaven. One cannot for a moment abstract the relationship between God and man from the way of humiliation, and hence one may not think of the relationship between revelation and humiliation *by itself* either. The incognito-theory is a principal divorce of the *unio personalis* from its purpose. When Paul refers to the attitude of Jews and Greeks toward the cross (I Cor. 1), he is talking about the *reactions* of those who view the cross as an offense or as folly. But at the same time he speaks of the power and wisdom of God visible in the cross to those who believe. Hence it is not permissible formally to relate the offense and folly to the concealment, as if there is a ground for this radical misunderstanding in the *form* of the revelation of God's love in the cross; for the offense issues from aversion to the explanatory Word. By the illumination of the Spirit this Word enables one to discover in the weakness and folly of God his wisdom and his power. One could say that Calvin always regarded the offense as a "noetic" problem, in the sense that the issue is the human reaction and response to the message.[38]

Calvin does speak with emphasis about the obscuration of Christ's glory, as it became evident when Christ was crucified with criminals. This was already a facet of Isaiah's picture of the Man of Sorrows (Isaiah 53:12), but in this connection Calvin always refers to the illumination of the eyes which could see his great love in this disgrace and, in this total desolation, the merciful fellowship of God with all those who believe in him. In the failure truly to listen, in the unbelieving and resistant human heart lies the reason why the humiliation of Christ is not understood. The "causa scandali" is unbelief in connection with the humiliation of Christ. When Christ speaks of the flesh and blood which he will give for the life of the world, many of his disciples murmur at this "saying" (John 6:60). "This is a hard saying; who can hear it?" And Christ answers: Does this cause you to stumble? Unbelief is the cause of their offense (Cf. John 6:64). Calvin has mentioned the "obstaculum" consisting in the humble condition of Jesus' life but it is plainly an obstacle only to the darkened mind. In the midst of general offense Christ spoke of the glory he would receive from the Father (John 6:62). For this reason Calvin has no difficulty with the message of Scripture concerning the miracles of Christ or with the "doxa" given him on the Mount of Transfiguration. Calvin's unbiased ear for the message of the entire Word shows us that he never approached the revelation in Christ in terms of a necessary dialectic between revelation and concealment.

---

38. See especially Calvin's exegesis of I Cor. 1.

*   *   *

We must still consider whether Reformed theology has
rightly used the word "occultatio" in its Christology. Is it possible in this manner to do justice to the mystery of Christ in his
inexpressible humiliation?   Must not we, in view of the idea
of substitution, proceed to draw Christ more deeply into the
flesh?   Must we not in any case give a deeper meaning to the
idea of "occultatio" than Calvin and Reformed theology allowed?   They, after all, still speak of a glory which, though
concealed, is still present. Can one still talk of a genuine kenosis on that basis?   And does not this idea of Reformed theology imply the idea of an incognito meaning that Christ was
really full of glory but that in the manner of his self-revelation
he assumed the *form* of a servant?   These are the objections
Korff has presented to the "occultatio"-view of Calvin and Reformed theology after him.   In his discussion of the so-called
"extra calvinisticum" he declares that if the deity really remains outside the humanity assumed by him and remains personally united with it, there is practically nothing left of a
kenosis, an emptying of the Logos. Against the background
of a permanently present deity the kenosis cannot be taken as
anything other than unreal.[39]   He does encounter in Calvin
a number of expressions which seem to imply a real kenosis:
Calvin speaks of a diminution [40] of God in Christ, for instance,
but Korff says these expressions are not meant literally. Korff
objects to the Lutheran conception, but he finds the Reformed
view of "occultatio" no more satisfying.   Again he asks the
question: "In what does the kenosis really consist?"   It is no
more than a metaphor for the concealment of the divine majesty while Reformed Christology adds that nothing is detracted from the heavenly glory and the Son loses nothing of
it. "This does not exactly make his coming in the form of a

39. Korff, *Christologie* I, page 237.
40. Korff is referring to Calvin's commentary on Hebrews 2:7.

servant more real to us. At bottom there is no kenosis at all.
At the Incarnation the Logos empties himself of exactly nothing."

Korff even goes so far as to agree with Schneckenburger
who says that in Reformed Christology everything is "as if."
With reference to a well-known statement he declares that he
is beginning to doubt whether the Son of God has *really descended.* Very little is left of the Pauline idea that this was the
grace of Christ that for our sakes he became poor. Nobody
becomes poor: "The Logos merely acquires a new mode of being by the assumption of a human nature but in no sense does
he become poor."

Of this criticism we must say that we could fully understand
it if Korff himself accepted the theory of kenosis as the laying
aside of divine attributes. In terms of this theory one might
indeed oppose the Reformed concept of concealment as a
"quasi-kenosis." The remarkable thing about Korff's point of
view is that he, with no less emphasis, rejects this kenotic theory. His ground is that on this view it is hard to see that God
himself comes to us. He even calls it a tragic case.[41] Indeed,
is not the prime intention of all Christology to give expression
to the fact that in Christ we have God? And that is something
we do not hear in a kenotic Christology. God, the only One
we are really concerned about, cannot be found in it.

Hence Korff rejects both the kenosis-doctrine of the nineteenth century and the concept of concealment as it occurs
in Reformed theology. He rejects both of them, as well as the
extra-calvinisticum, on the same grounds: both attempt logically to extend the Christology of the "vere Deus, vere homo."
But it should be plain that Korff, now that he has opposed the
kenosis-doctrine, can no longer, in the manner he once employed, criticize the idea of "occultatio." For this concept expresses that the glory of Christ, at his Incarnation, was hid-

41. *Ibid.,* page 289.

den beneath the flesh, without his laying aside his Deity. And
above all: Korff is not arguing *ad rem* when he says that this
view leaves no room for a genuine kenosis. He takes no account of the possibility that, since in Philippians 2 we encounter
the kenosis and humiliation of Christ as a transcription of the
fact that "God was manifest in the flesh," the idea of concealment teaches a concealment *in its own kind*. Korff, the man
who always sharply opposed the attempt to *understand* the Incarnation, obviously interpreted the Reformed idea of concealment as an attempt to understand the kenosis. But this interpretation is not at all correct. On the contrary: Reformed
theology merely tries to do justice to the testimony of Scripture concerning the self-emptying and humiliation of Christ—
the two being inextricably interrelated in Paul.

Korff's solution, we must object, is not plain in its antithesis to the kenosis-theory and Reformed Christology; it is
not plain in terms of the Scriptural revelation. What Korff
adduces as argument against the kenosis-doctrine of the nineteenth century constitutes the core of the extra-calvinisticum
and of the idea of concealment. When he opposes this latter
concept as a "quasi-kenosis," it must be because he believes that
this concealment is the mere putting on of an outer garment
which detracts nothing from the riches of the king. Korff
here teaches us how cautious we must be with the doctrine of
kenosis; if he had been cautious with the idea of concealment
he would have understood how "occultatio" in Calvin can be
accompanied by a confession of the deepest humiliation.

The emptying of his glory (in the form of God) is the aban-
donment of the glory which he had with the Father before the
world was (John 17:5). It takes place by way of the assumption of the form of a servant, the human nature, en route to the
most extreme humiliation, the death of the cross. The emptying at the beginning and the humiliation as a concomitant all
the way to the cross—the two belong together. One who
should wish to oppose the idea of concealment would forget

that this concealment is absolute, divine, earnestness. The question: what does it mean? can be answered only by reference to his suffering, desolation, and death. One may speak of this concealment only, as does the gospel, in terms of a dreadful curse and dreadful desolation and, at the same time, resist the logic of the nineteenth century doctrine of kenosis.[42]

The church with its confession has always skirted danger. To the left lies the ravine of theopaschitism (theory of the suffering God) and to the right that of the complete humanization of the Son of God; but the church knew that by using the word "concealment" it did not attempt to penetrate logically the Incarnation of the Word. The concept, so far from being used speculatively, was used with great sobriety by men who were intent on doing justice to the whole testimony of Scripture. Reformed theology made few inferences at this point. The word under discussion recurred, but always as a warning to honor the genuineness of the "vere Deus, vere homo." And when Reformed theology spoke of concealment, it was always thought of in reference to the darkness of the way of suffering. Hence Reformed exegesis or dogmatics did not, by speaking of concealment, cast a shadow upon the confession of Christ's true humiliation.

At the starting-point of the road which Paul pictures right up to the cross, we read of the Son of God in glory, "who counted not the being on an equality with God" a thing to cling to with all his might[43] but who emptied himself on a road which took him into desolation and death. And though the church has always rejected theopaschitism, it confessed nevertheless the *divine* love which caused the Son to go the whole way— as he himself summarized it: "For the Son of man also came not to be ministered unto, but to minister, and to give his life a ransom for many" (Mark 10:45).

---

42. See Greydanus, *Commentaar*, page 192; Kittel, *Th. W. B.*, IV, under "morphe."
43. See Kittel on "harpagmos."

* * *

If we now look backwards upon the road we have travelled we again become conscious of the auxiliary function of dogmatics. It does not intend to reach up into a gnosis higher than the simple faith of the church; there is no gnosis which would enable one to elevate himself above the "communio sanctorum" composed of those of whom the Savior said: "I thank thee, O Father, Lord of heaven and earth, that thou didst hide these things from the wise and understanding, and didst reveal them unto babes" (Matt. 11:25). Here too we read of revelation and concealment, but these words aim their sharp edge at the pride which imagines it can comprehend the mystery of Christ or which simply dismisses it all. When theology concerns itself with the problems of Christology its design is merely to point to that which is superior to all scientific reflection: the Holy Scriptures which witness to us concerning Jesus Christ. It does not supply a substitute for the reading of this inexhaustible Word, nor can it ever outreach the preaching out of this Word. On the contrary, it knows something of what John asserts at the end of his Gospel: "And there are also many other things which Jesus did, the which if they should be written every one, I suppose that even the world itself would not contain the books that should be written" (John 21:25).

A typical example of Jewish overstatement!—people have said. One who himself writes a relatively short Gospel, can only exaggerate when he speaks of books so numerous that the world would not contain them. But one can also read here the amazement and ecstatic delight which seized John, and others with him, at the appearance of Jesus Christ, whom they had learned to know through faith and love. In order to know a man and to describe him biographically, it is not necessary to report everything he has said and done. Life is full of events, actions, and words, and certainly not all of them are important enough to be preserved for future generations. But that it should occur to John—this possibility of total description, even though technically impracticable—indicates the unique significance of Jesus Christ.

In its age-long conflict the church understood something of this amazement and delight. It did not, surely, always do justice to the true confession of the Son of man, nor were its doxologies always harmonious; indeed, amidst the business of life, the coil and recoil of threatening forces, its doxologies sometimes ceased altogether. But always the old fires lit up again. Especially the rise of heresy reawakened the church's consciousness of the significance of Jesus Christ—the consciousness of his person and work inseparably united. Of this, theology may speak, when it ponders the Scriptures, and it reflects on the dogma of the church which was born and kept amidst much conflict. Of this valuable struggle theology may remind us. If there is anything of importance it can do, then it is to demonstrate that, in the struggle of the church for its confession of the Christ, the issue was not one of preserving subtle speculations concerning the mysteries of God, but one rather of resisting these subtleties and speculations.

For there is no stronger defense against speculation than the confession of this Lord as he comes to us in the revelation of God. Here speculation succumbs before the faith which overcomes the world. It is the same faith which listened to the stunning encouragement: " . . . be of good cheer; I have overcome the world" (John 16:33). This Lord is the living Lord of all times. In 1742 someone scribbled in the margin of the last page of John's Gospel these words: *"How much less* would the world contain the books which should describe what the *exalted* Lord has done."* We would not place this notation *next* to John's conclusion, because the exaltation of Christ is of one piece with the work he performed on earth in the years of which John is thinking. But this living Lord is the Lord of the church, and his work is indescribable, in governing it and in intercession for it, also after his exaltation. And the living faith of the church shall not yield, as long as it hears the ancient confession of Christian faith: "vere Deus, vere homo," as the echo of what prophets and apostles long ago testified, and as a summary of its faith—the faith which is irrevocably intertwined with the testimony of Scripture: "Jesus Christ the same yesterday and today, yea, and for ever" (Hebr. 13:8). To know him and to know his work is to know the life-giving word: "These things have I spoken unto you, that *in me* ye may have peace" (John 16:33).

Index of Persons and Subjects

Index of Texts